D0501328

# Never Eat More Than You Can Lift, and Other Food

Quotes and Quips

# Never Eat More Than You Can Lift, and Other Food

## Quotes and Quips

1,500
Notable
Quotables
About Edibles

and
Potables

## Sharon Tyler Herbst

Broadway Books
New York

# *To Julia Child . . .*

If ever I had a culinary hero, this energetic, generous
warm-hearted woman would be it. Thank you, Julia, for
never failing to make me laugh with your dry and witty
sense of humor and for inspiring me with your boundless
energy, creativity, courage, and kindness.

NEVER EAT MORE THAN YOU CAN LIFT, AND OTHER FOOD
QUOTES AND QUIPS. Copyright © 1997 by Sharon Tyler Herbst. All rights reserved. Printed in the United States of America. No part of this book may be reproduced or
transmitted in any form or by any means, electronic or mechanical, including photocopying,
recording, or by any information storage and retrieval system, without written permission from
the publisher. For information, address Broadway Books, a division of Bantam Doubleday
Dell Publishing Group, Inc., 1540 Broadway, New York, NY 10036.

Broadway Books titles may be purchased for business or promotional use or for special sales. For
information, please write to: Special Markets Department, Bantam Doubleday Dell Publishing Group, Inc., 1540 Broadway, New York, NY 10036.

BROADWAY BOOKS and its logo, a letter B bisected on the diagonal, are trademarks
of Broadway Books, a division of Bantam Doubleday Dell Publishing Group, Inc.

Library of Congress Cataloging-in-Publication Data
Herbst, Sharon Tyler.
   Never eat more than you can lift, and other food quotes and quips : 1,500 notable
quotables about edibles and potables / Sharon Tyler Herbst.
      p.    cm.        Includes bibliographical references and indexes.
   ISBN 0-553-06901-2
   1. Food—Quotations, maxims, etc.   2. Beverages—Quotations, maxims, etc.
   3. Cookery.   I. Title.
   TX357.H464  1997    641—dc21
   96-50017    CIP

FIRST EDITION

Designed by Terry Karydes
Illustrations by Beppe Giacobbe

97  98  99  00  01  10  9  8  7  6  5  4  3  2  1

# Contents

# Acknowledgments

*Every author knows that no book is written in a vacuum —
the support from family, friends, and colleagues is a vital and
indispensable part of the process. And so, with tremendous
gratitude and affection, I send a big hug with heartfelt
thanks to . . .*

**Ron Herbst,** my husband, hero, best friend, and soul-
mate—a man whose honesty and judgment I trust above
everyone else's. Not only is every day with this man pure joy,
but he's my anchor, business and creative consultant, research assistant, in-house computer expert, most-trusted
recipe tester . . . in short, my everything.

**Kay** and **Wayne Tyler** (Mom and Dad), two of my greatest fans, for instilling in me a love for food, a passion and respect for words and books, and the belief that I can
accomplish anything I set my heart and mind to. Thank you
for having me!

**Tia Leslie,** beloved sister, whose beauty and talent is ex-
ceeded only by her kindness, compassion, and wholehearted
love and support—how lucky I am to have a sister who's also
a dear friend.

**Harriet Bell,** consummate editor and wickedly funny
friend, who not only has brilliant ideas (like the title of this
book), but whose vision and guidance always make my
books better than they would have been without her. This is
our fourth book together, and I'm delighted that we're already working on our fifth.

**Bill Shinker** and **John Sterling,** Broadway Books presi-
dent-publisher and editor-in-chief, respectively, for their
great enthusiasm and support for this project. Seldom do
those "at the top" take such an active interest in individual

projects, and I'm thankful that these two remarkable men are noteworthy exceptions to that rule.

**Robert de Vicq de Cumptich** (also known as "the man with five names" and "emperor of design"), the brilliant creative director behind the look of this book, which I personally think is dazzling!

**Beppe Giacobbe,** the ingenious artist responsible for the cover design and illustration—my very favorite cover of *all* my books!

**Sonia Greenbaum,** consummate copy editor, with whom I've had the great pleasure of working on two books. She minds my p's and q's better than I do, and for that I'm eternally grateful.

**Daisy Alpert,** Harriet's right hand, who is always there with a smile in her voice and a ready response to all of my questions.

All the talented people at Broadway Books, who labored tirelessly behind the scenes and without fanfare on the design, layout, proofing, and dozens of other tasks to make this book all it could be.

The morning gang at Peet's Coffee (the best coffee in the world!)—**Christine, Cordelia, Erich, Ewa, Jeannine, Karen, Liz, Mark, Paymon,** and **Stella**—who defog my brain every morning with their tender, loving care and superlative D.A.C.s *(doppio alto cappuccinos)*.

And, of course, all the other branches on my support-system tree, including: Oscar Anderson, John and Mildred Arwood, Sue and Gene Bain, Tommie Bloemer, Leslie Bloom, Walt and Carol Boice, Michael and Mary Lynn Boyd, Dickie Brennan, Irena Chalmers, Phillip Cooke, Lisa Ekus, Holly Hartley, Joyce and Lew Herbst, Susan and Lee Janvrin, Jeanette and Tex Kinney, the Leslies, Daniel Maye, Mary Miller, Glen and Laura Miwa, Yei and Ken Miwa, and Emma Swain.

# Introduction

All these things here collected, are not mine,
But diverse grapes make but one sort of wine;
So I, from many learned authors took
The various matters printed in this book.
What's not mine own by me shall not be father'd,
The most part I in fifty years have gather'd,
Some things are very good, pick out the best,
Good wits compiled them, and I wrote the rest.
If thou dost buy it, it will quit thy cost,
Read it, and all thy labour is not lost.
— John Taylor

Two of the most powerful loves of my life are words and food. The fact that I was born at noon on Thanksgiving Day—America's most celebrated day of feasting—seems to have been a sign that I was destined to have a love affair with food. But I've also been an avid reader and ardent writer from the moment I was able to do both. And so it was a perfectly logical segue for me to make my twelfth tome a veritable feast of more than 1,500 quotes on my favorite subjects—food and drink.

What ensued was every writer's dream—the incredibly self-indulgent and extravagant assignment of reading book after book, gathering delicious quips and quotes on edibles and potables, subjects replete with emotional allusions. The selections in this book are, as they must be, intensely subjective, for I could only choose those aphorisms that intrigued me on some level because they're poetic, pithy, honest, disturbing, informative, historical, funny, or nostalgic. Some engender contemplative reflection, others are wickedly naughty or deliciously witty, many are insightful and erudite, and then there are those that are simply silly and nonsensical—pure fluff and frosting. Of course, such a collection wouldn't be complete without a few arrogantly pompous quotes by people who take themselves far too seriously—such citations earned inclusion simply because they make me snort at the author's insolence. And, because I've always been fascinated by the evolution of similar epigrams, I included the obvious parodies of certain quotes, as seen in those of Duncan Hines and Donald McCullough under DINNER.

There are quotes that make me grin or giggle, as with Fran Lebowitz's "Large naked raw carrots are acceptable as food only to those who lie in hutches eagerly awaiting Easter." Some I ardently agree with, like Irena Chalmer's biting bon mot, "Salt is what makes things taste bad when it isn't in them"; others I don't, as when Alice B. Toklas said, "As if a cookbook had anything to do with writing." Sometimes a phrase astonishes me because of who said it, such as Adolf Hitler, inarguably one of history's most contemptible monsters, with his seemingly humane sentiment: "I eat everything that nature voluntarily gives: fruits, vegetables, and the products of plants. But I ask you to spare me what animals are forced to surrender: meat, milk, and cheese."

Then there are those extraordinarily evocative passages that make me marvel at the writer's brilliance. One that jumps immediately to mind is Richard Atcheson's witty, irresistibly comical section on jalapeños.

Sometimes there's a line with a lilt and rhythm so lyrical, so euphonious that it's almost poetic, such as M. F. K. Fisher's "If Time, so fleeting, must like humans die, let it be filled with good food and good talk, and then embalmed in the perfumes of conviviality." Once in a while the speaker's plight makes an excerpt achingly poignant, as when Anne Frank said, "It's really disagreeable to eat a lot of sauerkraut for lunch and supper every day, but you do it if you're hungry." And then there are those word bites that ring so true for me I could have said them myself, such as Julia Child's "Food labels that say 'no fat, no cholesterol' might as well say 'no taste, no fun.'" Others I *wish* were true, like Beth Barnes's "What you eat standing up doesn't count." And, of course, there are those classic sayings, such as the one by my soul sister and eminent icon of porcine pulchritude, Miss Piggy, who said, "Never eat more than you can lift!" I thank her not only for such sage advice, but also for the title of this tome.

In the end, this collection became an appetizing feast of food- and drink-related quotes on more than two hundred subjects. I spent two hedonistically delicious years researching and writing the headnotes, anecdotes, etymologies, historical notes, and cooking tips, creating and testing the recipes and collecting the quotes. Tough work? Well, writing a book is never *easy,* but this one was pure pleasure. For it meant that I could immerse myself in a tantalizing assortment of food and words, devour books with unabashed greed and pleasure, and luxuriate in the happy symbiosis of the literary and the culinary worlds. Truth to tell, were it not for my publisher's deadline, I could happily have worked on this book for *at least* another two years. You see, I simply can't help myself, for—as may be the fate of one born on Thanksgiving Day—I am unequivocally hooked on literary grazing.

# A to Z Quips and Quotes on Edibles and Potables

# Abalone

It is said that abalone also makes good chowder, but I cringe at the thought. It would be too much like making an ordinary beef stew of filet mignon.

*— Euell Gibbons*

Abalone may be the one indestructible shellfish ... [it] seems to defy efforts to gussy it up. ... I once ordered something called Scalone—despite the fact that it sounded more like the Water Commissioner of Hoboken than something to eat—and what arrived, a sort of patty made out of abalone and scallops, was delicious.

*— Calvin Trillin*

*See also* FISH

# Airline Food

*According to Irena Chalmers in her inestimable tome* The Great Food Almanac, *one of the reasons airline food is so tasteless is that the cabin pressure at high altitude actually dulls one's taste buds. As a frequent flier who's been subjected to more than my share of dreck, I can only think such sensory deprivation is indeed a blessing.*

Do not accept any food from an airline that you would not accept from a vendor in Calcutta. If it's bottled or if you peel it yourself, it may be all right. Otherwise, it may stay with you for the rest of your life.

*— Roy Blount Jr.*

We do not demand good food in public, and when we eat upon an object that moves, such as a train or a boat, we expect, and generally get, absolute muck.

*— E. M. Forster*

The quality of food is in inverse proportion to the altitude of the dining room, with airplanes the extreme example.

*— Bryan Miller*

An airline is a great place to diet.

— *Wolfgang Puck*

Please take notice of these facial expressions when you're visiting a sick friend in a hospital at feeding time: closed eyes, narrowed nostrils, a downward curl of the lip, an extension of the tongue. You can see those same expressions on most airplanes at feeding time. Humans everywhere react similarly to foods that repel them.

— *Maggie Waldron*

*See also* DINING; RESTAURANTS

# Alcohol

*See* BEER; BRANDY; CHAMPAGNE; COCKTAILS; DRINKING; LIQUOR; PORT; TOASTS; WINE

# Almonds

*Did you know that an almond isn't really a nut but the kernel of a fruit of the almond tree? Not only that, but these delicious "kernels" contain the trace mineral boron, thought to be instrumental in preventing osteoporosis. Almonds also carry a healthy dose of oleic acid, an antioxidant. All nuts are high in fat (blanched unsalted almonds are about 170 calories per ounce; those that are dry-roasted and unsalted weigh in at about 150 calories), but most of the fat in almonds is monounsaturated — the same as in olive oil. So, to put it all in a nutshell, although only very thin people might want to eat handfuls at a time, almonds are a nutritional powerhouse, packed with calcium, fiber, folic acid, magnesium, potassium, riboflavin, and vitamin E.*

Don't eat too many almonds. They add weight to the breasts.

— *Colette*

The smell of almonds toasting in a metal pan . . . is the most agreeable incense I know. . . . I am decidedly addicted to the perfume of these nuts.

*— Bert Greene*

## Hot Nuts!

Toasting nuts intensifies their flavor and makes them crunchier—toasted nuts are also less likely to sink in cake or bread batters. To toast nuts, place them in a heavy, ungreased skillet over medium heat and stir often until golden brown. Or scatter the nuts on an ungreased shallow baking pan and bake at 350°F for 10 to 15 minutes, stirring occasionally. Then, like Bert Greene, bask in their evocative incense.

*See also* NUTS; PEANUTS

# American Food

*See* ETHNIC FOODS

# Apéritifs

*See* COCKTAILS

# Aphrodisiacs

*Named for Aphrodite, the Greek goddess of love, aphrodisiacs have been credited for eons with the ability to stimulate love and sex, not necessarily in that order. The fact that the aphrodisiac's reputation for libidinous arousal has little basis in scientific truth detracts little from its allure. Though everything from ground rhi-*

*noceros horns to spiders has been attributed with erotic powers, most agree that food is, by far, the most pleasurable form of ingested seduction. Almost every food has at one time or another been touted as an aphrodisiac (with the possible exception of rutabagas). No doubt about it — food is sexy, providing you look at it the right way. And isn't that the way of all things in life? Which leads us back to the fact that what's undoubtedly true is that the strongest, most sensuous aphrodisiac is one's imagination.*

Men become passionately attached to women who know how to cosset them with delicate tidbits.

*— Honoré de Balzac*

The right diet directs sexual energy into the parts that matter.

*— Barbara Cartland*

Wine is a precarious aphrodisiac, and its fumes have blighted many a mating.

*— Norman Douglas*

The truffle is not an outright aphrodisiac, but it may in certain circumstances make women more affectionate and men more amiable.

*— Alexandre Dumas*

The Elizabethans ascribed the power [of aphrodisiacs] to so many articles of diet that one suspects that in that virile but undernourished age all anyone needed was a square meal.

*— Bergen Evans*

At one time this [aphrodisiacal] quality was ascribed to the tomato. Reflect on that when you are next preparing the family salad.

*— Jane Grigson*

In one court of love or another, scores of different foods —
truffles, of course — have been believed to have aphrodisiac
powers, but nothing works as well to heighten romance as
the power of suggestion.

— *Evan Jones*

If your wife is old and your member is exhausted, eat onions
in plenty.

— *Martial*

Half past nine — high time for supper;
"Cocoa, love?" "Of course, my dear."
Helen thinks it quite delicious,
John prefers it now to beer.
Knocking back the sepia potion,
Hubby winks, says, "Who's for bed?"
"Shan't be long," says Helen softly,
Cheeks a faintly flushing red.
For they've tumbled on the secret
Of a love that never wanes,
Rapt beneath the tumbled bedclothes,
Cocoa coursing through their veins.

— *Stanley J. Sharpless*

It is the true believer who is going to get the most from an
aphrodisiac. How it works and what it does has a lot to do
with what one wants it to do.

— *Maggie Waldron*

The receptivity to romance probably comes from the general sense of relaxation and well-being good food induces.

— *Harry E. Wedeck*

Many of our Anglo-Saxons perhaps prefer their impotence
to the alternative of having to eat garlic.

— *Anonymous*

# Appetite

My son, Jaws II, had a habit that drove me crazy. He'd walk to the refrigerator-freezer and fling both doors open and stand there until the hairs in his nose iced up. After surveying two hundred dollars' worth of food in varying shapes and forms he would declare loudly "There's nothing to eat."

*— Erma Bombeck*

Of all living things that inhabit the earth, humans are the only species that lacks the ability to control appetite.

*— Irena Chalmers*

I can reason down or deny everything, except this perpetual Belly: feed he must and will, and I cannot make him respectable.

*— Ralph Waldo Emerson*

Appetite comes with eating.

*— French proverb*

All things require skill but an appetite.

*— George Herbert*

Appetite is a kind of passion, and bears the same relationship to food and drink as passion bears to the "loved object." Borne along irresistibly by the momentum of both, we never question our destination, still less its mysterious source. Nor should we.

*— Joyce Carol Oates*

'Tis not the meat, but 'tis the appetite makes eating a delight.

*— Sir John Suckling*

My stomach serves me instead of a clock.

*— Jonathan Swift*

# Apples

**Yet another myth conception.** *Although legend has it that the apple was the forbidden fruit offered by Eve to Adam in the Garden of Eden, archaeologists tell us that's not probable. You see, apples didn't grow in the Middle East during the time that Genesis is thought to have been written. Indeed, the Bible's words describing the tree of knowledge are not at all specific: ". . . good for food and pleasant to the eyes, and a tree to be desired to make one wise." For all we know, the fruit of temptation might more likely have been a luscious apricot.*

He that will not a wife wed must eat a cold apple when he goeth to bed.

*— Thomas Cogan*

If I think I'm about to get a cold and feel achy and chilled, I know it's time for hot [apple] cider with rum.

*— Joyce Goldstein*

The apple was the first fruit of the world, according to Genesis, but it was no Cox's orange pippin. God gave the crab apple and left the rest to man.

*— Jane Grigson*

You cannot sell a blemished apple in the supermarket, but you can sell a tasteless one provided it is shiny, smooth, even, uniform and bright.

*— Elspeth Huxley*

Coleridge holds that a man cannot have a pure mind who refuses apple-dumplings. I am not certain but what he is right.

*— Charles Lamb*

People have made a triumph of the Delicious apple because it doesn't taste like an apple and of the Golden Delicious because it doesn't taste like anything.

*— A. J. Liebling*

# The Legend of Johnny Appleseed

Oh, here am I, 'neath the blue, blue sky,
doing as I please,
Humming with the hummingbirds,
Buzzing with the bees . . .

I can still hear Dennis Day singing these words, part of a song on one of my favorite childhood records about the legend of Johnny Appleseed. To my young mind, this colorful folk character, who went barefoot and wore a tin saucepot for a hat, was fictional, as was Paul Bunyan. Imagine my surprise when, years later, I discovered that—although Johnny Appleseed was most certainly part of American frontier folklore—he was also a "real" person by the name of John Chapman. Massachusetts-born in 1774, Chapman, carrying apple seeds from Philadelphia cider presses, settled in the Ohio River valley around 1801 and devoted his life to the proliferation and care of apples. This eccentric free spirit, affectionately called Johnny Appleseed, wandered throughout Ohio, Illinois, and Indiana, planting apple-seedling nurseries, tending apple orchards, and spreading the Swedenborgian philosophy of love and wisdom. Before dying in 1845, he'd planted apple orchards over an estimated area of ten thousand square miles. What a gift he gave to us all. So let's all tip our tin hats to this gentle soul—thank you, Johnny Appleseed, for so generously sharing the fruits of your labor.

Hell is an idea first born on an undigested apple dumpling.
— *Herman Melville*

I have no truck with lettuce, cabbage, and similar chlorophyll. Any dietitian will tell you that a running foot of apple strudel contains four times the vitamins of a bushel of beans.

*— S. J. Perelman*

# Apple Talk

**APPLE CHEEKS:** Cheeks that have a healthy, rosy-red appearance

**APPLEJACK:** A potent brandy made from apple cider

**APPLEKNOCKER:** American slang for an unsophisticated country person; also for a fruit picker

**APPLE OF DISCORD:** A golden apple inscribed with "For the fairest," thrown by Eris, the Greek goddess of discord, among a gathering of the gods. Paris gave this infamous apple to Aphrodite because she offered him the most beautiful woman in the world—Helen of Troy—whose abduction by Paris caused the Trojan War.

**APPLE OF (ONE'S) EYE:** A person who's treasured above others

**APPLE-PIE BED:** One that's been short-sheeted; also called simply "pie bed"

**APPLE-PIE ORDER:** Neat, ordered, and everything in its place

**APPLE POLISHER:** One who fawns over someone in hopes of gaining favor or an advantage

**APPLESAUCE:** Nonsense

**BAD APPLE:** A person who's dishonest or a malcontent

**FULL OF APPLESAUCE:** One who's full of hot air, nonsense, or similar rubbish.

**LOVE APPLE:** A name once used for the tomato

**UPSET THE APPLECART:** To ruin someone's plans

**WISE APPLE:** A smart aleck

The friendly cow, all red and white,
I love with all my heart;
She gives me cream with all her might,
To eat with apple-tart.
— *Robert Louis Stevenson*

Adam was but human—this explains it all. He did not want the apple for the apple's sake, he wanted it only because it was forbidden.
— *Mark Twain*

*See also* FRUIT; PIES

## Spicy Fresh Applesauce

**A fresh-tasting, speedy applesauce that's wonderful drizzled with cream or spooned over pancakes, waffles, or warm gingerbread. A combination of red and green apples makes a festive Christmastime applesauce.**

$\frac{1}{2}$ teaspoon salt
4 medium-size crisp, tart apples, cored and cut into
    eighths (peeling optional)
freshly grated zest of 1 small orange
$\frac{1}{4}$ cup orange juice
$\frac{1}{4}$ teaspoon ground cinnamon
$\frac{1}{4}$ teaspoon ground allspice

Stir salt into a large bowl of cold water. Add apple chunks; soak 5 minutes to prevent discoloration. Thoroughly drain apples. In a blender or food processor fitted with the metal blade, process all ingredients until desired texture is obtained. Stop machine and stir down apples as necessary for even processing. Serve immediately. **Makes about 3 cups.**

# Apricots

**Is there an ape in apricot?** *Put another way: Do you say APE-rih-kaht or AP-rih-kaht? Well, according to Charles Harrington Elster in his brilliant tome* There Is No Zoo in Zoology, *the second (short-A) version has been preferred since about 1970, when dictionaries gradually began to shift to this more commonly used pronunciation. But don't worry if you're a longtime "ape"-ricot articulator — the variant pronunciation is perfectly acceptable.*

. . . apricots in whose golden pulp lay the core of long afternoons.

— *Bruno Schulz*

*See also* FRUIT

# Artichokes

*Legend has it that eating an artichoke before imbibing forestalls inebriation; consuming one after drinking hastens sobriety. Skeptics might logically assume that such wisdom is the result of creative advertising by some early (but enterprising) artichoke vendor.*

The artichoke, like the oyster, is a food that makes an indelible impression on the untried tongue.

— *Bert Greene*

The artichoke above all is a vegetable expression of civilised living, of the long view, of increasing delight by anticipation and crescendo. No wonder it was once regarded as an aphrodisiac. It had no place in the troll's world of instant gratification. It makes no appeal to the meat-and-two-veg. mentality.

— *Jane Grigson*

# Tartichoke Dunk

Parisian street vendors once used a sure advertising gimmick to sell artichokes (which some claim have aphrodisiacal powers) by shouting, "Artichokes to heat the body, the spirit, and the genitals." No shouting needed for this easy tomato-artichoke (tartichoke) dip, which isn't guaranteed to improve your sex life but is most definitely guaranteed to be good. A bonus with this dish is that it's absolutely fabulous spooned atop baked potatoes, on sandwiches, or over rice or scrambled eggs.

1 cup grated cheddar cheese
½ cup grated Swiss cheese
1 (14-ounce) can water-packed artichoke hearts, *well drained* and chopped
1 (14½-ounce) can ready-cut tomatoes, *well drained*
1 cup non- or low-fat mayonnaise
1 large clove garlic, minced
¼ to ½ teaspoon cayenne pepper
salt

Heat oven to 350°F. Lightly oil an 8 × 8-inch square baking pan. In a large bowl, combine cheeses; set aside ½ cup. Add remaining ingredients, except salt, to cheese in bowl; stir to combine. Salt to taste. Turn into prepared pan; sprinkle with reserved ½ cup cheese. Bake 20 minutes, or until bubbly around the edges. Serve hot as a spread for toast rounds or crackers. **Serves 6 to 8.**

The artichoke is, after all, an extremely civilized thistle with a very gastronomic beginning.

— *André Launay*

# Artichoke Apprehension

Are you intimidated when presented with a whole cooked artichoke? If so, you're not alone. Here's the way to handle it: Break off the leaves one by one, starting with the outer layer. Draw the base of the leaf through your front teeth to remove the soft portion. Discard the leaf on the side of your plate and go on to the next leaf. The edible part of the leaves may be dipped into melted butter or other sauce before eating. Once all the leaves have been removed, the inedible prickly "choke" should be carefully cut or scraped away and discarded. What's left is the tender artichoke heart and meaty bottom. M-m-m-m, heaven awaits!

After all the trouble you go to, you get about as much actual "food" out of eating an artichoke as you would from licking 30 or 40 postage stamps.

*– Miss Piggy*

*See also* VEGETABLES

# Asparagus

*One of the cultivated forms of the lily family, this extraordinarily popular vegetable comes in a variety of colors from creamy white to lush green to deep purple. Although the prime asparagus season is from February through June, hothouse versions are generally available year round. Dieters have long enjoyed the high-fiber asparagus in part because 94 percent of its weight is water.*

The three great stumbling blocks in a girl's education... *homard à l'Américaine*, a boiled egg, and asparagus.

*– Colette*

The Romans had a saying when they wanted something done quickly. "Do it," they said, "in less time than it takes to cook asparagus."

*– Alexandre Dumas*

## Asparagus Ardor

In the nineteenth century it was traditional to serve three courses of asparagus—thought to be a powerful aphrodisiac—to a French groom the night before the wedding. The modern Frenchman has discarded the noble asparagus for the more romantic passion prompter—champagne.

The air pulses with the warm smell of lilac, but as we pass each door, the lilac dominance is subdued by heady wafts of asparagus cooking.

*– Jane Grigson*

I stick to asparagus which still seems to inspire gentle thought.

*– Charles Lamb*

*See also* VEGETABLES

# Bacon

**Bringing home the bacon.** *In the United States, bacon is cured, smoked side pork (the pig's side). The ideal ratio of fat to lean is one half to two thirds. Bacon is sold in a variety of forms including:* **sliced bacon,** *which is trimmed of rind and sliced either thin (about 35 strips per pound) or thick (12 to 16 strips);* **slab bacon,** *which is usually sold unsliced with the rind, which should be removed before the bacon's sliced – dice and fry the rind and you have cracklings;* **Canadian bacon,** *which Canadians call "back bacon," is a lean, smoked meat from the loin and closer* to ham than American bacon; **canned bacon** needs no refrigeration because it's already cooked — a good choice for camping; **bacon bits** are preserved, dried, crispy pieces of bacon; **bacon-flavored bits** aren't really bacon at all but rather preformed bits of vegetable protein.

I've long said that if I were about to be executed and were given a choice of my last meal, it would be bacon and eggs. . . . Nothing is quite as intoxicating as the smell of bacon frying in the morning, save perhaps the smell of coffee brewing.

— *James Beard*

# Peppered Caramel Bacon

Sugar and spice makes everything nice—even bacon, which becomes ultracrispy with a thin coating of caramelized sugar. Perfect for special-occasion brunches.

1 pound thick-sliced, lean smoked bacon
3 tablespoons sugar
1 teaspoon ground allspice
1 teaspoon coarsely ground or cracked black pepper
2 tablespoons water

In a large skillet over medium heat, fry bacon until very crisp. Cook in two or three batches (depending on size of pan), pouring off excess fat as necessary. Drain cooked bacon on two layers of paper towel. In a small bowl, combine remaining ingredients. Drain skillet of all fat; return crisped bacon to pan. Drizzle sugar-spice mixture over bacon, tossing to coat. Cook over medium-high heat for 3 minutes, tossing often. Turn out onto a waxed-paper–lined baking sheet, separating pieces with two forks. Keep warm in a 250°F oven until ready to serve. **Serves 4 to 6.**

I myself know few Jews of my generation who, were it not for the taboo on cholesterol, wouldn't happily and guiltlessly dine daily on prosciutto and Canadian bacon.

— *Francine Prose*

*See also* HAM; PORK

# Bagels

*According to Leo Rosten's* The Joys of Yiddish, *bagels were first mentioned in print in Poland's 1610 Community Regulations of Cracow (Kraków). The document declared that bagels could be given as gifts only to women in childbirth, their midwives, and any women present during birthing. The reasoning behind such an odd edict? Why, everyone knew that bagels had mystical powers to ward off evil spirits and that therefore the gift of bagels must be reserved for life's most monumental moments. There are varying opinions as to the derivation of the word itself, with some experts claiming that it's from the Yiddish* beygl, *from the Middle High German* böugel, *which in turn is a diminutive of* bouc *(bracelet or ring). Other scholars declare the word "bagel" comes from the German* Beugel, *meaning "stirrup." Word origins aside, what's true today is that the bagel business is booming, with Americans annually consuming almost six million of these ring-shaped breads in renditions from sourdough to chocolate to cranberry. Bagel aficionados will tell you that the only true bagel is the water (eggless) bagel, which has the classic, chewy texture so beloved by purists (among which I count myself).*

The bagel is a lonely roll to eat all by yourself because in order for the true taste to come out you need your family. One to cut the bagels, one to toast them, one to put on the cream cheese and the lox, one to put them on the table and one to supervise.

— *Gertrude Berg*

The bagel, an unsweetened doughnut with rigor mortis . . .
— *Beatrice and Ira Freeman*

# Sesame Schmear

The word "schmear" is both a noun and a verb, and in this case, we're going to schmear *(spread)* our bagels with a sesame schmear (a dab of something to spread over a roll, bagel, etc.). Schmears are available in delis and supermarkets. They are flavored in myriad ways—with roasted garlic, sautéed onions, minced fruit . . . you name it. To toast the sesame seeds for this schmear, put them in an ungreased skillet and cook over medium-high heat, stirring often, until they're nicely browned. Cool the seeds, then grind them in a food processor or blender. Save on calories by using low-fat cream cheese—please, no nonfat cream cheese, which in this writer's humble opinion is more appropriate for a caulking agent than for eating.

1 (8-ounce) package cream cheese, softened
½ cup toasted sesame seeds, coarsely ground
1 to 2 tablespoons honey
salt (optional)

In a medium bowl, combine all ingredients, salting to taste. Use to "schmear" over toasted bagels.

A proper bagel is tough, firm, slightly doughy and should lie on your stomach for at least five hours after it has been consumed.

— *Mimi Sheraton*

Eating bagels leaves a hole in your pocket.

*– Yiddish proverb*

*See also* BREAD

# Barbecue

*Did you know that the word "buccaneer" – with its dashing Errol Flynn-like image – comes from the French boucanier, the base of which is boucaner ("to cure meat")? The word comes from Hispaniola and Tortuga island residents cooking and smoking their game in a wooden "barbecue" frame known as a boucan. So, it turns out these symbols of piratical romance – these buccaneers – were actually the original barbecuers until, that is, one of them decided that piracy made a lot more economic sense!*

[Barbecue is] a sort of savage rite, in fact, which consists of placing bloody portions of cattle on an open fire until they are charred beyond recognition and then smearing them with sauces that are not merely an abomination but a punishment.

*– Stanley Ellin*

To barbecue is a way of life rather than a desirable method of cooking.

*– Clement Freud*

There is no such thing as a bad barbecue place in Memphis. Some are just more equal than others.

*– Bruce Haney*

The story of barbecue is the story of America: Settlers arrive on great unspoiled continent, discover wondrous riches, set them on fire and eat them.

*– Vince Staten*

Barbecue is 99 percent perspiration and 1 percent sauce.

*– Vince Staten*

*See also* GRILLING

# Beans (and other legumes)

*Beans are among the oldest foods known to humanity, dating back at least four thousand years. Throughout the ages, people have used them for everything from ballots to warding off spirits to bringing luck. Famed trumpeter Louis Armstrong loved beans so much that he signed his letters with their praise. Others, however, felt differently about the venerable legume, as noted in some of the following quotes.*

> Beans, beans, the musical fruit
> The more you eat, the more you toot
> The more you toot, the better you feel
> So eat some beans at every meal!
> *— Martin and Sally Stone*

Red beans and ricely yours.
*— Louis Armstrong* (his sign-off on personal letters)

Boston runs to brains as well as to beans and brown bread.
*— William Cowper Brann*

We may not know beans, old bean, about this or that, and however much we may apply the old bean to a given notion, the notion itself may not amount to a hill of beans, although in our enthusiastic endorsement of our view we may be said to be full of beans . . . the less imaginative among us merely count beans, whether or not we're string-bean slender or skinny as bean poles.

*— Jay Jacobs*

# Toot Sweet

As the previous poem so aptly states, beans can be a problem for some people . . . in fact, for *most* people. The gas-producing troublemakers in dried beans are oligosaccharides—complex sugars that, because they're indigestible by normal stomach enzymes, proceed into the lower intestine, where they're fermented by friendly bacteria, a process that produces—you got it—*gas*.

There are ways to diminish this problem, but it takes a little extra effort. First of all, cover dried beans with water and bring to a boil. Pour off water and cover with at least 3 inches of fresh cold water. *(To quick-soak the beans, leave the boiling water on the beans for 3 hours, pouring off the old and replacing with new boiling water twice.)* Let beans soak about 6 hours, changing water twice during that time to help leach out those mischievous gas-generating sugars. You can further reduce the risk of flatulence by draining off the cooking liquid when the beans are halfway done and replacing it with fresh boiling water or other liquid.

Inhabitants of underdeveloped nations and victims of natural disasters are the only people who have ever been happy to see soybeans.

— *Fran Lebowitz*

Now hopping-john was [her] very favorite food. She had always warned them to wave a plate of rice and peas before her nose when she was in her coffin, to make certain there was no mistake; for if a breath of life was left in her, she would sit up and eat, but if she smelled the hopping-john, and did not stir, then they could just nail down the coffin and be certain she was truly dead.

— *Carson McCullers*

## Just What the Heck Is Hoppin' (Hopping) John, Anyway?

Hoppin' John is a dish of black-eyed peas (also called "cow-peas") and rice seasoned with spices, herbs, and a ham hock or salt pork. It's said to have originated with African slaves on southern plantations, and legend promises a year full of good luck for those who eat hoppin' John on New Year's Day.

If rationality were the criterion for things being allowed to exist, the world would be one gigantic field of soya beans!

— *Tom Stoppard*

All black-eyed peas are soulful . . .

— *Marvalene Styles*

# Beef

*You say you have a buff guy who's been beefing up to look good for a beefcake calendar . . . so what's your beef?!*

Beef is the soul of cooking.

— *Marie-Antoine Carême*

"Roast Beef, Medium" is not only a food. It is a philosophy . . . safe and sane, and sure.

— *Edna Ferber*

Veal is the quintessential Lonely Guy meat. There's something pale and lonely about it, especially if it doesn't have any veins. It's so wan and Kierkegaardian. You just know it's not going to hurt you.

— *Bruce Jay Friedman*

There are times when born hollandaise heads, as well as nouveaux turbot freaks and *recherché* escargotphiles alike, crave the *saignant* abundance of a New York steak.

*– Gael Greene*

Levin wanted friendship and got friendliness; he wanted steak and they offered Spam.

*– Bernard Malamud*

. . . I am a great eater of beef, and I believe that does harm to my wit.

*– William Shakespeare*

Steak tartare . . . not only one of the glories of great eating, but a possible cure-all for lethargy, obesity, hangovers and maybe even sexual impotence.

*– James Villas*

Being American is to eat a lot of beef steak, and boy, we've got a lot more beef steak than any other country, and that's why you ought to be glad you're an American. And people have started looking at these big hunks of bloody meat on their plates, you know, and wondering what on earth they think they're doing.

*– Kurt Vonnegut Jr.*

*See also* HAMBURGERS; MEAT

# Beer

*Around the world there are thousands of different types of beers, ranging in alcohol content from less than 2 percent (low-alcohol beer) to over 9 percent. The term "light beer" refers to a reduced-calorie brew made in the United States; in Europe it is used to distinguish between pale and dark lagers. Among the myriad beer varieties available today are:*

ALE: A light to dark amber-colored, malt-and-hops–based brew with a slightly bitter flavor

BOCK: A dark, slightly sweet, full-bodied German beer

FRUIT BEER: Mild ales flavored with fruit concentrates

LAGER: A golden, crystal-clear, light-flavored brew that's America's favorite

MALT LIQUOR: A relatively high-alcohol beer (up to 9 percent)

PORTER: A dark brown, heavy, strongly flavored brew made with roasted malt

STOUT: A strong, dark beer that gets its bittersweet flavor from dark-roasted barley

WHEAT BEER: A pale-colored, subtly flavored brew made from malted wheat

It is a known fact that beer drinkers will eat pretty much anything; Exhibit A is "Slim Jims." You could put a dish of salted mothballs in front of beer drinkers, and they would snork them up.

– *Dave Barry*

Life's not all beer and skittles [fun and games]!

– *British proverb*

Most people hate the taste of beer—to begin with. It is, however, a prejudice that many people have been able to overcome.

– *Winston Churchill*

It is said that beer drinkers are slow, and a little stupid; that they have an ox-like placidity not quite favourable to any brilliant intellectual display. But there are times when this placidity is what the labouring brain most needs. After the agitation of too active thinking there is safety in a tankard of ale.

– *Philip G. Hamerton*

Teetotallers seem to die the same as others, so what's the use of knocking off the beer?

– *A. P. Herbert*

# Like It or Not, Age Counts!

Unlike wine, beer should not be aged, but consumed as fresh as possible. Store it in an upright position—laying it on its side exposes more of the liquid's surface to air, which can diminish its flavor. The ideal serving temperature for light (lager-style) beers is 45° to 50°F, while ales, porters, and stouts are best in the 50° to 60°F range.

Nothing ever tasted better than a cold beer on a beautiful afternoon with nothing to look forward to but more of the same.

*– Hugh Hood*

Ale, man, ale's the stuff to drink
For fellows whom it hurts to think.

*– A. E. Housman*

She was . . . as beautiful as a tulip of beer with a high white collar.

*– A. J. Liebling*

Prohibition makes you
want to cry
into your beer and
denies you the beer
to cry into

*– Don Marquis*

What two ideas are more inseparable than beer and Britannia?

*– Sydney Smith*

You can't be a Real Country unless you have A BEER and an airline—it helps if you have some kind of a football team, or some nuclear weapons, but at the very least you need A BEER.

*– Frank Zappa*

*See also* BEVERAGES; BRANDY; CHAMPAGNE;
COCKTAILS; DRINKING; LIQUOR; PORT; TOASTS;
WINE

# Beets

*D*id *you know that the A*ustralians *and B*ritish *call this root veg-*
*etable "beetroot," rendered by some as* BEET-root, *a pronuncia-*
*tion that takes the A*merican *ear some getting used to.*

## Can't-Be-Beet Fudge Cake

1½ cups packed brown sugar
¾ cup butter, softened
1 tablespoon pure vanilla extract
½ teaspoon salt
5 ounces unsweetened chocolate, melted and cooled
4 large eggs
2 (15-ounce) cans water-packed beets, *thoroughly drained*
   and puréed
2 cups all-purpose flour
2½ teaspoons baking soda
6 ounces semisweet chocolate, finely chopped
⅓ cup heavy whipping cream
3 tablespoons butter

Heat oven to 350°F; grease and flour a 12-cup Bundt or tube
pan. In a large mixing bowl, beat sugar, butter, vanilla, and salt

The beet is the most intense of vegetables. . . . Beets are deadly serious.

*– Tom Robbins*

*See also* VEGETABLES

until light and fluffy, about 3 minutes. With mixer running, slowly drizzle in melted and cooled unsweetened chocolate, beating until thoroughly combined. Add eggs, one at a time, beating well after each addition. Beat in puréed beets (don't worry if mixture looks curdled). Combine flour and baking soda; add to chocolate mixture, a third at a time, beating on low speed *just* until dry ingredients are incorporated. Turn into prepared pan; smooth surface. Bake 40 to 50 minutes, or until a toothpick inserted in the center comes out clean. Cool 10 minutes in pan. Use a thin knife to loosen cake from center tube, if necessary. Invert cake onto a rack; cool to room temperature.

In a small pan over low heat, combine semisweet chocolate, cream, and butter; cook until chocolate is *almost melted*. Remove from heat; stir until smooth. Or combine ingredients in a 2-cup glass measure; microwave at HIGH for 1 minute. Stir until smooth. Leave cake on rack; place over waxed paper. Drizzle warm glaze over top, allowing it to drip down the sides. Let glaze set before serving. **Serves 10 to 12.**

# Berries

*A berry is not simply a berry. For instance, the surface of a straw-berry is coated with an average of two hundred tiny seeds. On the other hand, a raspberry is composed of many connecting drupelets (individual fruit sections), each one containing a single seed. Cranberries and blueberries have many tiny seeds in the center of the fruit. Talk about berryations on a theme!*

## Berry Tips

🍓Before buying berries, check the bottom of the container for unripe, bruised, or moldy fruit; if it's a cardboard box, look for juice stains, which signal crushed or spoiled berries.

🍓To store, refrigerate berries in a single layer, lightly covered with a paper towel.

🍓Wash berries, quickly and gently, just before using. Some, like strawberries, are porous and can become waterlogged easily.

🍓To freeze berries: Wash and thoroughly blot dry, then arrange in a single layer on a jelly-roll pan and freeze until hard. Then transfer the frozen berries to a freezerproof plastic bag and freeze up to 9 months.

*See also* BLACKBERRIES; BLUEBERRIES; FRUIT; HOLIDAYS; RASPBERRIES; STRAWBERRIES

# Beverages

Nectar, *n.* A drink served at banquets of the Olympian deities. The secret of its preparation is lost, but the modern Kentuckians believe that they come pretty near to a knowledge of its chief ingredient.

*– Ambrose Bierce*

*See also* BEER; BRANDY; CHAMPAGNE; COCKTAILS; COFFEE; DRINKING; LIQUOR; MILK; PORT; TEA; TOASTS; WATER; WINE

# Blackberries

*In some parts of America, blackberries are called "bramble-berries" because they grow on thorny (bramble) bushes.*

Oh, blackberry tart, with berries as big as your thumb, purple and black, and thick with juice, and a crust to endear them that will go to cream in your mouth, and both passing down with such a taste that will make you close your eyes and wish you might live forever in the wideness of that rich moment.

– *Richard Llewellyn*

*See also* BERRIES

# Blueberries

*The first written record of the native North American blueberry appears to have been made by Captain James Cook in the late eighteenth century. Indians used these silver-frosted indigo berries in savory dishes like stews, as well as in curing meat. They also sun-dried blueberries, a form that was popular with settlers.*

Blueberries as big as the end of your thumb,
Real sky-blue, and heavy, and ready to drum
In the cavernous pail of the first one to come!
All ripe together, none of them green
And some of them ripe! You ought to have seen!

– *Robert Frost*

*See also* BERRIES

## Maple-Kissed Blueberries

These maple-drizzled berries are great for breakfast—alone
or over pancakes or waffles—and make a lovely light dessert
for a summer meal.

3 cups fresh blueberries (about 1½ pints)
2 to 3 tablespoons pure maple syrup
1 tablespoon finely grated orange zest
pinch of freshly grated nutmeg
heavy whipping cream (optional)

In a medium bowl, combine blueberries, maple syrup, orange
zest, and nutmeg. Cover and refrigerate until ready to use, up
to 24 hours. Remove berries from refrigerator 30 minutes before serving. Drizzle with cream, if desired. **Serves 4.**

# Brandy

*Did you know that all cognacs are brandies, but not all brandies are
cognac? Brandy is a liquor distilled from wine and aged in wood,
which gives it flavor and color. The name "brandy" comes from the
Dutch brandewijin, meaning "burned (distilled) wine." The finest
of all brandies is cognac, which hails from in and around the town
of Cognac in western France. Cognac is double-distilled immediately after fermentation, then aged a minimum of three years in prized
Limousin oak.*

Brandy, *n.* A cordial composed of one part thunder-and-
lightning, one part remorse, two parts bloody murder, one
part death-hell-and-the-grave and four parts clarified Satan.

*– Ambrose Bierce*

For a treat you could drink two or three glasses of a nice little spiced brandy . . . better than champagne. After the first glass, your whole soul is enveloped by a fragrance, such a mirage, and you imagine that you aren't sitting at home in an armchair, but somewhere in Australia, on some sort of softest possible ostrich. . . .

*— Anton Chekhov*

Nothing sets a person up more than having something turn out just the way it's supposed to be, like falling into a Swiss snowdrift and seeing a big dog come up with a little cask of brandy round its neck.

*— Claud Cockburn*

Cognac . . . a sense of amusement, charm, excitement, all combined into the purest of pleasure.

*— Roy Andries de Groot*

Claret is the liquor for boys; port for men; but he who aspires to be a hero must drink brandy.

*— Samuel Johnson*

A mixture of brandy and water spoils two good things.

*— Charles Lamb*

Hell is full of musical amateurs: music is the brandy of the damned.

*— George Bernard Shaw*

Brandy, like man, should gain rather than lose in character with age, but its birth and upbringing determine its characteristics.

*— André Simon*

*See also* BEER; BEVERAGES; CHAMPAGNE;
COCKTAILS; DRINKING; LIQUOR; PORT;
TOASTS; WINE

# Bread

*Although man does not live by bread alone, this grainful suste-*
*nance has been a staple since prehistoric times. There are two ba-*
*sic types of bread — yeast and quick.* **Yeast breads** *are leavened*
*by — you guessed it — yeast. The doughs must be kneaded in order*
*to stretch the flour's gluten, which in turn creates the framework*
*that holds the yeast-produced gas that raises the dough. Batter*
*breads, which have a texture more like a heavy batter than a*
*dough, are yeast breads that are beaten vigorously rather than*
*kneaded.* **Quick breads** *are leavened with baking powder, bak-*
*ing soda, or eggs, and are quick to make because they require no*
*leavening. Then there's* **unleavened bread,** *such as matzo,*
*that is quite flat simply because it uses no leavening.*

After some dazzling flops, I assumed that breadmaking required a special talent, like limbo dancing, and I abandoned
the whole idea.

*— Peg Bracken*

Without bread all is misery.

*— William Cobbett*

She was so wild that when she made French toast she got
her tongue caught in the toaster.

*— Rodney Dangerfield*

Bread always falls on its buttered side.

*— English proverb*

The smell of good bread baking, like the sound of lightly
flowing water, is indescribable in its evocation of innocence
and delight.

*— M. F. K. Fisher*

# Devil Bread

Did you know that pumpernickel bread gets its name from the obsolete German word *pumper* (or breaking wind) plus the German *Nickel* (demon or goblin)? Knowing that, don't be surprised if a vision of a devil full of beans comes to mind the next time you eat pumpernickel!

The smell of buttered toast simply talked to Toad, and with no uncertain voice; talked of warm kitchens, of breakfasts on bright frosty mornings, of cosy parlour firesides on winter evenings. . . .

*– Kenneth Grahame*

Bread cast upon the water comes back eclairs.

*– Bert Greene*

Proust had his madeleines; I am devastated by the scent of yeast bread rising.

*– Bert Greene*

Bread, milk and butter are of venerable antiquity. They taste of the morning of the world.

*– Leigh Hunt*

Here with a Loaf of Bread beneath the Bough,
A Flask of Wine, a Book of Verse — and Thou
Beside me singing in the Wilderness —
And Wilderness is Paradise enow.

*– Omar Khayyám*

It requires a certain kind of mind to see beauty in a hamburger bun.

*– Ray Kroc*

Bread that must be sliced with an axe is bread that is too nourishing.

*– Fran Lebowitz*

Do you know on this one block you can buy croissants in five different places? There's one store called Bonjour Croissant. It makes me want to go to Paris and open a store called Hello Toast.

*– Fran Lebowitz*

Blues is to jazz what yeast is to bread—without it, it's flat.

*– Carmen McRae*

Bread is like dresses, hats and shoes—in other words, essential!

*– Emily Post*

Go pound some [bread] dough in your kitchen after work, and find out what tasty therapy it can be.

*– Wolfgang Puck*

Bread, Wine and Oil, that blessed trinity of the kindly fruits of the earth, have been, since Biblical times, the symbol of peace—and plenty, the reward promised by angels in heaven to men of goodwill upon earth.

*– André Simon*

What hymns are sung and praises said
For the home-made miracle of bread?

*– Louis Untermeyer*

*See also* BAGELS; MUFFINS; PANCAKES; PASTRY

# Breakfast

*Breakfasts around the world differ greatly. In the United States, for example, traditional fare might include cold or hot cereal, fruit, juice, pancakes, waffles, eggs, bacon or ham, and sundry bread* products ranging from muffins to coffee cake to bagels. That's not discounting in any way, however, more eclectic American tastes that run from leftover pizza to rice and beans, both honorable starts to any day. In other countries, the first meal of the day is decidedly different. For instance, Scandinavians favor herring or other fish, cheese, and hearty wholegrain breads. The Chinese are happiest with dim sum or a bowl of noodles, while the Japanese prefer grilled fish, salads, and, of course, the omnipresent rice. The standard in Britain is a huge breakfast of porridge, eggs, sausage, kippered herring, bread, and pots of jam, and Parisians are quite content with the simplicity of café au lait and a crisp croissant. But whether you prefer starting the day with a bowl of granola or, like Irena Chalmers, you fancy the occasional wedge of chocolate cake, breakfast is an intensely personal experience, which — depending on mood and personal taste — may be expanded or diminished by the company of others.

"There's no use trying," she said: "one can't believe impossible things."

"I daresay you haven't had much practice," said the Queen. "When I was your age, I always did it for half-an-hour a day. Why, sometimes I've believed as many as six impossible things before breakfast."

— *Lewis Carroll*

Chocolate cake, I find, is a splendid alternative to bran flakes, first thing in the morning. So is a bowl of cold spaghetti with a scattering of Parmesan cheese—slips down nicely and can be carried around while you dress.

— *Irena Chalmers*

My wife and I tried to breakfast together, but we had to stop or our marriage would have been wrecked.

— *Winston Churchill*

Once a woman has forgiven her man, she must not reheat his sins for breakfast.

*— Marlene Dietrich*

It was impossible for their joint imaginations to conjure up a world where anyone might object to anyone else having champagne for breakfast.

*— F. Scott Fitzgerald*

Breakfast is a notoriously difficult meal to serve with a flourish.

*— Clement Freud*

It takes some skill to spoil a breakfast—even the English can't do it.

*— John Kenneth Galbraith*

All happiness depends on a leisurely breakfast.

*— John Gunther*

The critical period in matrimony is breakfast-time.

*— A. P. Herbert*

A face on him as long as a late breakfast.

*— James Joyce*

He gave her a look you could have poured on a waffle.

*— Ring Lardner*

A simple enough pleasure, surely, to have breakfast alone with one's husband, but how seldom married people in the midst of life achieve it.

*— Anne Morrow Lindbergh*

The problem with marriage is that it ends every night after making love, and it must be rebuilt every morning before breakfast.

*— Gabriel García Márquez*

To eat well in England you should have breakfast three times a day.

— *W. Somerset Maugham*

There is a vast difference between the savage and the civilised man, but it is never apparent to their wives until after breakfast.

— *Helen Rowland*

I suppose the fact is that no friendship can stand the breakfast test. . . . Who can begin conventional amiability the first thing in the morning? It is the hour of savage instincts and natural tendencies; it is the triumph of the Disagreeable and the Cross. I am convinced that the Muses and the Graces never thought of having breakfast anywhere but in bed.

— *Elizabeth Russell*

Breakfast, an essentially unsociable meal, is an appropriate time to choose for disinheriting one's natural heirs.

— *P. Morton Shand*

I think breakfast so pleasant because no-one is conceited before one o'clock.

— *Sydney Smith*

Only dull people are brilliant at breakfast.

— *Oscar Wilde*

*See also* DINNER; PICNICS

# Lacy Corncakes

The extremely thin batter gives these pancakes their crispy, lacy edges, the maple syrup their evocative fragrance. Keep the finished corncakes warm in a 250°F oven while griddling the remaining batter. Or do as I do and bring an electric skillet to the table (with extension-cord assistance) and cook your cakes to order.

 2 large eggs, room temperature
 1½ teaspoons pure vanilla extract
 ½ teaspoon salt
 1⅔ cup milk
 ⅓ cup pure maple syrup
 6 tablespoons (¾ stick) unsalted butter, melted
 1 cup fine yellow cornmeal
 ½ teaspoon freshly grated nutmeg
 about 1 cup fresh blueberries or Maple-Kissed
     Blueberries, page 30 (optional)

In a large bowl, whisk eggs, vanilla, and salt until light. Gradually whisk in remaining ingredients (except blueberries) until batter is smooth. Heat a *very* lightly greased griddle or heavy skillet over medium-high heat. Pour a scant ¼ cup (about 3 tablespoons) batter onto griddle for each cake. Cook until bottom of cake is golden brown and top is set. Gently flip pancake and brown other side. Serve hot, topped with a few fresh blueberries and maple syrup (if desired). **Makes about 12 (5-inch) pancakes.**

NOTE: Batter will thicken as it sits. Stir well before making each batch of cakes, adding more milk if it becomes too thick.

# Broccoflower

**What the heck is a Broccoflower?** *It's a broccoli-cauliflower cross that looks like a light green cauliflower; it has a milder flavor than either of its parents. It also packs a nutritional punch with over 120 percent of the recommended daily allowance of vitamin C. This appealing vegetable originated in Holland, but the name "Broccoflower" is trademarked by Tanimura and Antle, a California company.*

*See also* BROCCOLI; VEGETABLES

# Broccoli

*This emerald-green beauty is the most popular member of the cruciferous (krew-SIH-fer-uhs) vegetable family (which also includes Brussels sprouts, cabbage, cauliflower, chard, kale, mustard greens, rutabagas, and turnips), which are known for their protection against certain cancers. These vegetables contain antioxidants (beta-carotene and the compound sulforaphane), and are high in fiber, vitamins, and minerals. Bottom line? No matter what past presidents like, broccoli is good for us!*

I do not like broccoli, and I haven't liked it since I was a little kid and my mother made me eat it. And I'm President of the United States, and I'm not going to eat any more broccoli.

— *George Bush*

Broccoli is one of the most amazing pharmaceutical packages in nature's food pharmacy.

— *Jean Carper*

## There's Nothing Like Excess

Unlike President Bush, myriad folks have been wild about broccoli since the vegetable was first discovered. For instance, the Roman emperor Tiberius's son, Drusus Caesar, so loved broccoli that he ate little else for more than a month and only stopped when his urine turned green.

If fresh broccoli is not cooked properly, then it becomes a big ugly thing, and I don't think any little kiddie or any big President would like it.

*– Julia Child*

## Talk About Ugly!

Julia's right—broccoli *can* become ugly, particularly when cooked with an acidic ingredient like lemon juice or vinegar, which turns it an unappetizing gray-green color. Also, the quicker you cook broccoli, the greener it will stay. One pound of fresh broccoli = 2 cups chopped; 1 (10-ounce) package frozen broccoli = about 1½ cups chopped.

Never, never trust a woman who would turn a perfectly respectable vegetable like broccoli into a *casserole* with cheese!

*– Minna Cohn*

When you eat broccoli, you're eating flower buds, a fact that always puts me in mind of the lotus-eaters, rather an exotic association for a good, wholesome, plain-and-simple vegetable.

*– Maggie Waldron*

*See also* VEGETABLES

# Butchers

*If you happen to shop at a market with a real, live, smiling butcher behind the counter, consider yourself lucky. A good butcher can make your life infinitely easier in all kinds of ways. He or she can suggest what cuts to buy, answer questions on how to cook them, personalize your meat cuts by boning them or cutting pockets into roasts or thick chops, and that's just a start. Unfortunately, most markets today have nary a butcher in sight. What they do have are rows and rows of shrink-wrapped cellophane packages of meat — all the better to confuse you, my dear. Oh, sure, the labels on all those packages are multiinformational, telling you what kind of meat you're buying, weight, price, fat content, and last date on which it should be purchased. But they sure as heck can't bone a roast or smile at you, can they?*

As he chops, cuts, slices, trims, shapes, or threads through the string, a butcher is as good a sight to watch as a dancer or a mime.

*— Colette*

To see the butcher slap the steak before he laid it on the block . . . to see him cut it off so smooth and juicy . . . it was a piece of art, high art; there was a delicacy of touch, clearness of tone, skilful handling of the subject, fine shading. It was the triumph of mind over matter; quite.

*— Charles Dickens*

# Butter

*It used to be that butter was butter, but all things change. The fact that markets now carry several types of butter can make things confusing, so here's a brief rundown.* **Unsalted butter** *(which means just what it says) is sometimes labeled "sweet butter" or "sweet cream butter," a misnomer because any butter made with sweet (as opposed to sour) cream is sweet butter. So know that* commercial **sweet cream butter** *contains salt.* **Whipped butter** *has had air beaten into it to increase its volume and create a soft, spreadable texture.* **Light** *or* **reduced-calorie butter** *contains water, skim milk, and gelatin, which results in about half the fat of regular butter. Never substitute reduced-fat butters for regular butter in frying and baking.*

I still like dishes made with cream and butter. I shouldn't have them, and I'm told it's unhealthy, but *tant pis* [never mind]!

– *Simone Beck*

Some folk want their luck buttered.

– *Thomas Hardy*

## Homemade Butter

The food processor makes homemade butter a snap! The liquid left over from making the butter can be used in soups and sauces or to make pastries.

2 cups cold heavy whipping cream (preferably
    unpasteurized)
1/4 teaspoon salt (optional)

Chill food processor bowl and metal chopping blade in freezer for 15 minutes. Pour cream into work bowl; add salt, if desired. Process 2 minutes; scrape down sides of bowl. Continue to process until solids separate from liquid, 3 to 5 minutes. Remove butter from work bowl, squeezing with your hands to remove excess liquid. Or place butter in a fine strainer and press with a rubber spatula to extract liquid. Spoon or pipe butter into a small bowl. Cover and refrigerate butter and liquid. Let butter stand at room temperature 30 minutes before serving. **Makes about 6 ounces butter; 1 cup liquid.**

She looked as though butter wouldn't melt in her mouth —
or anywhere else.
                                        *— Elsa Lanchester*

Many of us hope wanly for the day when butter, cream,
and cheese will be discovered to be better for us than their
pale and ascetic low-fat equivalents.
                                        *— Francine Prose*

Love is like butter, it's good with bread.
                                        *— Yiddish proverb*

*See also* MARGARINE

## Compound (Flavored) Butters

Compound butter (known in France as *beurre composé*) is
simply softened or melted butter combined with various flavorings. It's delicious as a spread for baked goods like
breads, waffles, and pancakes or atop meats, fish, or vegetables (particularly baked potatoes). Melted compound butters
can be brushed over corn-on-the-cob, used for basting meat or
fish, or drizzled over pancakes and the like. Additions for savory compound butters include minced herbs, grated cheese,
garlic, seeds (such as sesame or anise), spices (like pepper,
chili powder, or cumin), wine, and tomato paste. Flavorings
for sweetened butters include honey, liqueur, jam, orange
juice, maple syrup, and spices like cinnamon and nutmeg.

**To make compound butter:** Soften the butter and blend or
beat in the flavoring ingredients. Add any liquid ingredient
very gradually, beating constantly; adding too much liquid too
soon causes the mixture to separate. For every 4 ounces (1
commercial stick) of butter, use 2 to 4 tablespoons seeds or
minced fresh herbs; up to ¼ cup honey, maple syrup, or jam; 1
tablespoon mustard or tomato paste; or ½ to ¾ cup grated
cheese, or 4 ounces blue cheese.

# Cabbage

*The word "cabbage" is a derivation of the French caboche, a colloquial term for "head." The denigrating term "cabbagehead" refers to someone who's not too bright. Those in the know question this nomenclature — the American Cancer Society tells us that cabbage is definitely smart eating because it (along with other cabbage-family relatives) protects against colon, lung, rectal, and stomach cancers. So, go ahead — be a cabbagehead — you'll most likely live longer than "fat" heads!*

Cabbage, *n.* A familiar kitchen-garden vegetable about as large and wise as a man's head.

*— Ambrose Bierce*

"The time has come," the Walrus said,
"To talk of many things:
Of shoes—and ships—and sealing wax—
Of cabbages—and kings—
And why the sea is boiling hot—
And whether pigs have wings."

*— Lewis Carroll*

Cabbage as a food has problems. . . . It can smell foul in the pot, linger through the house with pertinacity, and ruin a meal with its wet flab. Cabbage also has a nasty history of being good for you.

*— Jane Grigson*

Cabbages, whose heads, tightly folded, see and hear nothing of this world, dreaming only of the yellow and green magnificence that is hardening within them.

*— John Haines*

The English have only three vegetables—and two of them are cabbage.

*— Walter Page*

# Sweetening the Pot

So you love cabbage but hate the smell that lingers after cooking it? Well, according to Maggie Waldron in her book *Cold Spaghetti at Midnight*, "The amount of hydrogen sulfide [the stinky stuff] produced in boiled cabbage doubles in the fifth through seventh minutes of boiling. . . ." Which makes it obvious that cooking cabbage in under 5 minutes will do the trick. Note that the smaller the cabbage is cut, the less cooking time it will need. If you absolutely *must* subject cabbage to lengthy cooking, try sweetening the pot by tossing a couple of thick bread chunks (slices will dissolve) into the cooking water; use a slotted spoon to retrieve the bread after the cabbage is cooked.

On a related subject, you can reduce the flatulence that often plagues cabbage eaters by boiling the vegetable for 5 minutes, then draining off the water, and finish cooking the cabbage in fresh boiling water. Of course, this technique only works with whole or large pieces of cabbage—preparing shredded cabbage this way would overcook it.

In the night the cabbages catch at the moon, the leaves drip silver, the rows of cabbages are series of little silver waterfalls in the moon.

*– Carl Sandburg*

Shed a tear for the lowly cabbage. Even as vegetables go, it is particularly friendless. The Department of Agriculture collects data on everything from asparagus to zucchini—but it stopped bothering with cabbage back in 1982.

*– Judith Valente*

*See also* SAUERKRAUT; VEGETABLES

# Cake

*Anyone who thinks it's* a piece of cake *to* have one's cake and eat it too *certainly* takes the cake *for having a* cakes-and-ale attitude.

The most dangerous food a man can eat is wedding cake.

— *American proverb*

While an eon, as someone has observed, may be two people and a ham, a fruitcake is *forever.*

— *Russell Baker*

To dream of cake foretells advancement for the laborer and enhancement for the industrious. . . . Layer cake denotes satisfaction. . . . A fluffy rich icing on a cake predicts gaiety.

— *Ned Ballantyne and Stella Coeli*

For me, the cinema is not a slice of life, but a piece of cake.

— *Alfred Hitchcock*

For months they have lain in wait . . . and now they are upon us, sodden with alcohol, their massive bodies bulging with strange green protuberances, attacking us in our homes . . . at our offices—there is no escape, it is the hour of the fruitcake.

— *Deborah Papier*

I don't like candies of any kind. I like cakes: they don't conceal any secret.

— *Pascal Quignard*

> Oh, cakes and friends we should choose with care,
> Not always the fanciest cake that's there
> Is the best to eat! And the plainest friend
> Is sometimes the finest in the end!

— *Margaret E. Sangster*

*See also* DESSERTS; SWEETS

# Candy

*Would you believe that Egyptian hieroglyphics in ancient pyramids depicted candy? Not Snickers or gumdrops, mind you, but confections made of honey-sweetened dried fruits and nuts. We've come a long way, baby, from those comparatively wholesome sweets. Now Americans are annually consuming an average of twenty-three pounds a person, and candy manufacturers are racing to produce treats with less candy and fat so they'll consume more. Talk about the sweet life!*

The great thing about candy is that it has no redeeming social characteristics. Its only purpose is to please—to taste so sweet and so good that we simply have to go back for more.
— *Irena Chalmers*

He was as round and sane as a butterscotch kiss.
— *M. F. K. Fisher*

## Sweet Talk

EAR CANDY: Music that's easy on the ears
CANDY ASS: A weakling or wimp
CANDY STRIPER: A hospital volunteer, so named for the red-and-white–striped uniforms that were once the norm
ROCK CANDY: A hard candy that resembles a cluster of clear crystals. It's made by dipping a string or stick into a concentrated sugar syrup, then letting it dry over a period of days until the sugar hardens and forms crystals

Candy
Is dandy
But liquor
Is quicker.
— *Ogden Nash* (sometimes misattributed to Dorothy Parker)

You can tell a lot about a fellow's character by his way of eating jelly beans.
— *Ronald Reagan*

*See also* DESSERTS; SWEETS

# Almond Toffee

This delicious, easy toffee makes a great gift any time of year. But "timing" is *important*—rainy days can ruin candymaking if you don't compensate for the added humidity by cooking the mixture about two degrees higher than called for in recipes. Some candies—like divinity—should never be attempted on a rainy day. Unless, of course, you particularly enjoy becoming frustrated.

2⅓ cups sugar
½ cup water
1¼ cups unsalted butter
1 teaspoon salt
2½ cups chopped almonds
2 teaspoons pure vanilla extract
½ teaspoon pure almond extract
8 ounces semisweet chocolate, melted

Generously butter a 10 × 15-inch jelly-roll pan; set aside. In a large, heavy saucepan, combine sugar, water, butter, and salt. Bring to a boil over medium heat. Continue to cook, stirring occasionally, until mixture reaches 300°F (hard-crack stage) on a candy thermometer. Remove from heat; stir in all but 1 cup of the almonds, then vanilla and almond extracts. Immediately pour toffee into prepared pan; quickly spread into even layer. Let stand in a cool place until toffee hardens. Spread melted chocolate over surface of cooled toffee; sprinkle with reserved almonds. Use the back of a spoon to lightly press almonds into surface of chocolate. Set aside in a cool place (may be refrigerated) until chocolate sets. Use a knife to break toffee into pieces. Store, tightly covered, in a cool place. **Makes about 3 pounds.**

# Carrots

*In the following quote, Will Rogers was definitely right about carrots on one count — they're extremely high in vitamin A! And now scientists have discovered that carrots contain calcium pectate, an extraordinary pectin fiber that has been found to have cholesterol-lowering properties. So hop on over to your market's produce section and load up on Bugs's favorite vegetable!*

These tasty roots [carrots] in a dream prophesy an unexpected legacy or money windfall.

— The Dreamer's Dictionary

No matter what time of day the carrot is picked, the temperature will be the same: warm at the skin from its earthly bed but chill as the night wind at the heart, a taste sensation unequaled by any other fresh-dug thing in the universe. . . .

— Bert Greene

## Carrot Common Sense

Fresh carrots will keep a long time in the refrigerator—2 to 3 weeks if stored in a plastic bag. If they become limp, you can revive them by covering them with iced water for about 30 minutes. Some of the carrot's flavor and nutrients are removed with the peel, so, if possible, simply give carrots a good washing and use them *au naturel.* One pound of carrots = 3 cups chopped or sliced, or about 2½ cups shredded.

Large naked raw carrots are acceptable as food only to those who lie in hutches eagerly awaiting Easter.

— Fran Lebowitz

Some guy invented Vitamin A out of a carrot. I'll bet he can't invent a good meal out of one.

— *Will Rogers*

*See also* VEGETABLES

# Catfish

If I go down for anything in history, I would like to be known as the person who convinced the American people that catfish is one of the finest eating fishes in the world.

— *Willard Scott*

*See also* FISH

# Cauliflower

Cauliflower is nothing but cabbage with a college education.

— *Mark Twain*

*See also* VEGETABLES

# Caviar

*For many people, caviar is the ultimate indulgence, while for others it's nothing but a mouthful of fish eggs. If you're a neophyte at the caviar game and haven't made up your mind yet, the terms on the next page should help you out.*

Caviar is to dining what a sable coat is to a girl in evening dress.

— *Ludwig Bemelmans*

There is more simplicity in the man who eats caviar on impulse than in the man who eats Grapenuts on principle.

— *G. K. Chesterton*

# A Caviar Primer

BELUGA: The best and costliest, from the Caspian and Black seas' beluga sturgeon, which produce soft, extremely large (the size of small peas) eggs

OSETRA AND SEVRUGA: From smaller sturgeon that produce medium-size to small eggs; prized second only to beluga

STERLET: Small, golden eggs that are so rare they were once reserved for Russian czars, Iranian shahs, and Austrian emperors

WHITEFISH (also called AMERICAN GOLDEN): Small yellow-gold eggs from the Great Lakes

SALMON (or RED): Medium-size eggs that can range in color from pale orange to deep red, primarily from Alaska

LUMPFISH: Tiny, hard black eggs

MALOSSOL: Not a *type* of caviar, but a designation for roe that has been preserved with a minimum amount of salt

PASTEURIZED CAVIAR: Roe that's been partially cooked, which slightly changes the texture of the eggs and makes them less perishable

PRESSED CAVIAR: Damaged or fragile eggs that are treated, salted, and pressed. The result is a thick, concentrated caviar conserve—extremely rich and delicious

NOTE: Although only a spoonful of caviar supplies the adult daily requirement of vitamin B-12, it's also high in cholesterol and loaded with sodium.

When I was young and poor, my favorite dish was caviar accompanied by a half bottle of Bollinger. But repetition destroys any pleasure, gastronomic or sexual. . . .

*— A. J. Cronin*

No food's name or presence breathes the extravagant life in quite the same way as caviar.

*– Barbara Kafka*

The play, I remember, pleased not the million; 'twas caviare to the general.

*– William Shakespeare*

The cream and hot butter mingled and overflowed separating each glaucose bead of caviar from its fellows, capping it in white and gold.

*– Evelyn Waugh*

*See also* FISH

# Champagne

*True champagne comes only from France's Champagne region, just ninety miles northeast of Paris. Most countries bow to this tradition by calling their bubbling wines by other names, including spumante in Italy, Sekt in Germany, and vins mousseux in other regions of France, or by simply using the term "sparkling wine." Although it's legal to use the term "champagne" in the United States, most top-quality producers simply label their sparkling wines* méthode champenoise, *indicating that the wine was made by the French method. Seventeenth-century Abbey of Hautvillers cellarmaster Dom Pérignon is credited both for developing the art of blending wines to create superior champagnes and for using thicker bottles and tie-down corks to help retain their explosive pressure.*

I drink [champagne] when I'm happy and when I'm sad. Sometimes I drink it when I'm alone. When I have company I consider it obligatory. I trifle with it if I'm not hungry and drink it when I am. Otherwise I never touch it—unless I'm thirsty.

*– Lily Bollinger*

Burgundy makes you think of silly things, Bordeaux makes you talk of them and Champagne makes you do them.

*— Jean-Anthelme Brillat-Savarin*

Champagne is exciting in its first effects and stupefying in its later ones, in other words it acts exactly like the carbonic acid gas it contains.

*— Jean-Anthelme Brillat-Savarin*

I like [champagne] because it always tastes as though my foot is asleep.

*— Art Buchwald*

Champagne with foaming whirls, as white as Cleopatra's pearls.

*— Lord Byron*

Even for those who dislike Champagne . . . there are two Champagnes one can't refuse: Dom Pérignon and the even superior Cristal, which is bottled in a natural-coloured glass that displays its pale blaze, a chilled fire of such prickly dryness that, swallowed, seems not to have been swallowed at all, but instead to have been turned to vapours on the tongue, and burned there to one sweet ash.

*— Truman Capote*

A single glass of champagne imparts a feeling of exhilaration. The nerves are braced; the imagination is stirred, the wits become more nimble. A bottle produces the contrary effect. Excess causes a comatose insensibility. So it is with war: and the quality of both is best discovered by sipping.

*— Winston Churchill*

## Champagne Terms

*In wine parlance, the term "dry" describes a wine that isn't sweet; its French counterpart is sec.*

BRUT: bone dry to almost dry—less than 1.5 percent sugar
EXTRA-SEC or EXTRA-DRY: slightly sweeter—1.2 to 2 percent sugar
SEC: medium sweet—1.7 to 3.5 sugar
DEMI-SEC: sweet—3.3 to 5 percent sugar
DOUX: very sweet—over 5 percent sugar

There comes a time in every woman's life when the only thing that helps is a glass of champagne.

*— Bette Davis (in the film Old Acquaintance)*

Champagne . . . takes its fitting rank and position [at a ball] amongst feathers, gauzes, lace, embroidery, ribbons, white satin shoes, and eau-de-Cologne, for champagne is simply one of the elegant extras of life.

*— Charles Dickens*

I was enjoying myself. . . . I had taken two finger-bowls of Champagne, and the scene had changed before my eyes into something significant, elemental, and profound.

*— F. Scott Fitzgerald*

Champagne, if you are seeking the truth, is better than a lie detector.

*— Graham Greene*

Champagne has the taste of an apple peeled with a steel knife.

*— Aldous Huxley*

What is the special quality of sparkling wine? Why does the very sight of its bulky bottle, the muffled pop of its cork coming out, act as the starting pistol for smiles and laughter?

*— Hugh Johnson*

# Champagne Savvy

Champagne and other sparkling wines should be served very cold, between 39° and 50°F. Since cold mutes flavor, inexpensive potables should be chilled to a lower temperature; vintage champagnes—with their complexity and delicate flavor balance—are better served between 45° and 50°F. Excess refrigeration can dull a wine's flavor and bouquet, so don't chill sparklers for much more than 2 hours before serving. You can speed-chill wine by submerging the bottle in a bucket filled with equal amounts of ice and cold water, which chills it faster than ice alone.

**Stop That Pop!** Contrary to what the movies portray, champagne shouldn't be uncorked with a loud bang, the cork flying across the room, the wine foaming out of the bottle. When that happens, you not only lose a lot of the effervescence, but some of the wine as well. Here's how to do it: After removing the foil, untwist and remove the wire cage enclosing the cork—cover the cork with your hand in case it pops prematurely (which rarely happens). Hold the bottle at a 45-degree angle (be sure it's not pointed at anyone) with the fingers of one hand over the cork; gently rotate the bottle (not the cork) with your other hand. As you feel the cork begin to loosen and lift, use your thumb to ease it gently from the bottle. The cork should release from the bottle with a muted *poof*, not a loud POP. Although properly opened champagne should never gush from the bottle, it's a good idea to have a glass standing by, just in case. Don't use the shallow "saucer" champagne glasses, which allow both effervescence and bouquet to escape twice as fast as the tall, slender *flutes*, with their small surface area that retains both bubbles and bouquet.

If the aunt of the vicar
Has never touched liquor
Look out when she finds the champagne.
— *Rudyard Kipling*

**I**f you're given champagne at lunch, there's a catch somewhere.

— *Lord Lyons*

**F**or some reason, you can't just pick up champagne and drink it — someone has to be very witty and give a toast.

— *Hugh Marlowe (in the film* All About Eve*)*

**O**h, come quickly, I am drinking stars!

— *Dom Pérignon*

**I** like to start off my day with a glass of champagne. I like to wind it up with champagne, too. To be frank, I also like a glass or two in between. It may not be the universal medicine . . . but it does you less harm than any other liquid.

— *Fernand Point*

**Y**ou can have too much champagne to drink, but you can never have enough.

— *Elmer Rice*

**C**hampagne is the wine-lover's luxury.

— *Jancis Robinson*

**T**he advantage of champagne consists not only in the exhilarating sparkle and play of its mantling life, where the beads that airily rise ever in pursuit of those that have merrily passed; but in the magnetism it possesses above all other wines — of tempting the fair sex to drink an extra glass.

— *St. Ange*

**I**'m only a beer teetotaler, not a champagne teetotaler.

— *George Bernard Shaw*

Champagne's funny stuff. I'm used to whiskey. Whiskey is a slap on the back, and champagne's a heavy mist before my eyes.
— *Jimmy Stewart (in the film* The Philadelphia Story*)*

He took a large tablet of beet sugar . . . and soaked it in Angostura Bitters and then rolled it in Cayenne pepper. This he put into a large glass which he filled up with champagne. . . . Each bubble as it rises to the surface carries with it a red grain of pepper, so that as one drinks one's appetite is at once stimulated and gratified, heat and cold, fire and liquid, contending on one's palate and alternating in the mastery of one's sensations. I sipped this almost unendurably desirable drink.
— *Evelyn Waugh*

Bubbles are the gracenotes of champagne.
— *Anonymous*

*See also* BEER; BEVERAGES; BRANDY; COCKTAILS; DRINKING; LIQUOR; PORT; TOASTS; WINE

## Chambord Royale

Chambord is a heady liqueur with an intense black raspberry flavor. Start with just a little—you can always add more.

1/4 to 1/2 teaspoon Chambord
4 ounces cold champagne or other sparkling wine
1 whole raspberry

Pour the liqueur into a flute glass; slowly add champagne. Do not stir. Drop raspberry into glass. **Serves 1.**

# Cheese

*The world is lucky indeed to be favored with thousands of cheeses. There are fresh (unripened) cheeses (like ricotta, cottage, and cream) and*

*ripened cheeses, which come in various textures from hard (Parmesan and pecorino) to semihard (cheddar and Edam) to semisoft (Monterey Jack, Gouda, and Tilset). And there are soft-ripened treasures (like Brie and Camembert), blue cheeses (Roquefort and Stilton), and pasta filata, "spun paste," specialties (mozzarella and provolone). But it's not often that you hear someone asking for some quark on their sandwich. What? Isn't a quark an elementary subatomic particle that goes into creating protons and neutrons? Well, yes, but quark is also a cheese, and unlike its scientific sister, which is enunciated QWORK, it's pronounced just as it looks — QWARK. This rich, soft cheese is unripened — like cream cheese — and has a flavor and texture akin to that of sour cream. Quark's thick, creamy texture makes it perfect for dips, salads, sauces, and the like, and it makes a great spread for bread (like bagels and sandwiches). Quark comes in both low-fat and nonfat versions, and, as with cream cheese, the low-fat rendition tastes better. Low-fat quark and low-fat sour cream have about 35 calories per ounce, but quark's texture is richer, its flavor milder. So the next time someone asks you if a quark is something with which you're familiar, tell them yes! And you particularly like it on baked potatoes.*

An apple pie without some cheese
Is like a kiss without a squeeze.

— *American proverb*

Cheese is probably the friendliest of foods. It endears itself to everything and never tires of showing off to great advantage.

— *James Beard*

The great Norman cheeses were served as well: Camembert, Pont-l'Evèque, and the stinky Livarot. But my father warned: "Not for Mademoiselle Simone, the strong cheeses." He thought young girls shouldn't be allowed to pollute their mouths with smelly odors.

— *Simone Beck*

Never try to eat the holes in Swiss Cheese.

*— Robert Campbell*

## Cheese Talk

BIG CHEESE: A person who's influential or important
CHEESY: Someone or something that's cheap or chintzy
CHEESED, CHEESED OFF: Upset or disgusted
CHEESE EATER: A rat (informer)
CHEESE HEAD: Green Bay Packers fan
CHEESE IT!: A warning to look out, usually because the cops are coming
HARD CHEESE: Tough luck; an unpleasant situation

Poets have been mysteriously silent on the subject of cheese.

*— G. K. Chesterton*

How can you be expected to govern a country [France] that has 246 kinds of cheese?

*— Charles de Gaulle*

Never commit yourself to a cheese without having first examined it.

*— T. S. Eliot*

A cheese may disappoint. It may be dull, it may be naive, it may be oversophisticated. Yet it remains cheese, milk's leap toward immortality.

*— Clifton Fadiman*

Age is not important unless you are a cheese.

*— Helen Hayes (in the play New Woman)*

Richard Nixon . . . committed unspeakable acts with cottage cheese.

*— Jay Jacobs*

Cheese that is compelled by law to append the word "food" to its title does not go well with red wine or fruit.

– *Fran Lebowitz*

# The "Fake" Factor

I agree completely with the witty Ms. Lebowitz—processed cheese should definitely not be paired with fine food and drink. The reason it bears little resemblance to the real thing is that United States government standards only require that 51 percent of a processed cheese's final weight need actually be cheese! And the word "food" appended means that liquid has been added to create a more spreadable mixture. No wonder the taste and texture seem so . . . well, so . . . fake!

# Hot Brie Velvet

Drizzle this fragrant sauce over crisp, chilled salad greens, warm vegetables, or grilled chicken. It's also a great warm dip for crudités.

⅓ cup chicken broth
2 tablespoons olive oil
2 tablespoons white wine vinegar
¼ cup minced leeks, white portion only
1 large clove garlic, minced
1½ teaspoons Dijon mustard
3 tablespoons heavy whipping cream, room temperature
8 ounces Brie, rind removed, cut into ½-inch chunks
    and softened
salt and white pepper

A bad accent is the cinematic equivalent of a festering Limburger cheese planted on a sumptuous dinner table, making it pointless for the gourmand to try thinking about anything other than that peculiar odor.

— *Joe Queenan*

It is a bit of a mystery why so many aspiring American hosts — gourmet and otherwise — came to think of mass quantities of cheese *before* dinner as an appropriate hors d'oeuvre; but cheese for dessert was strictly for the sophisticated set.

— *Jane and Michael Stern*

If you've ever tried to scour a sink with Parmesan cheese, you know the wisdom of reading labels first. . . .

— *Dereck Williamson*

In a small saucepan over high heat, combine chicken broth, oil, vinegar, leeks, garlic, and mustard; bring to a boil. Reduce heat to low; simmer for 10 minutes. Stir in cream; heat 1 minute. Stirring constantly, add 3 or 4 pieces of cheese at a time to simmering mixture. Stir until cheese is melted before adding more cheese. If sauce begins to bubble, remove from heat for a few seconds. Do not let boil. Remove from heat when cheese is melted. Pour hot mixture into a blender jar; cover securely. Beginning at LOW speed and gradually increasing to HIGH, process for 1 minute on HIGH. Salt and pepper to taste. If using within an hour, return sauce to pan and keep warm in a hot-water bath. Or cool to room temperature, cover, and refrigerate. Rewarm in a small saucepan over low heat. Or reheat in a 2-cup glass measuring cup by microwaving at MEDIUM (50 percent power) for about 2½ minutes, stirring halfway through. The microwave time depends on how cold the mixture is to begin with. **Makes about 1 cup.**

# Cherries

*Cherries, which date at least back to 300 B.C., were named after the Turkish town of Cerasus. There are two main types of this fruit — the larger sweet cherries, which range in color from the darkest purple-red to red-blushed gold, and the smaller sour cherries, which range from bright red to mahogany red. Among the more popular sour cherries are Early Richmond, Montmorency, and Morello. Favorite sweet-cherry varieties include Bing, Lambert, Tartarian, and Royal Ann.*

If Life Is a Bowl of Cherries, What Am I Doing in the Pits?
— *Erma Bombeck (book title)*

I have seen hogs devour cherries by the bucketful and not show discomfort, but then, I can't tell a discomforted hog grunt from a comfortable grunt.

— *Grace Firth*

## Cherrier Cherries

Believe it or not, almond extract makes cherries taste more like cherries in baked desserts like pies, cobblers, and cheesecakes. Add about $1/4$ teaspoon almond extract and experience the magic.

... shiny pink cherries full of juice under their transparent skins, the mysterious black morellos that smelled so much better than they tasted. ...

— *Bruno Schulz*

So we grew together,
Like to a double cherry, seeming parted,
But yet an union in partition;
Two lovely berries molded on one stem.
— *William Shakespeare*

One must ask children and birds how cherries and strawberries taste.

*— Johann Wolfgang von Goethe*

## Cherry Bomb

As hard as it is to believe, the luscious, red-blushed, golden
Royal Ann cherry is the variety that is most often used to make
those neon-red (and green) abominations that perch perkily
atop sundaes and tropical drinks—the ubiquitous maraschino
cherry, or, as my friend Kate calls it, the *cherry bomb*. The word
"maraschino" comes from the Italian *marasca*, a bitter wild
cherry used to make an Italian liqueur. Today's maraschino
cherries, however, which are macerated in a flavored sugar
syrup (almond for red cherries, mint for green) and then
brightly dyed, bear absolutely no resemblance to the original
liqueur. Oh, and one last little tidbit—if you've been pro-
nouncing the word mar-uh-SHEE-noh, don't. Why? Because
the Italian "sch" is pronounced *sk*, which makes the correct
enunciation mar-uh-SKEE-noh.

# Chicken

For many years, nobody ate chicken wings, and for good
reason: They are inedible. They are essentially meat-free
bones. You might as well chew on a plate of toenails. But one
day a shrewd restaurant owner came up with the idea of
serving the wings "Buffalo-style," which means "to people
who have been drinking beer."

*— Dave Barry*

We didn't starve, but we didn't eat chicken unless we were
sick, or the chicken was.

*— Bernard Malamud*

A good many things taste like chicken except, nowadays, chicken, which tastes like damp cardboard—a small price to pay for the triumph of having produced the battery-fed square-foot chicken reared on scientifically compounded foods which bring it to a weight of two pounds on four pounds of feed instead of yesterday's six and a half.

*— Waverley Root*

[Chicken] is a more important article of food, all the world over, than any other domesticated fowl, and its claim to being the best of them all rests upon the fact that, like bread, potatoes and rice, Chicken may be eaten constantly without becoming nauseating.

*— André Simon*

Of all indigenous American culinary triumphs, probably the most put-upon, misunderstood, and generally abused is the Southern fried chicken which in its pure state almost no one ever gets to eat. . . . Southern fried chicken can be sublime . . . [but it] is ruined in the home by inattentiveness, by insouciance, by the idea of—well, it's just a chicken to fry, I'll throw it in the pan. No attitude could be more disastrous. . . .

*— William Styron*

To know about fried chicken you have to have been weaned and reared in the South. Period.

*— James Villas*

I don't know which is more discouraging, literature or chickens.

*— E. B. White*

*See also* DUCK; MEAT; POULTRY; TURKEY

# Children and Food

*I don't know anyone who doesn't have memories, fond or otherwise, of food they ate as a child. I myself have always been rather focused on food, a condition I assume may have been predestined, having been born just before noon on Thanksgiving Day. To tell the truth, I don't really have any awful food memories, since my parents didn't insist that I try everything whether I liked it or not. They didn't have to insist – I liked almost everything. Some of my earliest fond food memories include autumn days in the loft of an old barn surrounded by an apple orchard, where my friend Susan and I would carry our payload of tiny, tart apples still warm from the sun, tasting of sunshine, shared secrets, and adventure. And of dill pickle–peanut butter sandwiches, which at the time I considered one of my mother's most ingenious creations. And of standing on tiptoe, eyes level with the kitchen countertop, gazing in wonderment as my mother formed magical swirls with the back of a teaspoon in frosting as thick and white and fluffy as a summer cloud. It was all I could do to keep my fingers from reaching out for a swipe. But it was not entirely willpower – Mom and I had a deal: If I resisted temptation, I got to lick both the bowl and beaters. Needless to say, I was a very good little girl.*

Remember when you were a child, and your mom wouldn't let you leave the dinner table until you ate all your Brussels sprouts, and so you took your fork and mashed them into smaller and smaller pieces in hopes of eventually reducing them to individual Brussels-sprout molecules that would be absorbed into the atmosphere and disappear?

*– Dave Barry*

In general, my children refused to eat anything that hadn't danced on TV.

*– Erma Bombeck*

. . . with food . . . [children] control the agenda, and they know it. All they have to do is put a single green pea in their mouths and pretend to gag. Sometimes once will do. If not, they can keep it up until the cows come home. There are no parents on earth who can sit calmly at a table, watch this charade for more than ten seconds, and not declare an immediate cease-fire. "OK, OK," they surrender. "You can try it again some other time." The child relaxes. The parents relax. And under the table, the dog relaxes. He doesn't think much of green peas either.

*– H. Jackson Brown Jr.*

Probably some of everyone's most dismal nursery memories are connected with food. . . . The miseries of fish days were hardest to overcome because the food looked so terrifying even before it was put on your plate. Egg sauce didn't do much to compensate for the black skin and monstrous head of boiled cod; fish pudding, a few spiteful bones inevitably lying in wait in that viscous mass, and whitings biting their own tails were frightening dishes for children.

*– Elizabeth David*

When a man is small, he loves and hates food with a ferocity which soon dims. At six years old his very bowels will heave when such a dish as creamed carrots or cold tapioca appears before him. His throat will close, and spots of nausea and rage swim in his vision. It is hard, later, to remember why, but at the time there is no pose in his disgust. He cannot eat; he says, "To hell with it!"

*– M. F. K. Fisher*

As a child my family's menu consisted of two choices: take it, or leave it.

*– Buddy Hackett*

The highlight of my childhood was making my brother laugh so hard that food came out his nose.

*– Garrison Keillor*

Ask your child what he wants for dinner only if he's buying.

*– Fran Lebowitz*

"There's no such thing as bad food," Mama used to say. "There are only spoiled-rotten children."

— *Sam Levenson*

Animal crackers, and cocoa to drink,
That is the finest of suppers, I think,
When I'm grown up and can have what I please
I think I shall always insist upon these.

— *Christopher Morley*

A food isn't necessarily essential just because your child hates it.

— *Katharine Whitehorn*

*See also* MOM'S COOKING

# Chiles; Chile Peppers

*Touch your eyes after handling chile peppers and you'll shed tears, all right, but not of joy. Talk about pain! The bad guy here is an irritant known as capsaicin (kap-SAY-ih-sin), 80 percent of which is contained in a chile's seeds and veins. So caution is the by-word — to be perfectly safe, wear disposable plastic gloves, which can be found in most drugstores. Barring that, be sure to wash your hands thoroughly with hot, soapy water as soon as you're through handling chiles.*

So I popped [a jalapeño] into my mouth and chomped down. As my teeth met I had a spiritual experience. Every cell in my body flipped over, tucked in, and said "Yaaah!" Tears gushed from my eyes, sweat exploded all over me tip to toe, I couldn't speak. . . . For a long time I sweated vigorously, gasped, wept—I think I was with the angels.

— *Richard Atcheson*

Chilies—the soul of the sauce.

*— Huntley Dent*

## Put Out the Fire!

Contrary to popular belief, an icy-cold beer or margarita *is not* the best remedy to cool a chile-scorched mouth. In fact, alcohol increases the absorption of capsaicin, the source of a chile's fiery nature. The best fire quenchers are starches like bread, rice, or potatoes or something fatty, like butter, milk, or ice cream.

# Chili

*Texans, who claim origination of the dish, call their* chili con carne *(chili with meat) a "bowl of red." They also favor beef over other meats in chili and consider the addition of beans a sacrilege. But Texas does not rule the chili world (don't tell them), and there are hundreds of delicious chili styles using various meats (lamb, sausage, game, chicken, to name a few) and beans. There are even vegetarian chilis. And chili's not simply a stand-alone dish — for years it's been used to top nachos, baked potatoes, hot dogs, and burgers (in which case it's called a "chili size" — no one knows why). In Ohio, "Cincinnati chili" is a dish of spaghetti smothered with chili, grated cheese, and chopped onions. Talk about comfort food!*

Wish I had time for just one more bowl of chili.

*— Kit Carson* (alleged last words)

Chili is not so much food as a state of mind. Addictions to it are formed early in life and the victims never recover.

*— Margaret Cousins*

Chili is much improved by having had a day to contemplate its fate.

— *John Steele Gordon*

Next to jazz music, there is nothing that lifts the spirit and strengthens the soul more than a good bowl of chili.

— *Harry James*

My social instincts are primitive, centering around a fireplace and a pot of chili and beans.

— *Adela Rogers St. John*

Heaven is a pot of chili simmering on the stove.

— *Charles Simic*

*See also* SOUPS

# Chives

*Although chives are related to both onions and garlic, they are, in fact, an herb. If you can find them with their powder-puff lavender flowers attached, by all means buy them. Not only do these edible flowers taste good, but they also make a stunning garnish.*

He who bears chives on his breath
Is safe from being kissed to death.

— *Martial*

*See also* GARLIC; ONIONS

# Chocolate

*The word "chocolate" comes from the Aztec xocolatl (transliterated to chocolatl), meaning "bitter water," undoubtedly an apt description of the unsweetened drink the Aztecs made with pounded cacao beans (from a tree they held divine), vanilla, and spices.*

*Taste aside, Aztec emperor Montezuma purportedly consumed up to fifty golden goblets of the potion daily, probably not, pundits say, because he was wild about the flavor but more likely because the brew was reputedly an aphrodisiac. After all, he had a royal reputation to maintain.*

*Historians tell us that cocoa beans were an Aztecan secret until the sixteenth century, when Hernando Cortés returned to Spain from conquering Montezuma's empire, his ships laden with Aztecan treasures, including cocoa beans and their cuttings. The Spanish were impressed with the health and restorative properties attributed to chocolate but not with its bitter flavor — until they found that a little sugar could make a delicious difference. Chocolate soon became all the rage in Europe, and Thomas Jefferson introduced it to eighteenth-century America. A mid–nineteenth-century British confectioner developed a technique for creating extravagantly smooth eating chocolate, and that, as they say, was definitely the start of something BIG.*

The Spanish ladies of the new World are madly addicted to chocolate, to such a point that, not content to drink it several times each day, they even have it served to them in church.

*— Jean-Anthelme Brillat-Savarin*

Watching a small child consume a chocolate bar could tempt even a rational man like me to consider the notion that the delectable stuff has a narcotic potency.

*— Bert Greene*

My favorite word is "chocolate." It's the most delicious word I know. . . . The word—if I read it or write it or say it—tastes just great to me.

*— Maida Heatter*

Chocolate is a passionate, sensuous connection to all my hedonistic yearnings.

*— Herself*

To the so-called chocoholic, chocolate epitomizes gastronomic bliss, but the ultimate indulgence undergoes an exponential enhancement, at least conceptually, when a mere bonbon, explosive as its flavor may be, is termed a "chocolate truffle," with nothing but a deliberately contrived physical resemblance to the genuine article to justify the nomenclature.

— *Jay Jacobs*

## That Lovin' Feeling

Down through the ages, chocolate's reputation as an aphrodisiac has been affirmed by legions—from the Aztecan emperor Montezuma to Casanova (who purportedly favored it over champagne for seduction) to millions of romantics who give chocolates to their heart's desire on Valentine's Day. Fact or fiction? The truth is that chocolate contains theobromine, a bitter, colorless alkaloid that has a mild stimulant effect that, among other things, dilates blood vessels and stimulates heart muscles. Another natural component in chocolate is phenylethylamine, an antidepressant that acts as a mood elevator, creating a feeling of elation and well-being akin to the heady sensation engendered by new love. The bottom lines? *Whatever works for you . . . and, if it feels good, do it!*

The word "chocolate" has a beautiful sound, and when I hear it, the juices start to flow and I simply must find a piece of Fanny Farmer, Godiva, or Nestle. If none of these is available, I will settle for those rather ordinary Hershey's Kisses.

— *Ann Landers*

After eating chocolate you feel godlike, as though you can conquer enemies, lead armies, entice lovers.

— *Emily Luchetti*

Milk chocolate is a yokel taste.

*— Neiman Marcus*

It seems to me that chocolate eaten early in the day does not tend to turn to fat as readily as does an evening's chocolate binge, but I might be wrong about this.

*— Judith Olney*

Always serve too much hot fudge sauce on hot fudge sundaes. It makes people overjoyed, and puts them in your debt.

*— Judith Olney*

# Meltingly Delicious

Melting chocolate can be tricky—the key is to use a low heat so it doesn't scorch. Here are some tricks to keep your melted chocolate perfect:

Use nonstick vegetable spray to coat the container you'll use for melting chocolate and the cleanup will be a cinch.

Various chocolates have different consistencies when melted—unsweetened chocolate becomes runny, whereas semisweet, sweet, and white chocolates generally hold their shape until stirred.

To expedite melting, cut chocolate into relatively small pieces. Chocolate chips melt faster than squares.

Chocolate scorches easily (which completely ruins its flavor), so should be melted slowly. White chocolate is particularly sensitive to scorching and so should be handled with extra care.

To melt chocolate in the microwave oven: Put it in a microwave-safe container and heat at MEDIUM (50 percent) power. Four ounces of chocolate will take about 3 minutes in a 650- to 700-watt oven; timing will vary depending on the oven and the

There's no metaphysics on earth like chocolate.

*— Fernando Pessoa*

Life is like a box of chocolates. You never know what you're gonna get.

*— Eric Roth (from the screenplay for Forrest Gump)*

An intensely chocolate dessert will activate any endorphin known to man.

*— Grant Showley*

*See also* APHRODISIACS; DESSERTS; SWEETS

type and amount of chocolate. One-ounce, paper-wrapped squares of chocolate can easily be microwaved right in the paper to save on cleanup—1 square takes $1\frac{1}{2}$ to 2 minutes, 2 squares about 3 minutes, and 3 squares about 4 minutes.

🌿Chocolate can also be melted in the top of a double boiler over simmering water. Remove the top of the pan from the heat when the chocolate is a little more than halfway melted and stir until it's completely smooth.

🌿Although chocolate can be melted *with* liquid (at least $\frac{1}{4}$ cup liquid per 6 ounces of chocolate), a single drop of moisture added to already melted chocolate will make it seize (clump and harden); heating chocolate above 120°F will produce the same problem. While the texture will be affected, seized chocolate can be saved: Stir in a small amount (1 tablespoon per 6 ounces of chocolate) of vegetable oil, clarified butter, or cocoa butter and slowly remelt the mixture, stirring until smooth.

🌿Cool melted chocolate to room temperature before adding to cookie doughs or cake batters. Adding hot melted chocolate could cause a textural change in the baked product.

# Black Satin Sauce

This thick, shiny sauce, from my *Food Lover's Guide to Chocolate and Vanilla*, makes a seductive topping for everything from ice cream to cake to bread pudding. If you don't have whipping cream on hand, substitute ³/₄ cup milk and ¹/₃ cup butter (in addition to the 4 tablespoons butter called for in the recipe).

¹/₂ cup unsweetened cocoa powder
1 cup sugar
¹/₈ teaspoon salt
³/₄ cup heavy whipping cream
4 tablespoons butter, cut into 4 pieces
1 teaspoon pure vanilla extract

In a medium, heavy saucepan, stir together cocoa, sugar, and salt. Slowly stir in cream, blending until smooth. Add butter; cook over medium-low heat, stirring constantly, until mixture comes to a boil. Reduce heat to low; cook, stirring constantly, for 2 minutes. Remove from heat. Cool for 15 minutes before stirring in vanilla. Serve warm or at room temperature. Sauce becomes very thick when it cools. Store, tightly covered, in refrigerator for up to 2 weeks. To reheat after refrigeration, warm in top of double boiler over simmering water. Or heat in a microwave oven at HIGH for about 1 minute (stirring after 30 seconds), or until sauce reaches desired texture. **Makes about 1³/₄ cups.**

# Chowder

*See* SOUPS

# Christmas

*See* HOLIDAYS

# Chutney

Chutney is marvelous. I'm mad about it. To me, it's very imperial.

— *Diana Vreeland*

# Clams

*American Indians once used clam shells to make* wampum—*different-colored beads used for many purposes, including ornamental (belts that have pictographic designs), ceremonial, spiritual (white beads), and as a currency for barter. The word "wampum" is Algonquian for "white string of beads."*

Recently I sat across from a person who was deliberately eating clams; she'd open up a shell, and there, in plain view, would be this stark naked clam, brazenly showing its organs . . . if a restaurant is going to serve these things it should put little loincloths on them.

— *Dave Barry*

I simply cannot imagine why anyone would eat something [a clam] slimy served in an ashtray.

— *Miss Piggy*

Some husbands would be happy as a clam if their wives would simply clam up.

— *Anonymous*

## A Clam Is a Clam, You Say?

Not so! These bivalve mollusks can be soft-shell or hard-shell, and range in size from slightly less than 2 inches in diameter (littlenecks) to the huge geoduck (GOO-ee-duck), which—with a neck (siphon) that can reach up to 18 inches—also takes the prize for the funniest-looking clam.

*See also* FISH

# Cocktail Parties

The cocktail party has the form of friendship without the warmth and devotion. It is a device for getting rid of social obligations hurriedly en masse.

*— Brooks Atkinson*

. . . cocktail parties . . . are an anathema. They are expensive. They are dull. They are good for a time, like a dry Martini, and like that all-demanding drink they can lift you high and then drop you hideously into a slough of boredom, morbidity, and indigestion.

*— M. F. K. Fisher*

Memorial services are the cocktail parties of the geriatric set.

*— Harold Macmillan*

I misremember who first was cruel enough to nurture the cocktail party into life. But perhaps it would be not too much to say, in fact it would be not enough to say, that it was not worth the trouble.

*— Dorothy Parker*

The cocktail party—a device for paying off obligations to people you don't want to invite to dinner.

*— Charles Merrill Smith*

# Cocktails

*Cocktails and cocktailing are back in a big way. No, the three-martini lunch hasn't returned yet, but the Wall Street Journal tells us that businesspeople are drinking at lunch again, and not just wine. I don't know about you, but I've endured a few deadly business lunches where an icy cold martini might not have been a bad idea at all. Make mine with olives.*

> The cocktail is a pleasant drink;
> It's mild and harmless I don't think,
>     When you've had one you call for two,
>     And then you don't care what you do.
>
> *– George Ade*

The decline of the apéritif may well be one of the most depressing phenomena of our time.

*– Luis Buñuel*

If you were to ask me if I'd ever had the bad luck to miss my daily cocktail, I'd have to say that I doubt it; where certain things are concerned, I plan ahead.

*– Luis Buñuel*

Alcohol is like love. The first kiss is magic, the second is intimate, the third is routine. After that you take the girl's clothes off.

*– Raymond Chandler*

An umbrella is of no avail against a Scotch mist.

— *James Russell Lowell*

*See also* BEER; BEVERAGES; BRANDY; CHAMPAGNE; COCKTAIL PARTIES; DRINKING; LIQUOR; MAI TAI; MARTINI; PORT; TOASTS; WINE

# Cod; Codfish

The codfish lays ten thousand eggs,
The homely hen lays one.
The codfish never cackles
To tell you what she's done.
And so we scorn the codfish,
While the humble hen we prize,
Which only goes to show you
That it pays to advertise.

— *Anonymous*

*See also* FISH

# Coffee

*Coffee has never been more popular than it is today, a fact made obvious by the proliferation of retail coffee stores and coffee houses popping up around the nation. To some, coffee is coffee, but to others it's an experience unto itself. I know people who consider a restaurant déclassé if it doesn't serve cappuccinos, espressos, and lattes — terms that can be intimidating to coffee neophytes. If you're new at the coffee game, you might be interested in the following menu of terms.*

# Coffee Carte

CAFÉ AU LAIT [ka-fay oh-LAY]: French for "coffee with milk"; equal portions of scalded milk and coffee

CAFÉ BRÛLOT [ka-fay broo-LOH]: Coffee blended with spices, orange and lemon peel, and brandy, then flamed and served in demitasse cups

CAFÉ LATTE [ka-fay LAH-tay]: Espresso with a liberal amount of foamy steamed milk, usually served in a tall glass mug

CAFÉ MACCHIATO [ka-fay mah-kee-YAH-toh]: Espresso with a dollop of steamed-milk foam, served in an espresso cup

CAFÉ MOCHA [ka-fay MOH-kah]: A café latte with chocolate added

CAPPUCCINO [kap-poo-CHEE-noh]: Espresso topped with foamy steamed milk, served in a regular-size cup or glass mug

ESPRESSO [ehs-PREHS-soh]: A very strong brew made with dark-roasted coffee under pressure, served in a tiny espresso cup

GREEK COFFEE: A rich, intensely strong boiled coffee

IRISH COFFEE: A mélange of strong coffee, Irish whiskey, and sugar, usually served in a glass mug with a dollop of whipped cream

THAI COFFEE: Coffee mixed with sweetened condensed milk

TURKISH COFFEE: An extremely strong brew made by boiling finely ground coffee, sugar, and water together

VIENNESE COFFEE: Strong, usually sweetened coffee served in a tall glass and topped with whipped cream

Coffee is the common man's gold, and like gold, it brings to every man the feeling of luxury and nobility.

*– Abd-al-Kadir*

Dig up some dirt from your backyard, add a teaspoon of mud, a drop of fertilizer, add hot water, presto! instant Turkish coffee.

*– Joey Adams*

Coffee glides down into one's stomach and sets everything in motion.

*– Honoré de Balzac*

Coffee has two virtues: It is wet and warm.

*– old Dutch proverb*

Coffee in England is just toasted milk.

*– Christopher Fry*

The best proof that tea or coffee are favourable to intellectual expression is that all nations use one or the other as aids to conversation.

*– Philip G. Hamerton*

The morning cup of coffee has an exhilaration about it which the cheering influence of the afternoon or evening cup of tea cannot be expected to reproduce.

*– Oliver Wendell Holmes Sr.*

Do you know how helpless you feel if you have a full cup of coffee in your hand and you start to sneeze?

*– Jean Kerr*

Actually, this seems to be the basic need of the human heart in nearly every great crisis—a good hot cup of coffee.

*– Alexander King*

Only Irish coffee provides in a single glass all four essential food groups: alcohol, caffeine, sugar, and fat.

*– Alex Levine*

# The Consummate Cup

✎Make sure the coffeepot and filter are absolutely clean — residual coffee oils from previous brews will give subsequent pots a bitter, rancid flavor.

✎Use freshly drawn cold water that tastes good. Your coffee will only be as good as the water it's made with — highly chlorinated or distinctively mineral-tasting water can produce bitter, off-tasting coffee. Use bottled water if necessary.

✎Use the correct amount, grind, and brewing time for your coffeemaker.

✎For a full-flavored cup of coffee, use 2 level tablespoons (1 coffee measure, $1/8$ cup) for each 6 ounces ($3/4$ cup) of water. Keep in mind that a standard coffee cup holds 6 ounces, whereas a mug's capacity is often 10 to 12 ounces. For stronger coffee, use 2 level tablespoons for each 4 ounces ($1/2$ cup) of water.

✎If coffee seems acidic to you, try adding a pinch of salt to the grounds before brewing.

✎Within 15 minutes after it's brewed, coffee flavor begins to deteriorate, and leaving the coffee on a heating element expedites the process — as the aromatic oils evaporate, the coffee begins to taste bitter and flat. Retain first-cup freshness by transferring coffee to a preheated (with hot water), vacuum-insulated carafe. These thermos carafes are available in a wide variety of attractive colors and styles.

✎Remember that reheating coffee just makes it bitter.

The smell of coffee cooking was a reason for growing up, because children were never allowed to have it and nothing haunted the nostrils all the way out to the barn as did the aroma of boiling coffee.

*– Edna Lewis*

**I**f this is coffee, please bring me some tea; if this is tea, please bring me some coffee.

*— Abraham Lincoln*

**I**'ll have a half double decaffeinated half cap with a twist of lemon.

*— Steve Martin (ordering cappuccino in the film L.A. Story)*

**C**offee is a fleeting moment and a fragrance.

*— Claudia Roden*

## Poison, Anyone?

Oscar Wilde (known to his mum as Oscar Fingal O'Flahertie Wills Wilde) once said, "Moderation is a fatal thing. . . . Nothing succeeds like excess." Of course, much of what this witty Irishman said was tongue in cheek, but his philosophy was dead wrong when applied to Honoré de Balzac. In fact, this great French writer purportedly died from caffeine poisoning because of his lack of moderation in drinking over fifty cups of coffee a day. One wonders if he'd have written so brilliantly while drinking tea.

**T**he best maxim I know in life is to drink your coffee when you can, and when you cannot, to be easy without it.

*— Jonathan Swift*

Coffee:
Black as the devil,
Hot as hell,
Pure as an angel,
Sweet as love.

*— Count Charles Talleyrand*

# Café Brûlot

Café Brûlot is a tradition in New Orleans. In French, the word *brûlot* means "burnt brandy." Making this grand finale at the table is dramatic, but it'll be just as delicious if made in a saucepan in the kitchen.

½ cup brandy
3 tablespoons Curaçao or Grand Marnier
¼ cup finely julienned lemon zest
¼ cup finely julienned orange zest
1 tablespoon brown sugar
1 (2-inch) cinnamon stick, broken in half
4 whole cloves
4 whole allspice
3 cups hot, strong coffee

In a chafing dish or medium saucepan over medium heat, combine all ingredients except coffee. Stir often while mixture heats. Just when bubbles begin to form around edge of pan, use a long-handled match to ignite. (If making in saucepan, pour mixture into warm, heatproof 1½- to 2-quart serving bowl before igniting.) Gradually add coffee so flame lingers as long as possible. Ladle into demitasse cups; serve immediately. **Makes 6 to 8 servings.**

Coffee should be black as Hell, strong as death and sweet as love.
— *Turkish proverb*

After a few months' acquaintance with European "coffee," one's mind weakens, and his faith with it, and he begins to wonder if the rich beverage of home, with its clotted layer of yellow cream on top of it, is not a mere dream after all, and a thing which never existed.
— *Mark Twain*

I think if I were a woman I'd wear coffee as a perfume.

*– John Van Druten*

*See also* BEVERAGES; TEA

# Cognac

*See* BRANDY

# Comfort Food

*Dictionaries tell us the word "comfort" means to soothe, console, cheer up, or reassure. So the phrase "comfort food" would seem to be self-explanatory — a comforting comestible deliciously evocative of a gentler, perhaps happier, time. Just what is a comfort food? Intensely personal, that's what it is. For me, comfort foods include maple-laced oatmeal, billowy mashed potatoes, and spiced chocolate chip cookies, still warm from the oven — as you can see, something soft and warm pushes my buttons. I have one friend, however, who swears by mayo-slathered Spam-and-Velveeta sandwiches in dire times, and another who reaches for Oreo cookies but only eats the middle. And so it is with your personal comfort food — something you reach for when you just want a hug.*

When you are feeling sick . . . you want loving care and comfort. The foods that fill that need are simple, easy to eat, and cooked with love.

*– Joyce Goldstein*

Food is the most primitive form of comfort.

*– Sheila Graham*

Give me hashed browns off a griddle and flapjacks browned beside them that are not made from a mix. What has happened to the crisp waffle with warm maple syrup? On comfort days in sloppy clothes, I don't want macadamia waffles with exotic grains.

*— Barbara Kafka*

Food, like a loving touch or a glimpse of divine power, has that ability to comfort.

*— Norman Kolpas*

## Chocolate-Cinnamon Toast

My mother used to make me cinnamon toast when I had a cold or was feeling sad. As a confirmed chocoholic, I've added cocoa powder here, and I must confess that this fragrant comforter still makes blue days better. Since this mixture keeps a long time, you might want to double the recipe so you'll have plenty on hand "in case of emergency."

1 tablespoon unsweetened cocoa powder
3 tablespoons sugar
½ teaspoon ground cinnamon
toasted bread
softened butter

In a small bowl, combine cocoa powder, sugar, and cinnamon. Store, tightly sealed, at room temperature. **Makes enough topping for about 8 slices of toast,** depending on the size.

*For each serving:* Spread 1 slice of toasted bread with butter; sprinkle evenly with a rounded teaspoon of chocolate mixture. Broil 3 inches from heat source until top is bubbly—watch carefully, it only takes a few seconds.

# Condiments

*Henry Miller once said: "Americans can eat garbage, provided you sprinkle it liberally with ketchup, mustard, chili sauce, Tabasco sauce, cayenne pepper, or any other condiment which destroys the original flavor of the dish." A statement that would seem to condemn not only condiments but the American palate as well. That's not to say I don't cringe upon seeing some poor misguided soul smother a perfectly good steak with ketchup. Seems to me that if one likes ketchup that much, why not just eat it alone, which would certainly be better for the arteries than meat. But, unlike Henry Miller, I think condiments enhance rather than destroy a food's flavor, provided, of course, a light touch is used. A light touch is not something I always possessed, however. I'll never forget the time my new husband (the same one I have today) went off to work, my "Sharon's special" scrambled eggs in his tummy. That night when he got home I reared back from his kiss. "Whew, garlic!" I said. "What on earth did you have for lunch?" He smiled ruefully and explained that he hadn't had time for lunch and what I was smelling was the garlic-powdered eggs he'd had for breakfast. Ohmigod, I could see the writing on the proverbial wall:* NEW BRIDE DESTROYS HUSBAND'S CAREER BY GIVING HIM GARLIC DRAGON BREATH. *At that very instant my "more is better" mentality vanished. That's not to say that was the last time I used too much of a flavoring or condiment — experimentation is the springboard of creative cooking — but it is to say I haven't touched garlic powder since.*

Condiments are to food what jewelry and makeup are to clothing. They are not essential . . . but they definitely "dress up" your food and make eating a lot more interesting.

*– Kathy Gunst*

Condiments are like old friends—highly thought of, but often taken for granted.

*— Marilyn Kaytor*

Eat safely—use condiments.

*— Vinnie Tonelli*

*See also* CHUTNEY; GRAVY; KETCHUP; MAYONNAISE; MUSTARD; PEPPER, BLACK; SALT; SALSA; SAUCES; SEASONINGS

## Balsamic Nectar

This sweet-and-sour amalgam adds intriguing flavor to myriad dishes. Drizzle it over greens, rice, grilled meat, or fish, or add it to salad dressings, stir-frys, or sautés for a touch of pizzazz. For the uninitiated, balsamic vinegar gets its dark color and pungent sweetness from being aged in barrels over a period of years—the longer it's aged, the more expensive (and delicious) it becomes. Balsamic nectar keeps forever in the refrigerator.

1 cup balsamic vinegar
½ cup sugar

Combine ingredients in a small saucepan; bring to a boil over high heat. Cook until reduced by half. Cool to room temperature. Pour into a screwtop jar and refrigerate. **Makes about ½ cup.**

# Cookbooks

*I can't count the times I've heard someone say, "I've been collecting recipes for years . . . maybe I should do a cookbook. . . ." It seems like everybody — whether secretly or openly — thinks they "have a cookbook in them." And many do. But few realize that writing a good cookbook is extremely hard work. (I speak from ex-*

*perience.) I'm not saying it isn't fun, but a "collection of recipes" won't make it, at least not so you'd notice. First of all, editors want new angles, snappy headnotes and subtext writing, and, most of all, original recipes. That doesn't mean new recipes, for as famed French chef Anton Mosimann once said: "There is really nothing new in [cooking]. I have four thousand cookbooks dating back to 1503 and everything that is in 'nouvelle cuisine' was there two hundred years ago." What most editors definitely do not want are your favorite recipes collected from other cookbooks or the backs of boxes (although there is a "back-of-the-box" cookbook). All of which is food for thought before submitting a cookbook idea to an editor. And who knows? With the right approach, exciting, well-constructed recipes, lively writing, and generous measures of talent and passion, you may just become the next Julia Child, although, truth to tell, I can't imagine anyone ever living up to the standard set by the re-markable Julia.*

One man's cookbook is another woman's soft porn: there's a certain Sybaritic voyeurism involved, an indulgence by proxy.

*— Margaret Atwood*

Anyone who eats three meals a day should understand why cookbooks outsell sex books three to one.

*— L. M. Boyd*

Anyone who wants to write about food would do well to stay away from similes and metaphors, because if you're not careful, expressions like "light as a feather" make their way into your sentences and then where are you?

*— Nora Ephron*

Central heating, French rubber goods and cookbooks are three amazing proofs of man's ingenuity in transforming ne-cessity into art, and, of these, cookbooks are perhaps the most lastingly delightful.

*— M. F. K. Fisher*

The [cookbook] was a backbreaking thousand-odd pages thick and generously larded with color plates of presumably edible rococo and Byzantine ornamentation, any subject of which would have taken a fairly accomplished home cook, working with tweezers and magnifying glass, a month to replicate.

*– Jay Jacobs*

The primary requisite for writing well about food is a good appetite.

*– A. J. Liebling*

I did toy with the idea of doing a cook-book. . . . The recipes were to be the routine ones: how to make dry toast, instant coffee, hearts of lettuce and brownies. But as an added attraction, at no extra charge, my idea was to put a fried egg on the cover. I think a lot of people who hate literature but love fried eggs would buy it if the price was right.

*– Groucho Marx*

The two biggest sellers in any bookstore are the cookbooks and the diet books. The cookbooks tell you how to prepare the food and the diet books tell you how not to eat any of it.

*– Andy Rooney*

Next to eating good dinners, a healthy man with a benevolent turn of mind must like, I think, to read about them.

*– William Thackeray*

As if a cookbook had anything to do with writing.

*– Alice B. Toklas*

*See also* RECIPES

# Cookies

**Crazy cookie logic.** *When* a tough cookie *gets caught with his* hand in the cookie jar, *it's enough to make him* toss his cookies *until, that is, his* cookie-cutter *mentality reminds him that* that's the way a cookie crumbles, *at which point he becomes* a smart cookie.

I suppose I could have stayed home and baked cookies and had teas, but what I decided to do was fulfill my profession.

– *Hillary Rodham Clinton*

Shortbread has beneficial effects on the soul. The warm glow it gives is better than alcohol, and more readily available than sex.

– *Lucy Ellman*

# That's the Way the Cookie Crumbles

Ever sent a box of cookies you'd spent hours making and baking only to have them arrive cookie *crumbs*? Here are a few tips for mailing cookies:

🍪You definitely *won't* end up with crumbs if you send soft cookies; if sending crisp cookies, avoid those with pointed edges. Don't send frosted cookies.

🍪Wrap soft and crisp cookies separately—otherwise you'll end up with soft crisp cookies and dry soft cookies.

🍪Use heavy-duty foil to wrap cookies in pairs (flat sides together) or in small stacks.

🍪Use sheets of waxed paper or plastic wrap to separate layers of soft cookies.

🍪The best containers for shipping cookies are rigid—cookie tins, plastic or cardboard boxes, coffee or shortening cans with plastic lids, or half-gallon cardboard milk cartons are all good choices.

🍪Pack cookies close together so they'll have less room to move and break.

*[How to eat chocolate chip cookies like a child:]* Half-sit, half-lie on the bed, propped up by a pillow. Read a book. Place cookies next to you on the sheet so that crumbs get in the bed. As you eat the cookies, remove each chocolate chip and place it on your stomach. When all the cookies are consumed, eat the chips one by one, allowing two per page.

*— Delia Ephron*

Shrink-wrapping very large cookies or stacks of three to four cookies is a great way to stabilize them for mailing. Here's how: Preheat the oven to 325°F; line a baking sheet with two layers of heavy-duty paper towel. Wrap cookie stacks or large single cookies firmly in a good-quality plastic wrap (bargain brands melt!), overlapping the edges at the bottom middle of the cookie. Cut away any excess plastic wrap at the overlap. Place the paper-towel–lined baking sheet in the oven for 5 minutes. Remove from oven and arrange wrapped cookies, folded side down and 1 inch apart, on hot baking sheet. Return sheet to oven, leaving the door ajar so you can watch the cookies closely. The plastic wrap will shrink tightly around the cookies in just a few seconds. Cool the wrapped cookies on racks.

Pack cookie containers in a sturdy, corrugated box with plenty of room for a cushion of filler (crumpled newspaper or other paper, Styrofoam pellets, popcorn, or plastic bubble-wrap). Pad the bottom of the box with several inches of filler, add the cookie container(s), then more filler on the sides and top.

Mail cookies first class so they won't be stale by the time they get there.

# Bodacious Brownie Thins

These one-bowl, mix-in-minutes brownies are rich, spicy, chewy, and thin (which you won't be if you eat too many). Don't worry about the pepper—it adds pizzazz to the sweetness. Peppers have different degrees of heat (for instance, older pepper has less heat than fresh), so taste before you add it.

1¼ cups sugar

½ cup unsweetened cocoa powder

1 cup all-purpose flour

½ teaspoon *each* ground cinnamon and allspice

½ teaspoon salt

¾ to 1 teaspoon ground black pepper

½ cup (1 stick) butter, melted and cooled

2 eggs, lightly beaten

2 teaspoons pure vanilla extract

¾ cup chopped pecans, walnuts, or almonds

Adjust oven rack to center position; preheat oven to 375°F. Grease a 9 × 13-inch baking pan; set aside. In a medium bowl, stir sugar and cocoa until well combined. Stir in flour, spices, salt, and pepper. Add butter, eggs, and vanilla; beat by hand until smooth. Turn into prepared pan; spread evenly, pushing batter all the way to the edges. Sprinkle evenly with nuts. Bake about 13 minutes, or until a toothpick inserted in the center comes out clean. Cool completely in pan. Use a sharp, pointed knife to cut into 24 (approximately 1½ × 3-inch) rectangles, cutting 6 strips lengthwise and 4 strips crosswise. **Makes 2 dozen brownies.**

When I was four years old, my mother used to bring me a cookie every time she came home from the market. I always went to the front yard and took my time eating it, sometimes half an hour or forty-five minutes for one cookie. I would take a small bite and look up at the sky. Then I would touch the dog with my feet and take another small bit. I just enjoyed being there, with the sky, the earth, the bamboo thickets, the cat, the dog, the flowers. . . . I was entirely in the present moment with my cookie.

*– Thich Nhat Hanh*

And when all of the flourless chocolate cakes and chocolate mousse or ganache cakes have come and gone, there will still be nothing like a fudgy brownie, dry and crackled on top, moist and dense within, with a glass of cold milk.

*– Richard Sax*

*See also* DESSERTS; SWEETS

# Cooking

When my mother had to get dinner for eight she'd just make enough for sixteen and only serve half.

*– Gracie Allen*

I wanted for Christmas what Phyllis Diller always wanted . . . an oven that flushed.

*– Erma Bombeck*

Cookery is not chemistry. It is an art. It requires instinct and taste rather than exact measurements.

*– X. Marcel Boulestin*

Cooking is a way of giving and making yourself desirable.

*– Michel Bourdin*

You don't get over hating to cook, any more than you get over having big feet.

— *Peg Bracken*

. . . the sauerbraten tasted like fly spray. Thinking a simple admission of error was in order, I said philosophically, "Well, cooking is full of ups and downs," and my ten-year-old said, "It comes up right after it goes down."

— *Peg Bracken*

Don't use a metal fork for fishing something out of a plugged-in electrical appliance like a toaster, or you can end up dead with a permanent wave.

— *Peg Bracken*

The discovery of a new dish does more for the happiness of mankind than the discovery of a new star.

— *Jean-Anthelme Brillat-Savarin*

When we no longer have good cooking in the world, we will have no literature, no high and sharp intelligence, nor friendly gatherings, nor social harmony.

— *Marie-Antoine Carême*

Until I got into cooking, I was never *really* interested in anything.

— *Julia Child*

Noncooks think it's silly to invest two hours' work in two minutes' enjoyment; but if cooking is evanescent, well, so is the ballet.

— *Julia Child*

I'm not interested in dishes that take three minutes and have no cholesterol.

— *Julia Child*

Cooking is often one disaster after another. What you learn is the only thing you can't fix is a soufflé.

— *Julia Child*

For those who love it, cooking is at once child's play and adult joy. And cooking done with care is an act of love.

*— Craig Claiborne*

If you aren't up to a little magic occasionally, you shouldn't waste time trying to cook.

*— Colette*

If you throw a lamb chop in the oven, what's to keep it from getting done?

*— Joan Crawford (in the film* The Women*)*

In cooking, as in all the arts, simplicity is the sign of perfection.

*— Curnonsky*

Summer cooking implies a sense of immediacy, a capacity to capture the essence of the fleeting moment.

*— Elizabeth David*

All culinary tasks should be performed with reverential love. . . .

*— Norman Douglas*

Cookery is naturally the most ancient of the arts, as of all arts it is the most important.

*— George Ellwanger*

What I love about cooking is that after a hard day, there is something comforting about the fact that if you melt butter and add flour and then hot stock, it will get thick! It's a sure thing! It's a sure thing in a world where nothing is sure; it has a mathematical certainty in a world where those of us who long for some kind of certainty are forced to settle for crossword puzzles.

*— Nora Ephron*

The accepted way to test the heat of an oven was to thrust in the hand and count seconds till one had to pull it out with a faint scream.

*– J. C. Furnas*

Sensuality is what I love best about cooking. It is the frizzle of bacon on the back burner and the froth of scalded cream whisked into vanilla and sugar until the pans, sink, cook and even the walls are pale, polka-spotted that make a kitchen kitchenly. Remove the mess and, for me, you dispel a measure of the magic.

*– Bert Greene*

If you go back far enough [in cookery], you realize that you are not an inventor, only a recreator.

*– Michel Guérard*

If cooking becomes an art form rather than a means of providing a reasonable diet, then something is clearly wrong.

*– Tom Jaine*

Cooking demands attention, patience, and, above all, a respect for the gifts of the earth. It is a form of worship, a way of giving thanks.

*– Judith B. Jones*

People have been cooking and eating for thousands of years, so if you are the very first to have thought of adding fresh lime juice to scalloped potatoes try to understand that there must be a reason for this.

*– Fran Lebowitz*

The most indispensable ingredient of all good home cooking: love for those you are cooking for.

*– Sophia Loren*

What is literature compared with cooking? The one is shadow, the other is substance.

*– E. V. Lucas*

Kissing don't last: cookery do.

— *George Meredith*

Cooking is a fickle and faltering art. Didn't Rembrandt ever ruin a picture? Then why shouldn't I have the right to ruin a dish?

— *Raymond Oliver*

To the old saying that man built the house but woman made of it a "home" might be added the modern supplement that woman accepted cooking as a chore but man has made of it a recreation.

— *Emily Post*

I never see any home cooking. All I get is fancy stuff.

— *Prince Philip, Duke of Edinburgh*

Cookery is my one vanity and I am a slave to any guest who praises my culinary art.

— *Marjorie Kinnan Rawlings*

Long before institutionalized religions came along — and temples and churches — there was an unquestioned recognition that what goes on in the kitchen is *holy*. Cooking involves an enormously rich coming-together of the fruits of the earth with the inventive genius of the human being.

— *Laurel Robertson*

What does cookery mean? It means the knowledge of Medea and of Circe, and of Calypso, and Sheba. . . . It means the economy of your great-grandmother and the science of modern chemistry, and French art, and Arabian hospitality. It means, in fine, that you are to see imperatively that everyone has something nice to eat.

— *John Ruskin*

When men reach their sixties and retire they go right to pieces. Women just go right on cooking.

— *Gail Sheehy*

Cooking for someone is like a love affair. You cook to make someone happy. . . . I'm sure someone with a bitter personality cannot be a good chef.

– *André Soltner*

The fricassee with dumplings is made by a Mrs. Miller whose husband has left her four times on account of her disposition and returned four times on account of her cooking. . . .

– *Rex Stout*

Cooking is a lot like making love. It just takes a little longer to clean up.

– *Michael Tucker*

Cooking is like love — it should be entered into with abandon, or not at all.

– *Harriet Van Horne*

There is no sight on earth more appealing than the sight of a woman making dinner for someone she loves.

– *Thomas Wolfe*

*See also* COOKS AND CHEFS; MOM'S COOKING

# Cooks and Chefs

*So just what is the difference between a cook and a chef? I surveyed several of my fellow food pros on this one and to a person they agreed that all chefs are cooks but not all cooks are chefs. A chef is someone who's formally (or informally) trained in the culinary arts and — here's the distinction — whose profession is cooking in a dining establishment, whether restaurant, cruise ship, or health spa. Now, I cook for a living and have been trained to do so, but I would never call myself a "chef" — I'm a home cook who creates recipes for my fellow food lovers. None of this is exceptionally important unless, of course, a dinner becomes particularly boring, in which case you now have new fodder with which to fuel the conversation.*

A good cook is not necessarily a good woman with an even temper. Some allowance should be made for artistic temperament.

*– X. Marcel Boulestin*

I like a cook who smiles out loud when he tastes his own work. Let God worry about your modesty; I want to see your enthusiasm.

*– Robert Farrar Capon*

All good cooks learn something new every day.

*– Julia Child*

She spends much time with me in the kitchen and carries with her always the sweet scent of something pleasant bubbling on the stove.

*– Jacqueline Deval*

The true cook . . . is the perfect blend, the only perfect blend, of artist and philosopher.

*– Norman Douglas*

. . . everyone filled up on caviar because Mrs. Roosevelt, who cooked on Sunday nights, was "the worst cook in the world, you know. When she put the chafing dish full of scrambled eggs on the table, they'd be heavier than lead and Mr. Roosevelt would look so depressed."

*– Maureen Dowd*

There is no hope for a cook who will not learn his own as well as other gourmets' limitations, and a man who has made one good Béchamel by rote . . . and then goes on to make impossible ones because of his lack of balance, perspective and plain common sense and modesty, is, to be blunt again, past recall.

*– M. F. K. Fisher*

There is one thing more exasperating than a wife who can cook and won't and that's a wife who can't cook and will.

*— Robert Frost*

I was a frightfully excessive child-chef, and only strongly scented dishes seemed to enflame my culinary sensibilities.

*— Bert Greene*

Approaching the stove, she would don a voluminous apron, toss some meat on a platter, empty a skillet of its perfectly cooked *à point* vegetables, sprinkle a handful of chopped parsley over all, and then, like a proficient strip-tease artist, remove the apron, allowing it to fall to the floor with a shake of her hips. . . .

*— Bert Greene*

Often, admiring a chef and getting to know him is like loving goose liver and then meeting the goose.

*— George Lang*

Some people's food always tastes better than others, even if they are cooking the same dish at the same dinner . . . because one person has more life in them—more fire, more vitality, more guts—than others. A person without these things can never make food taste right, no matter what materials you give them . . . they have nothing in themselves to give. You have got to throw feeling into cooking.

*— Rosa Lewis*

One glance at her and I knew at once the sort of things that Dorcas would cook, that Dorcas was born to cook. Never, in later life, have I sat down to dinner without saying to myself, "Ah! things look Dorcassy tonight!" or, "Alas! there is nothing Dorcassy here."

*— Don Marquis*

Good taste [in cooking] is innate, and knowing with certainty when and how to break the rules (and when not to) is a talent few possess.

*— Michael McLaughlin*

The secret to good cooking resides in the cook's ability to say "the hell with the basic recipe" and improvise freely from it. If you haven't got this kind of moxie, you might as well hang up your apron.

*– James Alan McPherson*

We may live without poetry, music
and art;
We may live without conscience, and live
without heart;
We may live without friends; we may
live without books;
But civilized man cannot live without
cooks.

*– Owen Meredith*

Bad cooks—and the utter lack of reason in the kitchen—have delayed human development longest and impaired it most.

*– Friedrich Nietzsche*

. . . our "chef saucier" told me that by the time a chef is forty he is either dead or crazy.

*– David Ogilvy*

No mean woman can cook well. It calls for a generous spirit, a light hand, and a large heart.

*– Eden Phillpotts*

The cook was a good cook, as cooks go; and as cooks go she went.

*– Saki*

A good cook is like a sorceress who dispenses happiness.

*– Elsa Schiaparelli*

'Tis an ill cook that cannot lick his own fingers.

*– William Shakespeare*

The true Muses are cooks.

— *Charles Simic*

All cooks, like all great artists, must have an audience worth cooking for.

— *André Simon*

Cooks are in some ways very much like actors; they must be fit and strong, since acting and cooking are two of the most exacting professions. They must be blessed—or cursed, whichever way you care to look at it—with what is called the artistic temperament, which means that if they are to act or cook at all well, it cannot be for duds or dummies.

— *André Simon*

Americans, more than any other culture on earth, are cookbook cooks. . . .

— *John Thorne*

A cook is creative, marrying ingredients in the way a poet marries words.

— *Roger Vergé*

I always ask at once, "Do you drink?" and if she says "No," I bow politely and say I am sorry but I fear she will not suit. All *good* cooks drink.

— *James Abbott McNeill Whistler*

The British cook is a foolish woman—who should be turned for her iniquities into a pillar of salt, which she never knows how to use.

— *Oscar Wilde*

*See also* COOKBOOKS; COOKING; MOM'S COOKING; RECIPES

# Corn

*In his tome* Greene on Greens, *Bert Greene shared an old New England adage: "You may stroll to the garden to cut the corn but you had darn well better run back to the kitchen to cook it!" So true! As soon as an ear of corn is picked, its sugar immediately begins its gradual conversion to starch. This natural process lessens the corn's natural sweetness and eventually turns the juicy, sweet kernels into starchy, mealy bites. That's why it's important to buy corn as soon after it's picked as possible, preferably from a farmer's market or specialty produce market where you know the turnover is brisk. Choose ears with bright green, snugly fitting husks and golden silk. The kernels should be plump and milky — pierce one with your fingernail and if it squirts juice, you're in business!*

## Cornsational!

As I said in the corn introduction, it's simply a fact that corn should be eaten just as soon as possible after it's picked to keep the sugar from converting to starch. Which is why I find so intriguing the research of Don Schlimme, a University of Maryland professor of food science, who's come up with a way to keep corn tasting fresher longer. Here's his technique: Put a cooler with ice in your car and, as soon as you leave the market, place the fresh corn inside. At home, prepare a solution of 1 drop of lemon juice and 2 drops of Clorox for each gallon of ice water, a mixture that curbs starch conversion and significantly reduces the possibility of bacteria and mold. Remove the corn's husk and silk and plunge the corn into the water. Remove the corn from the water, shaking off excess moisture; place five ears into a 1-gallon plastic freezer bag that's at least .8 mil. thick. Remove as much air as possible, sealing tightly and refrigerating immediately. According to Schlimme, processing and storing corn this way will keep it fresh-tasting for two weeks.

I expand and live in the warm day like corn and melons.
                                                    — *Ralph Waldo Emerson*

# Grilled Corn "Off" the Cob

Marinated corn kernels with a kiss of smoke—it just may be the quintessential way to cook corn!

1/4 cup olive oil
2 tablespoons balsamic vinegar or red wine vinegar
1/2 teaspoon salt
6 large ears corn, kernels removed (about 5 cups kernels)
2/3 cup finely snipped herbs (basil, fennel, chives, etc.)
freshly ground black pepper
sour cream (optional)

In a 13 × 9-inch metal baking pan, combine oil, vinegar, salt, and herbs. Add corn, tossing to coat. Season with freshly ground pepper to taste. Cover and refrigerate for 3 hours. At least 1 hour before grilling, soak 2 cups wood chips in water to cover. When ready, light fire in outdoor grill according to manufacturer's directions. Just before grilling, sprinkle wood chips over heat source. Stir corn well. Place uncovered pan of corn in center of grill rack; cover grill. Cook over high heat for 3 minutes; stir corn. Cover grill and continue to cook for 3 minutes, or until corn is sizzling slightly. Serve hot, accompanied by sour cream, if desired. **Serves 6.**

People have tried and they have tried, but sex is not better than sweet corn.

— *Garrison Keillor*

I believe in the forest, and in the meadow, and in the night in which the corn grows.

— *Henry David Thoreau*

There is no dignity in the bean. Corn, with no affectation of superiority, is however, the child of song. It waves in all literature. But mix it with beans and its high tone is gone. Succotash is vulgar.

— *Charles Dudley Warner*

*See also* VEGETABLES

# Crab

*In Irena Chalmers's* The Great Food Almanac, *Sandra Soehngen and Melanie Young tell us that crab passion is a killer: "Female blue crabs mate only once. Only during this brief period when the female or 'Sook' sheds her shell can she be mated to the 'Jimmy' or male crab. The mating session can last up to 48 hours [no wonder they're crabby!]. Afterward, the male cradles his female partner until she regenerates a hard shell. Once the female's shell hardens, she proceeds to attack and eat her male partner unless he makes a quick getaway. Talk about 'till death us do part'!" I don't know about you, but if I were a guy, I'd breathe a sigh of relief — mating rituals like that make single bars and blind dates seem almost innocent.*

The kind of crabbing my wife likes to do is to return from an afternoon's swim or sunbathing session, open the refrigerator door, and find a generous plate of Crab Cakes all ready to cook.

— *Euell Gibbons*

There are three species of creatures who when they seem coming are going, when they seem going they come: diplomats, women, and crabs.

— *John Hay*

When we have crab meat to spare, I make a crab Newburg so superlative that I myself taste in wonder, thinking, "Can it be I who has brought this noble thing into the world?" ... We do not desecrate this dish by serving any other. .... We just eat crab Newburg. My friends rise from the table, wring my hand with deep feeling, and slip quietly and reverently away. I sit alone and weep for the misery of the world that does not have blue crabs and a Jersey cow. . . .

*— Marjorie Kinnan Rawlings*

Canned crabmeat tastes like Styrofoam. A bad version of she-crab soup in Charleston tastes like the sauce used on lobster Newburg by the third fanciest French restaurant in Tulsa.

*— Calvin Trillin*

*See also* FISH

# Cranberries

*See* HOLIDAYS

# Crime

*See* MURDER AND FOOD

# Cucumbers

*Ever wonder where the phrase "cool as a cucumber" came from? Some say it's because the internal temperature of a cucumber is always several degrees cooler than its surroundings. And no wonder the cucumber has a "cool" attitude — it's about 96 percent water, which translates to a very slim calorie count of about 40 for a medium cuke. Filling, satisfying (no matter what Samuel Johnson says), and low in calories and sodium . . . perfect for dieters!*

To see cucumbers in a dream denotes that you will speedily fall in love. Or, if you are in love, then you will marry the object of your affection.

*— Richard Folkard*

# Cucumber Slaw

Most markets carry two basic types of cucumber—the regular variety with seeds, and the English (or hothouse) cucumber, which is sealed in plastic, contains many fewer seeds, and costs many more pennies. To seed a cucumber easily, cut it lengthwise in half, then run a teaspoon (tip down) along the center, scooping out the seeds. In this recipe, it's important to squeeze as much liquid from the cucumbers as possible because excess liquid produces soggy slaw. I put the shredded cucumber into a colander and press out the liquid, then wrap it in paper towel and twist until it's as dry as possible.

2½ pounds cucumbers, seeded if necessary
salt
½ cup low-fat sour cream or mayonnaise
1 tablespoon balsamic vinegar
2 teaspoons Dijon mustard
¾ teaspoon ground coriander
¾ teaspoon celery seeds
2 tablespoons minced chives
freshly ground black pepper to taste

Several hours before serving, shred cucumbers (peeling is optional). Place in a colander, pressing with your fingers to drain as much liquid as possible. Transfer cucumbers to a large bowl; sprinkle with 1 teaspoon of salt, then toss with 8 ice cubes. Cover and refrigerate for 1 hour. Remove ice cubes; drain cucumbers thoroughly, squeezing dry in paper towel. Return cucumbers to bowl; add remaining ingredients, salting and peppering to taste; toss to combine thoroughly. Cover and refrigerate until ready to serve. **Serves 4 to 6.**

A cucumber should be well-sliced, dressed with pepper and vinegar, and then thrown out.

*— Samuel Johnson*

## To Peel or Not to Peel . . .

Cucumbers are often coated with an edible wax to seal in moisture and extend shelf life. This coating, though not particularly pleasant on the palate, is not generally harmful. Washing the cucumber with soapy water (rinse well!) will remove most of the wax—don't wash until just before using. Bottom line: Taste the peel before deciding if you should leave it on—waxed or not, if the peel's bitter, remove it.

He had been eight years upon a project for extracting sunbeams out of cucumbers, which were to be put in vials hermetically sealed, and let out to warm the air in raw inclement summers.

*— Jonathan Swift*

*See also* VEGETABLES

# Curry

*See* SEASONINGS

# Custard

She had a strong sweetish odor that all her rose water and soap could not subdue, an odor I loved because it made me think of warm custard.

*— Isabel Allende*

Custard, *n.* A detestable substance produced by a malevolent conspiracy of the hen, the cow, and the cook.

*— Ambrose Bierce*

# Custard Care

It's easy to run into trouble when making a custard because too high a temperature can coagulate the eggs and curdle what should be a silky smooth texture. Here are a few tips to keep that from happening:

Stir the mixture constantly so the egg's protein coagulates evenly and smoothly. Recipes often call for egg yolks only because egg whites coagulate at a lower temperature than the yolks.

Raising the heat to hurry a custard will only curdle the mixture.

If your custard begins to curdle, quickly pour it into a blender jar, cover, and process until smooth (start blender at LOW speed and gradually increase to HIGH). Return it to a clean pan and continue cooking.

Custard is done when it leaves a thick coating on the back of a metal spoon. Dip a spoon into the custard and run your finger across the back of it; it should leave a definitive track. Custard is also ready when it registers 170°F on a candy thermometer.

Immediately remove cooked custard from the heat or it will continue to cook.

For a perfectly smooth result, pour custard through a fine sieve into a bowl.

Quick-cool custard by placing the pan in a large bowl of ice water and stirring the custard until it's cool.

Place a piece of plastic wrap or waxed paper right on the custard's surface and refrigerate.

*See also* DESSERTS; PUDDING

# Desserts

*The word "dessert" comes from the French* desservir, *which means "to clear away," as in clearing the plates before the grand finale. For centuries, desserts were luxuries because sugar was scarce and therefore expensive; hence, it was sometimes referred to as "white gold." Thankfully — at least for those of us with a sweet tooth — sugar is no longer expensive, which means that indulging ourselves is easier than ever!*

Comedy just pokes at problems, rarely confronts them squarely. Drama is like a plate of meat and potatoes, comedy is rather the dessert, a bit like meringue.

*— Woody Allen*

Bring on the dessert. I think I am about to die. *(Alternatively:* I feel the end approaching. Quick, bring me my dessert, coffee, and liqueur.)

*— Pierette Brillat-Savarin* (often attributed to Jean Anthelme Brillat-Savarin, when in fact it was said by his aunt!)

The dessert is said to be to the dinner what the madrigal is to literature—it is the light poetry of the kitchen.

*— George Ellwanger*

[People] come to me with their heads held high and announce that they do not eat sugar anymore, as though they have tackled one of life's deadly sins. My response is to ask them how long they have had this problem and if they have considered seeing a psychiatrist. *— Emily Luchetti*

One of the goldenest of the golden rules in making up a menu . . . is to pay special attention to the dessert course . . . nobody seems able to resist a delicious dessert.

*— Wolfgang Puck*

*See also* CAKES; CANDY; CHOCOLATE; COOKIES; CUSTARD; ICE CREAM; PASTRY; PIES; PUDDING; SWEETS

# Baked Caramel Apples

What could be more comforting on a crisp autumn evening than baked apples, gooey with caramel sauce? The next morning coarsely chop and warm the leftovers to spoon over pancakes or waffles.

Ooey-Gooey Caramel Sauce, page 299
6 large tart apples
about ¾ cup apple juice or apple cider
1 cup heavy whipping cream
2 drops pure almond extract
2 tablespoons confectioners' sugar
2 tablespoons amaretto liqueur (optional)

Prepare caramel sauce; set aside (may be done up to a week in advance). Preheat oven to 350°F. Grease a shallow baking pan large enough to hold apples. Core apples from the top, cutting to within ½ inch of the bottom. Use a vegetable peeler or sharp paring knife to remove about a ½-inch strip of peel around top of each apple. Arrange apples upright in pan; pour in apple juice or cider to cover bottom of pan. Using about 1 cup of the caramel, fill each apple cavity with sauce; spread some of the sauce around the peeled rim to prevent discoloration. Bake, uncovered, for 30 to 40 minutes, or until apples are tender when pierced with a fork. Whip cream and almond extract to soft-peak stage. Add sugar, beating until cream forms firm peaks. If desired, slowly drizzle in amaretto while mixer is running; be careful not to overbeat cream. Serve apples hot, topped with additional caramel sauce (let excess sauce drizzle down sides); pass whipped cream for guests to serve themselves. **Serves 6.**

# Dieting and Diets

**Sorry, guys, calories** do **count.** *With all the hooplah about reducing fat in our diets (definitely a good idea), a lot of people seem to think that calories simply don't count anymore — or at least that they're not as important as they were once thought to be. Recently in a restaurant I actually overheard a rather Rubenesque woman proclaiming that she was on a reduced-fat diet. "I don't get hungry," she said, "because I snack on red-licorice twists, which contain absolutely no fat!" HEL-LOHHHHH . . . It's clear that this woman probably glanced at the package, saw "o fat grams," and thought she was home free. In fact, calories definitely do count, but to confuse the issue further, all calories are not alike. To begin with, calories come from four sources — alcohol, carbohydrates, fats, and proteins — and they don't all count in the same way. Here's the breakdown: Fat packs a hefty 9 calories per gram, over twice as much as the 4 calories per gram carried by both carbohydrates and proteins. And, if you're like me and enjoy wine with dinner, you should know that alcohol contains 7 calories per gram, almost as many as fat! All of which is food for thought the next time you have to choose between ice cream and an apple.*

If you want to feel important, go on a diet.

*— Joey Adams*

For when we lose twenty pounds, dear reader . . . we may be losing the twenty best pounds we have! We may be losing the pounds that contain our genius, our humanity, or love and honesty.

*— Woody Allen*

No diet will remove all the fat from your body because the brain is entirely fat. Without a brain you might look good, but all you could do is run for public office.

*— Covert Bailey*

What you eat standing up doesn't count.

*– Beth Barnes*

If there's life after whipped cream, it's in Thigh City.

*– Erma Bombeck*

Life is too short for cuisine minceur and for diets. Dietetic meals are like an opera without the orchestra.

*– Paul Bocuse*

The [liquid diet] powder is mixed with water and tastes exactly like powder mixed with water.

*– Art Buchwald*

It's not women's fault that diets don't work. It's not perversity of lack of willpower. God did this — in Her great wisdom.

*– Dr. Wayne Callaway*

Worrying about calories and cholesterol takes the fun out of food.

*– Julia Child*

Those food labels that say "no fat, no cholesterol" might as well say "no taste, no fun."

*– Julia Child*

The further I travel in search of the ideal slimming method the more I am convinced that food is one of the oldest and greatest comforters . . . a secret return to the womb. . . .

*– Roy Andries de Groot*

> It's a very odd thing — as can be —
> That whatever Miss T. eats
> Turns into Miss T.

*– Walter de la Mare*

So far I've always kept my diet secret but now I might as well tell everyone what it is. Lots of grapefruit throughout the day and plenty of virile young men.

*– Angie Dickinson*

If you want to look young and thin, hang around old fat people.

*— Jim Eason*

'Tis a superstition to insist on a special diet. All is made at last of the same chemical atoms.

*— Ralph Waldo Emerson*

I've been on a diet for two weeks and all I've lost is two weeks.

*— Totie Fields*

It is wonderful, if we chose the right diet, what an extraordinarily small quantity would suffice.

*— Mohandas K. Ghandi*

Your body is the baggage you must carry through life. The more excess baggage, the shorter the trip.

*— Arnold Glasgow*

Most people eat as if they were fattening themselves for the market.

*— E. W. Howe*

We never repent of having eaten too little.

*— Thomas Jefferson*

Overweight is one of America's major health problems; I think that is because we love our food too little, not too much. If it tastes fabulous, if every bite delights, if we really pay attention, we will end up eating less, not to deprive ourselves, but because we will be satisfied.

*— Barbara Kafka*

I feel about airplanes the way I feel about diets. It seems to me they are wonderful things for other people to go on.

*— Jean Kerr*

If you have formed the habit of checking on every new diet that comes along, you will find that, mercifully, they all blur together, leaving you with only one definite piece of information: French-fried potatoes are out.

*– Jean Kerr*

An optimist is a girl who mistakes a bulge for a curve.

*– Ring Lardner*

If you wish to grow thinner, diminish your dinner,
    And take to light claret instead of pale ale;
Look down with an utter contempt upon butter,
    And never touch bread till it's toasted—or stale.

*– H. S. Leigh*

I told my doctor I get very tired when I go on a diet, so he gave me pep pills. Know what happened? I ate faster.

*– Joe E. Lewis*

"How long does getting thin take?" Pooh asked anxiously.

*– A. A. Milne*

A seafood diet . . . if you see food, eat it!

*– Miss Piggy*

Young misses whut eats heavy mos' gener'ly doan never ketch husbands.

*– Margaret Mitchell (Mammy to Scarlett O'Hara
in the film Gone With the Wind)*

I refuse to spend my life worrying about what I eat. There is no pleasure worth forgoing just for an extra three years in the geriatric ward.

*– John Mortimer*

The toughest part of being on a diet is shutting up about it.

*– Gerald Nachman*

How easy for those who do not bulge
To not overindulge!

— *Ogden Nash*

The reason fat people are happy is that the nerves are well protected.

— *Luciano Pavarotti*

A diet is a plan, generally hopeless, for reducing your weight, which tests your will power but does little for your waistline.

— *Herbert B. Prochnow*

The chief excitement in a woman's life is spotting women who are fatter than she is.

— *Helen Rowland*

Hank Fonda . . . was also very skinny, and someone told him that milk mixed with brandy was a very good way to add pounds. We started with a lot of milk and a little bit of brandy. Then some more. Soon the color got darker and darker. We used to drink that concoction for breakfast and by 8 A.M. we were half stoned. Anyway, I gained some weight.

— *Jimmy Stewart*

I have gained and lost the same ten pounds so many times over and over again my cellulite must have déjà vu.

— *Jane Wagner*

I never worry about diets. The only carrots that interest me are the number you get in a diamond.

— *Mae West*

I went to a fat farm to lose some weight. Then I got a call saying, "If you lose 1 pound, you will lose this part," so I immediately left and went to the Dairy Queen.

— *Oprah Winfrey*
(*regarding her role in the film* The Color Purple)

Nobody wants protein. The best-educated, most affluent people in America want to pay top dollar to eat a third-world diet.

— *Clark Wolf*

To ask women to become unnaturally thin is to ask them to relinquish their sexuality.

— *Naomi Wolf*

A waist is a terrible thing to mind.

— *Ziggy (by Tom Wilson)*

Diets are for those who are thick and tired of it.

— *Anonymous*

Eat, drink and have fun, for tomorrow we shall diet.

— *Anonymous*

*See also* EXERCISE

# Digestion

*Digestive enzymes are a boon to those who find that eating beans, broccoli, cabbage, cauliflower, grains, and onions is best done behind closed doors. For those unfortunate souls (and if misery loves company there are plenty of us out there), such foods produce gas because they contain almost-impossible-to-digest complex sugars that sit in the large intestine zealously bubbling and fermenting away, creating humiliating situations at the worst possible moments. But take heart, there's a simple solution known as digestive enzymes, which help break down those miscreant complex sugars into more easily digested simple sugars. These lifesavers come in tablet form, and some — like the immensely popular Beano — also come in liquid form. They're commonly available at health-food stores, drugstores, and supermarkets. So now that you know how to alleviate those particular embarrassing moments, you can enjoy beans and veggies without "fear of flatulence"!*

Digestion, *n.* The conversion of victuals into virtues. . . .

— *Ambrose Bierce*

The healthy stomach is nothing if it is not conservative. Few radicals have good digestions.

— *Samuel Butler*

Because of the media hype and woefully inadequate information, too many people nowadays are deathly afraid of their food, and what does fear of food do to the digestive system? I am sure that an unhappy or suspicious stomach, constricted and uneasy with worry, cannot digest properly. And if digestion is poor, the whole body politic suffers.

— *Julia Child*

I feel a very unusual sensation—if it is not indigestion, I think it must be gratitude.

— *Benjamin Disraeli*

Indigestion is charged by God with enforcing morality on the stomach.

— *Victor Hugo*

Unquiet meals make ill digestions.

— *Shakespeare*

To eat is human, to digest divine.

— *Mark Twain*

# Dining

*What's the difference between "dining" and "eating"? Well, to my way of thinking, the word "eating" describes the simple mechanical act of chewing and ingesting nourishment, sans ceremony or accoutrements. The word "dining," on the other hand, implies a certain care given to the process — an ambience, a mood, perhaps the pleasure of good company, although one can certainly dine alone. The act of dining intimates a grace absent in the simple pro-*

*cedure of* eating. *Frank Lloyd Wright called dining "a great artistic opportunity" — something that is most certainly lacking in drive-through hamburger stands or fast-fix diners.*

Animals feed, man eats; only a man of culture knows how to dine.

*— Jean-Anthelme Brillat-Savarin*

The table is the only place where a man is never bored for the first hour.

*— Jean-Anthelme Brillat-Savarin*

It's a lovely thing—everyone sitting down together, sharing food.

*— Alice May Brock*

There is a universe between the meal set brusquely before you and that on which thought and careful planning have been spent.

*— Edward Bunyard*

Given the choice, most people would prefer to dine with an inspired companion than to dine on inspired food.

*— Irena Chalmers*

I never eat when I can dine.

*— Maurice Chevalier*

Sharing food with another human being is an intimate act that should not be indulged in lightly.

*— M. F. K. Fisher*

There is a communion of more than our bodies when bread is broken and wine is drunk.

*— M. F. K. Fisher*

It isn't so much what's on the table that matters, as what's on the chairs.

*— W. S. Gilbert*

Spread the table and the quarrel will end.
*— Hebrew proverb*

The art of dining well is no slight art, the pleasure not a slight pleasure.
*— Michel Eyquem de Montaigne*

A chief maxim in dining with comfort is to have what you want when you want it.
*— Thomas Walker*

. . . though one can dine in New York one could not dwell there.
*— Oscar Wilde*

One cannot think well, love well, sleep well, if one has not dined well.
*— Virginia Woolf*

Dining is and always was a great artistic opportunity.
*— Frank Lloyd Wright*

*See also* AIRLINE FOOD; EATING, GENERAL

# Dining Out

*See* RESTAURANTS

# Dinner

Everything ends this way in France, everything. Weddings, christenings, duels, burials, swindlings, diplomatic affairs— everything is a pretext for a good dinner.
*— Jean Anouilh*

I have always thought that there is no more fruitful source of family discontent than badly cooked dinners and untidy ways.
*— Isabella Beeton*

. . . at the end of a good dinner, body and soul both enjoy a remarkable sense of well-being.

*— Jean-Anthelme Brillat-Savarin*

Americans are just beginning to regard food the way the French always have. Dinner is not what you do in the evening before something else. Dinner is the evening.

*— Art Buchwald*

All human history attests
That happiness for a man—the hungry sinner!
Since Eve ate apples, much depends on dinner.

*— Lord Byron*

Music with dinner is an insult both to the cook and the violinist.

*— G. K. Chesterton*

I personally prefer a nice frozen TV dinner at home because it's so little trouble. All you have to do is have another drink while you're throwing it in the garbage.

*— Jack Douglas*

The cold truth is that family dinners are more often than not an ordeal of nervous indigestion. . . .

*— M. F. K. Fisher*

If the soup had been as warm as the wine; if the wine had been as old as the turkey; and if the turkey had had a breast like the maid, it would have been a swell dinner.

*— Duncan Hines*

A man seldom thinks with more earnestness of anything than he does of his dinner.

*— Samuel Johnson*

A man is in general better pleased when he has a good dinner upon his table, than when his wife talks Greek.

*— Samuel Johnson*

Civilized adults do not take apple juice with dinner.

*— Fran Lebowitz*

If the soup had been as warm as the claret . . .
If the claret had been as old as the chicken . . .
If the chicken had been as fat as our host . . .
It would have been a splendid meal.
— *Donald McCullough*

**S**trange to see how a good dinner and feasting reconciles everybody.
— *Samuel Pepys*

**D**inner at the Huntercombes' possessed only two dramatic features—the wine was a farce and the food a tragedy.
— *Anthony Powell*

**H**ell was to him . . . a little eternity of family dinners.
— *Philippa Pullar*

**A** freeloader is a confirmed guest. He is the man who is always willing to come to dinner.
— *Damon Runyon*

**A** dinner lubricates business.
— *William Scott, Lord Stowell*

**S**how me another pleasure like dinner which comes every day and lasts an hour.
— *Count Charles Talleyrand*

**H**e planned dinners, of enchanting aromatic foods . . . endless dinners, in which one could alternate flavour with flavour from sunset to dawn without satiety, while one breathed great draughts of the bouquet of old brandy.
— *Evelyn Waugh*

**A**fter a good dinner, one can forgive anybody, even one's own relatives.
— *Oscar Wilde*

*See also* BREAKFAST; DINNER PARTIES; PICNICS

# Dinner Parties;
# Dinner Invitations

Punctuality is the most important quality of the cook, and it should also be that of the guests.

*– Jean-Anthelme Brillat-Savarin*

I had rather munch a crust of brown bread and an onion in a corner, without any more ado or ceremony, than feed upon turkey at another man's table, where one is fain to sit mincing and chewing his meat an hour together, drink little, be always wiping his fingers and his chops, and never dare to cough nor sneeze, though he has never so much a mind to it, nor do a many things which a body may do freely by one's self.

*– Miguel de Cervantes*

Dining-out is a vice, a dissipation of spirit punished by remorse. We eat, drink and talk a little too much, abuse all our friends, belch out our literary preferences and are egged on by accomplices in the audience to acts of mental exhibitionism. Such evenings cannot fail to diminish those who take part in them.

*– Cyril Connolly*

The best number for a dinner party is two—myself and a dam' good head waiter.

*– Nubar Gulbenkian*

The formal Washington dinner party has all the spontaneity of a Japanese imperial funeral.

*– Simon Hoggart*

If you are the hostess and you have a well-raised Southern boy at the table, please pick up your fork and eat. Otherwise, he'll sit there, starving, waiting for you to begin.

*– Barbara Kafka*

# Entertaining at Home— What Goes Where?

Entertaining the boss or other important-to-impress notable and not sure of just how the table should be set? Here are a few tips:

🌿Forks go on the left, knives and spoons on the right; the knives positioned with the cutting side toward the plate. No more than three pieces of silverware should be placed on each side of the plate. Arrange the silver in the order it will be used, from the outside working in—if soup is your first course, put the soupspoon at the far right position. Dessert utensils should be positioned at the top of the plate—the spoon should be closest to the plate, the handle facing right; the fork above the spoon, facing in the opposite direction.

🌿Glasses go on the right: the water glass directly above the knife, and the wine or other glasses to its right. The bread plate goes opposite the glasses, above the forks, with a butter knife sitting diagonally across the top of the plate. If a salad plate is used, position it to the left of the forks.

🌿The water should be poured and candles lit when the guests sit down. Pour the wine after they're seated.

🌿When serving food to seated guests, serve from the left; remove plates from the right. Since glasses are on the right side of a table setting, it's appropriate to pour beverages while standing to the right of your guest.

🌿Pass food around the table in a clockwise direction (from right to left).

At a dinner party one should eat wisely but not too well, and talk well but not too wisely.

— *W. Somerset Maugham*

A dinner invitation, once accepted, is a sacred obligation. If you die before the dinner party takes place, your executor must attend.

— *Ward McAllister*

One should never refuse an invitation to lunch or dinner, for one never knows what one may have to eat the next day.

— *Edouard de Pomiane*

A man who can dominate a London dinner table can dominate the world.

— *Oscar Wilde*

If you accept a dinner invitation you have a moral obligation to be amusing.

— *Wallis Warfield Windsor (Duchess of Windsor)*

A dinner invitation is a terrible thing to waste.

— *Anonymous*

*See also* DINNER; ENTERTAINING; MANNERS

# Drinking

*Most of us can't remember it, but Prohibition — a four-letter word to many a drinker — lasted from 1920 to 1933, a remarkable thirteen years! To the joy of drinkers and chagrin of prohibitionists, Prohibition ended on December 5, 1933, when Utah ratified the Twenty-first Amendment. Though eight states remained "dry," I'm told that the sound of clinking glasses could be heard throughout the rest of North America as celebrations commenced in earnest. One of my favorite drinking-related remarks comes from anatomist and teacher Florence Sabin, who wittily summed up Prohibition when she said, "The prohibition law, written for weaklings and derelicts, has divided the nation, like Gaul, into three parts — wets, drys, and hypocrites."*

If all be true that I do think
There are five reasons we should drink;
Good wine—a friend—or being dry—
Or lest we should be by and by—
Or any other reason why.

*— Henry Aldrich*

When men drink, then they are rich and successful and win lawsuits and are happy and help their friends.

*— Aristophanes*

Drinking makes such fools of people, and people are such fools to begin with, that it's compounding a felony.

*— Robert Benchley*

The trouble with the world is that everybody in it is three drinks behind.

*— Humphrey Bogart*

Gazing at the typewriter in moments of desperation, I console myself with three thoughts: alcohol at six, dinner at eight and to be immortal you've got to be dead.

*— Gyles Brandeth*

If the devil were to offer me a resurgence of what is commonly called virility, I'd decline. "Just keep my liver and lungs in good working order," I'd reply, "so I can go on drinking and smoking!"

*— Luis Buñuel*

What's drinking?
A mere pause from thinking!

*— Lord Byron*

Man, being reasonable, must get drunk;
The best of life is but intoxication.

*— Lord Byron*

I think a man ought to get drunk at least twice a year just on principle, so he won't let himself get snotty about it.

*– Raymond Chandler*

[Americans] have a sort of permanent intoxication from within, a sort of invisible champagne . . . [they] do not need to drink to inspire them to do anything, though they do sometimes, I think, need a little for the deeper and more delicate purpose of teaching them how to do nothing.

*– G. K. Chesterton*

Drink because you are happy, but never because you are miserable.

*– G. K. Chesterton*

. . . my rule of life prescribed as an absolutely sacred rite smoking cigars and also the drinking of alcohol before, after, and if need be during all meals and in the intervals between them.

*– Winston Churchill*

When I was younger, I made it a rule never to take strong drink before lunch. It is now my rule never to do so before breakfast.

*– Winston Churchill*

I have taken more out of alcohol than alcohol has taken out of me.

*– Winston Churchill*

There is nothing wrong with sobriety in moderation.

*– John Ciardi*

Some men are like musical glasses—to produce their finest tones you must keep them wet.

*– Samuel Taylor Coleridge*

Conversation did not flow with the drink; it drowned in it.

*– Quentin Crisp*

## Almonds, Anyone?

Legend has it that eating a handful of almonds before imbibing will forestall drunkeness and the ensuing hangover. Pity there aren't warning labels attached to such tales that say just what a handful of nuts might do to your waistline—a very large person could easily hold almost 1,000 calories' worth in one very large hand!

Drinking when we are not thirsty and making love at any time, madam, is all that distinguishes us from the other animals.

*— Pierre de Beaumarchais*

A Drunkard cannot meet a Cork
Without a Revery. . . .

*— Emily Dickinson*

No other human being, no woman, no poem or music, book or painting can replace alcohol in its power to give man the illusion of real creation.

*— Marguerite Duras*

The man that isn't jolly after drinking
Is just a drivelling idiot, to my thinking.

*— Euripedes*

My first wife drove me to drink. I shall always be grateful to her for that.

*— W. C. Fields*

What contemptible scoundrel stole the cork from my lunch?

*— W. C. Fields*

We frequently hear of people dying from too much drinking. . . . But the blame is always placed on whiskey. Why this should be I could never understand. You can die from drinking too much of anything—coffee, water, milk, soft drinks. . . . And so long as the presence of death lurks with anyone who goes through the simple act of swallowing, I will make mine whiskey.

*– W. C. Fields*

It's a great advantage not to drink among hard-drinking people. You can hold your tongue and, moreover, you can time any little irregularity of your own so that everybody else is so blind that they don't see or care.

*– F. Scott Fitzgerald*

There are more old drunkards than old doctors.

*– Benjamin Franklin*

He that drinks fast, pays slow.

*– Benjamin Franklin*

A drinker has a hole under his nose that all his money runs into.

*– Thomas Fuller*

Inebriation is the great equalizer.

*– Paul Kelly*

Even though a number of people have tried, no one has yet found a way to drink for a living.

*– Jean Kerr*

Drink! for you know not whence you came
nor why:
Drink! for you know not why you go,
nor where.

*– Omar Khayyám*

The rapturous, wild, and ineffable pleasure
Of drinking at somebody else's expense.
— *H. S. Leigh*

**O**ne can drink too much, but one never drinks enough.
— *Gotthold Ephraim Lessing*

**I** don't drink; I don't like it — it makes me feel good.
— *Oscar Levant*

**I** envy people who drink — at least they know what to blame everything on.
— *Oscar Levant*

**I** drink to forget I drink.
— *Joe E. Lewis*

**A**s a cure for the cold, take your toddy to bed, put one bowler hat at the foot, and drink until you see two.
— *Sir Robert Bruce Lockhart*

**I** drink only to make my friends seem interesting.
— *Don Marquis*

**B**y the time a bartender knows what drink a man will have before he orders, there is little else about him worth knowing.
— *Don Marquis*

**I**f you drink, don't drive. Don't even putt.
— *Dean Martin*

**A** prohibitionist is the sort of man one wouldn't care to drink with — even if he drank.
— *H. L. Mencken*

**I**t is, of course, true that we can be intemperate in eating as well as in drinking, but the results of the intemperance would appear to be different. After a fifth helping of rice-pudding one does not become over-familiar with strangers, nor does an extra slice of ham inspire a man to beat his wife.
— *A. A. Milne*

Of old all invitations ended
With the well-known R.S.V.P.,
But now our [Prohibition] laws have been amended
The hostess writes B.Y.O.B.
— *Christopher Morley*

It is an odd but universally held opinion that anyone who doesn't drink must be an alcoholic.
— *P. J. O'Rourke*

Being sober for so many years is getting interesting.
— *Peter O'Toole*

There are two reasons for drinking: one is, when you are thirsty, to cure it; the other when you are not thirsty, to prevent it. . . . Prevention is better than cure.
— *Thomas Love Peacock*

It's all right to drink like a fish—if you drink what a fish drinks.
— *Mary Pettibone Poole*

I drink no more than a sponge.
— *François Rabelais*

Drunkenness . . . is temporary suicide.
— *Bertrand Russell*

Of all vices, drinking is the most incompatible with greatness.
— *Sir Walter Scott*

Anybody that can't get drunk by midnight ain't trying.
— *Toots Shor*

At the punch bowl's brink
Let the thirsty think
What they say in Japan:
"First the man takes a drink,
Then the drink takes a drink,
Then the drink takes the man!"
— *Edward Rowland Sill*

The ancient Goths of Germany had a wise custom of debating everything of importance to their state twice; that is, once drunk and once sober. Drunk, that their councils might not want vigor; and sober, that they might not want discretion.

*– Laurence Sterne*

I never drink —wine.

*– Bram Stoker* (said by Count Dracula)

We were to do more business after dinner; but after dinner is after dinner —an old saying and true, "much drinking, little thinking."

*– Jonathan Swift*

There are two things that will be believed of any man whatsoever, and one of them is that he has taken to drink.

*– Booth Tarkington*

An alcoholic is someone you don't like who drinks as much as you do.

*– Dylan Thomas*

I hate to advocate drugs, alcohol, violence, or insanity to anyone, but they've always worked for me.

*– Hunter S. Thompson*

"I think this calls for a drink," has long been one of our national slogans.

*– James Thurber*

I don't have a drinking problem except when I can't get one.

*– Tom Waits*

Once in every lifetime one should experience a hangover, so as to abstain from immoderate imbibing for the rest of one's life.

*– Maggie Waldron*

Give me another drink and I'll tell you all you want to know.

*– Fats Waller*

A drinking man's someone who wants to forget he isn't still young and believing.

*— Tennessee Williams*

The worst thing about some men is that when they are not drunk they are sober.

*— William Butler Yeats*

*See also* BEER; BEVERAGES; BRANDY; CHAMPAGNE; COCKTAILS; LIQUOR; PORT; TOASTS; WINE

## Blond Bombshell

This bloody Mary rendition is perfectly wonderful in the summer months when yellow tomatoes are rife. I prefer gin in this drink, but vodka or tequila work as well. Cheers!

1½ cups yellow tomato purée (about 1 pound
    tomatoes)
¾ cup gin
¼ cup freshly squeezed lemon or lime juice
2 tablespoons white wine Worcestershire sauce
½ to 1 teaspoon green Tabasco sauce
celery salt and white pepper to taste
4 yellow tomato wedges for garnish (optional)

In a blender jar, combine tomato purée, gin, lemon or lime juice, Worcestershire sauce, and Tabasco sauce. Process 15 seconds. Add 8 ice cubes; process 15 seconds (ice will break into large chunks). Season to taste with celery salt and pepper. Pour into 4 stemmed glasses; garnish each serving with tomato wedge, if desired. **Serves 4.**

# Duck

We ate to the music of the [duck] press — the crunch of the bones, the drip of blood and marrow, the tap of the spoon basting the thin slices of breast.

*— Evelyn Waugh*

## Duck Talk

BOMBAY DUCK: A term originated by the British Raj in India for dried salted fish, most often used as a condiment with curries

DUCK: Used as a verb, to duck can refer to lowering one's head or body, or moving fast to avoid being seen, or submerging under water, or dodging one's obligations

DUCK AND RUN: To escape to freedom; make a break

DUCKBOARD: A board that's laid across wet or muddy ground

DUCKING STOOL: A sixteenth-century teetertotter-like device with a chair on one end in which some poor transgressor was tied and ducked (dunked) into water

DUCK SOUP: A slang term for a simple or easily accomplished job or assignment

DUCKTAIL: A hairstyle in which the long side hair is slicked down and combed back, to meet at an unturned point in the back at the nape of the neck

DUCK THE ISSUE: To avoid something you don't want to do or discuss

DUCKY: British slang for "most excellent"

*See also* MEAT; POULTRY

# Eating, General

*I'd have loved to have lived in France in the first quarter of the eighteenth century (who knows, maybe I did), for I would certainly have made it a point to know Jean-Anthelme Brillat-Savarin. I like the man's style, his brilliant wit, his dry sense of humor. In this century, of course, I must make do with his writings, specifically, Physiologie de Goût, translated so beautifully in M. F. K. Fisher's The Physiology of Taste. This section on "eating" brings to mind one of my favorite Brillat-Savarin quotes, in which one can almost see the twinkle in his eye as he so teasingly wrote: "Those . . . from whom nature has withheld the legacy of taste, have long faces, and long eyes and noses, whatever their height there is something elongated in their proportions. Their hair is dark and unglossy, and they are never plump; it was they who invented trousers." Delicious!*

A crust eaten in peace is better than a banquet partaken in anxiety.

— *Aesop*

The secret of staying young is to live honestly, eat slowly, and lie about your age.

— *Lucille Ball*

Why so many different dishes? Man sinks almost to the level of an animal when eating becomes his chief pleasure.

— *Ludwig van Beethoven*

Edible, *adj.* Good to eat and wholesome to digest, as a worm to a toad, a toad to a snake, a snake to a pig, a pig to a man, and a man to a worm.

— *Ambrose Bierce*

Tell me what you eat, and I shall tell you what you are.

— *Jean-Anthelme Brillat-Savarin*

In eating we experience a certain special and indefinable well-being.

*— Jean-Anthelme Brillat-Savarin*

All things being equal, those who know how to eat look ten years younger than those who are ignorant of that science.

*— Jean-Anthelme Brillat-Savarin*

What you eat and drink is 50 percent of life.

*— Gérard Depardieu*

Probably no strychnine has sent as many husbands into their graves as mealtime scolding has, and nothing has driven more men into the arms of other women as the sound of a shrill whine at table.

*— M. F. K. Fisher*

Almost every person has something secret he likes to eat.

*— M. F. K. Fisher*

Between the ages of twenty and fifty, John Doe spends some twenty thousand hours chewing and swallowing food, more than eight hundred days and nights of steady eating. The mere contemplation of this fact is upsetting enough.

*— M. F. K. Fisher*

Eating and sleeping are a waste of time.

*— Gerald Ford*

He that never eats too much will never be lazy.

*— Benjamin Franklin*

> Gobble your food however you might,
> Never eat a dish that is trite.

*— Greek proverb*

If you are ever at a loss to support a flagging conversation, introduce the subject of eating.

*— Leigh Hunt*

The whole of nature is a conjunction of the verb *to eat,* in the active and passive.

— *Willian Inge*

Statistics show that of those who contract the habit of eating, very few ever survive.

— *William Wallace Irwin*

For my part, I mind my belly most studiously and very carefully; for I look upon it that he who does not mind his belly will hardly mind anything else.

— *Samuel Johnson*

## Taste Bud Byways

How food tastes depends on many things including its smell, temperature (too cold and the flavor will be muted; too hot and the flavor is lost), texture, sound (yes!, we perceive crunchy or crispy foods differently than those that are soft), and of course what our tongue tells us about flavor. And what a miraculous organ is the tongue — small, powerfully perceptive, and packed with receptor cells just waiting to tell us what's what. In fact, you could call it a taste-bud map, with pathways in different areas sensing different things — sweetness is detected at the tip of the tongue, bitterness at the far back, sourness along the forward edges, and saltiness overall, but primarily up front. Food for thought: The next time you lick an ice-cream cone, notice that subtle shock of sweetness at the tip of your tongue, and know that all's right with the world.

Eating takes a special talent. Some people are much better at it than others. In that way, it's like sex, and as with sex, it's more fun with someone who really likes it. I can't imagine having a lasting friendship with anyone who is not interested in food.

— *Alan King*

He who eats for two must work for three.

— *Kurdish proverb*

One of the great disadvantages of being a coward is that one is constantly having to eat things that one does not wish to eat.

— *Robert Lynd*

There are some sad facts concerning eating and drinking. One is that the best foods are unwholesome: an arrangement doubtless made by the authors of our being in order to circumvent gluttony.

— *Rose Macaulay*

Why put off till tomorrow what you can eat today?

— *Miss Piggy*

Never eat more than you can lift.

— *Miss Piggy*

## Tongue-Tied

HOLD (ONE'S) TONGUE: To be quiet, even when you don't want to

LOSE (ONE'S) TONGUE: To become temporarily speechless from embarrassment, shock, surprise, etc.

ON THE TIP OF (ONE'S) TONGUE: Usually something you want to say if only you could remember it

SLIP OF THE TONGUE: A remark you wish you hadn't said

TONGUE IN CHEEK: A disingenuous or mocking comment

I never met a meal I didn't like!

— *Miss Piggy*

One must eat to live, and not live to eat.

— *Molière*

... the smell and taste of things remain poised for a long time, like souls, ready to remind us, waiting and hoping for their moment, amid the ruins of all the rest; and bear unfaltering, in the almost palpable drop of their essence, the vast structure of recollection.

*— Marcel Proust*

> Eat slowly: only men in rags
> And gluttons old in sin
> Mistake themselves for carpet-bags
> And tumble victuals in.
>
> *— Sir Walter Raleigh*

It is the mark of a mean, vulgar and ignoble spirit to dwell on the thought of food before meal times or worse to dwell on it afterwards, to discuss it and wallow in the remembered pleasures of every mouthful.

*— Saint Francis de Sales*

Eating well gives a spectacular joy to life.

*— Elsa Schiaparelli*

If you wish for anything like happiness in the fifth act of life, eat and drink about one-half what you could eat and drink.

*— Sydney Smith*

Bad men live that they may eat and drink, whereas good men eat and drink that they may live.

*— Socrates*

Without the assistance of eating and drinking the most sparkling wit would be as heavy as a bad soufflé, and the brightest talent as dull as a looking-glass on a foggy day.

*— Alexis Soyer*

Most people love to eat. There's a real celebratory aspect to a great meal—a sensuality and a sexuality and a theatricality to it.

*— Stanley Tucci*

Part of the secret of success in life is to eat what you like and let the food fight it out inside.

*— Mark Twain*

Nothing would be more tiresome than eating and drinking if God had not made them a pleasure as well as a necessity.

*— Voltaire*

Thought depends absolutely on the stomach, but in spite of that, those who have the best stomachs are not the best thinkers.

*— Voltaire*

I believe eating well with an ear attuned to the body's language satisfies an unconscious hunger.

*— Maggie Waldron*

The lunches of fifty-seven years had caused his chest to slip down to the mezzanine floor.

*— P. G. Wodehouse*

*See also* AIRLINE FOOD; APPETITE; DIGESTION; DINING

# Eels

*Throughout the ages, folklore has been rife with legends of eels. Some Philippine tribes honor eels as souls of the dead, while in parts of Europe it's believed that rubbing the skin with eel oil will* enable one to see fairies. *Because* of their somewhat phallic shape, eels have also been attributed with aphrodisiacal powers. *My fa-vorite* tidbit about this snakelike fish is what baby eels are called – "*elvers.*" *Elvers* . . . there's something sweet, and small, and innocent about that word, and *I* like the way it feels when *I* say it. *But* there's a fact about eels that most people don't know, and that's the rather remarkable journey they take before even becom-ing elvers. *The* minuscule, transparent eel larvae drift on ocean currents from the *Sargasso Sea* (part of the north *Atlantic Ocean* between the *West Indies* and the *Azores*) to *European* waters, a pilgrimage that can take up to three years. *Once* they reach coastal areas they metamorphose into tiny elvers (also called "glass eels"), at which time they begin wriggling up inland waterways and across boggy grounds to reach the small ponds and streams where they'll take up residence. *All* of which is food for thought the next time you see eel on a menu – *I* know they've certainly earned my respect!

*I* think the eels prefer to be eaten by someone who loves them.

– *Samual Applebaum*

*I*f eels only looked a little less like eels more people would want to eat them.

– *Clement Freud*

## Anagramatically Yours

An anagram for "elver" is "revel," something these baby eels undoubtedly do when they reach their freshwater destination and settle down to the business of being eels.

*See also* FISH

# Eggplant

*Anyone watching their calories knows better than to fry eggplant because it soaks up fat like a sponge. That's the bad news . . . and the good news. You see, when you eat fatty foods with eggplant, the result is that the eggplant absorbs some of those fats before they can do any harm. So broil your eggplant and let it sponge up the bad guys in your system.*

Over-the-hill eggplant betrays its age precisely in the same manner as over-the-hill debutantes: slack skin and slightly puckered posteriors.

*— Dione Lucas*

*See also* VEGETABLES

# Eggs

*The answer to which came first, the chicken or the egg, seems obvious. Early Phoenicians thought that a primeval egg split open to form heaven and earth; Egyptians believed that their god Ptah created the egg from the sun and the moon; and American Indians thought that the Great Spirit burst forth from a giant golden egg to create the world. See any chickens mentioned?*

Be content to remember that those who can make omelettes properly can do nothing else.

*— Hilaire Belloc*

The French way of preserving eggs is to dissolve beeswax, mix a little olive oil with it, and use it to paint the eggs all over. If they are kept cool and unjostled, they will stay good for two years, which is probably true of most of us.

*— Peg Bracken*

A hen is only an egg's way of making another egg.

*— Samuel Butler*

There are entire nations that have never learned how to scramble eggs. One has only to travel in Great Britain.

*— Jon Carroll*

In Australia, what they do to eggs is incomprehensible — they serve them with spaghetti at breakfast. They cook the eggs for nine hours until all moisture is removed, then they cozy them up to thick chewy noodles warmed in the can not moments before.

*— Jon Carroll*

Eggs are very much like small boys. If you overheat them or overbeat them, they will turn on you, and no amount of future love will right the wrong.

*— Irena Chalmers*

A boiled egg raised its little lid and revealed its buttercup yolk.

*— Colette*

I never see an egg brought on my table but I feel penetrated with the wonderful change it would have undergone but for my gluttony; it might have been a gentle, useful hen, leading her chickens with a care and vigilance which speaks shame to many women.

*— St. John de Crèvecoeur*

Egg dishes have a kind of elegance, a freshness, an allure, which sets them quite apart from any other kind of food, so that it becomes a great pleasure to be able to cook them properly and to serve them in just the right condition.

*— Elizabeth David*

It was obvious that the egg had come first. There was something dignified about a silent passive egg, whereas Aunt Irene found it difficult to envisage an angel bearing a hen — which despite its undoubted merits, was a foolish and largely intractable bird.

*— Alice Thomas Ellis*

# The Perfect Hard-Cooked Egg

First of all, according to the American Egg Board, the term hard- or soft-"boiled" is inappropriate because boiling eggs makes them tough and rubbery. Now that that's settled, here are some tips for hard-"cooked" eggs.

✎Very fresh eggs (less than a week old) will be harder to peel after cooking than their older kin. To cook, place a single layer of eggs in a saucepan and top with at least 1 inch of water. Cover and bring to a *gentle* boil, stirring occasionally to keep the yolk centered (if you care), then remove from heat and let stand for 15 to 17 minutes. Drain hot water; immediately cover with cold water, adding a few ice cubes, and let stand until completely cool. The ice-water cooling method prevents the formation of a dark gray-green halo on the yolk.

✎Eggshells won't crack during cooking (and the eggs will be easier to peel) if you pierce the large end with a needle, thumbtack, or egg piercer.

There is always a best way of doing everything, if it be to boil an egg.

— *Ralph Waldo Emerson*

Probably one of the most private things in the world is an egg until it is broken.

— *M. F. K. Fisher*

Of course, the finest way to know that the egg you plan to eat is a fresh one is to own the hen that makes the egg.

— *M. F. K. Fisher*

You can't make an omelet without breaking eggs.

— *French proverb*

🌿Refrigerate cooled, hard-cooked eggs (preferably in their original carton) and use within 1 week.

🌿To help distinguish hard-cooked eggs from raw ones in the refrigerator, add a few drops of food coloring to the cooking water. Or use a crayon to mark hard-cooked eggs. If you haven't marked a hard-cooked egg and aren't sure if it's raw, give it a spin on the countertop—cooked eggs spin easily, raw eggs wobble because the liquid inside is moving.

🌿Hard-cooked eggs are easier to peel and slice when they're cold. Before peeling, gently roll an egg between your palm and the countertop, creating dozens of hairline cracks in the shell. Peel under cold running water, starting at the large end.

🌿Egg slicers, available at many supermarkets, hardware stores, and gourmet shops, make slicing a cinch. Otherwise, use a sharp, thin-bladed knife, dipping it into cold water every few slices.

I don't know how long I like my egg boiled, but it's exactly right by the time I finish my hair.

— *Betty Furness*

. . . it might seem that an egg which has succeeded in being fresh has done all that can reasonably be expected of it.

— *Henry James*

Who can help loving the land [France] that has taught us six hundred and eighty-five ways to dress eggs?

— *Thomas Moore*

To innovate in cooking, it is more difficult to attack a boiled egg than a pheasant mousse.

— *Raymond Oliver*

# Egg Talk

BAD EGG: A good-for-nothing; one who's unreliable or dishonest

DON'T PUT ALL YOUR EGGS IN ONE BASKET: Don't invest all your time, energy, or money in only one investment, activity, or person

EGGHEAD: An intellectual, a "brain"

EGG ON ONE'S FACE: Embarrassment or humiliation after saying or doing something foolish

GOOD EGG: A likable, trustworthy person

GOOSE EGG: Zero

INNOCENT AS A NEW-LAID EGG: Fresh, unspoiled

LAY AN EGG: To fail miserably, usually in front of others

NEST EGG: Money or other investments set aside for the future

ROTTEN EGG: A "bad egg," only worse

WALKING ON EGGS: To move with caution, whether verbally or physically

Love and eggs are best when they are fresh.

— *Russian proverb*

The eggs do not teach the hen.

— *Russian proverb*

I have never regretted Paradise Lost since I discovered that it contained no eggs-and-bacon.

— *Dorothy Sayers*

It may be the cock that crows, but it is the hen that lays the eggs.

— *Margaret Thatcher*

Put all your eggs in one basket and—WATCH THAT BASKET.

— *Mark Twain*

An unhatched egg is to me the greatest challenge in life.
— *E. B. White*

... having decapitated an egg, [he] peered sharply into its interior as if hoping to surprise guilty secrets.
— *P. G. Wodehouse*

The egg is to cuisine what the article is to speech.
— *Anonymous*

*See also* BACON; COOKBOOKS; FOOD, GENERAL

# Chocolate Eggnog

This nog is seriously chocolaty and not for the timid. If you prefer, substitute Kahlúa, Frangelico, or brandy for the rum.

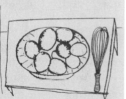

4 eggs, separated
½ cup packed brown sugar
⅔ cup unsweetened cocoa powder
1 tablespoon pure vanilla extract
1½ cups milk
½ cup light rum
⅛ teaspoon salt
1½ cups heavy whipping cream, whipped to soft-
  peak stage
about ⅓ cup grated semisweet chocolate

In a large bowl, beat together egg yolks, sugar, cocoa, and vanilla until thick and smooth. Gently stir in milk and rum; refrigerate until just before serving, at least 2 hours, so mixture becomes very cold. Beat egg whites and salt until soft peaks form. Fold whipped cream into chocolate mixture, then gently fold in egg whites. Serve immediately, garnished with grated chocolate. **Serves 8 (about 6-ounce servings).**

# English Food

*See* ETHNIC FOODS

# Entertaining

Hostesses who entertain much must make up their parties as ministers make up their cabinets, on grounds other than personal liking.

— *George Eliot*

A host is like a general: calamities often reveal his genius.

— *Horace*

Tempting things often seem better when they are shared. Good food is good enough alone, but it takes on eminence when there is host, or hostess — preferably both — with undiluted love for the act of hospitality, and guests to match.

— *Evan Jones*

The best host is not he who spends the most money to entertain his guests, but he who takes the most intelligent interest in their welfare and makes sure that they will have a good time, something good to drink, something that is both good and new, if possible.

— *André Simon*

It is a very poor consolation to be told that the man who has given one a bad dinner, or poor wine, is irreproachable in private life. Even the cardinal virtues cannot atone for half-cold entrées.

— *Oscar Wilde*

The hostess must be like the duck — calm and unruffled on the surface, and paddling like hell underneath.

— *Anonymous*

*See also* DINNER PARTIES; MANNERS

# Epicures

*See* GOURMETS, GASTRONOMES, GOURMANDS, GLUTTONS, AND EPICURES

# Ethnic Foods

*Culinary patriotism aside, most of us enjoy — sometimes lust after — cuisines of other lands. But some nations consistently get a bad rap for their food — the British come immediately to mind and often seem to get the worst of it. The reality is that delicious dishes abound in every country — a truism that's not particularly shared by some of the following notables.*

Germans . . . if they can't shove it into an animal casing, they don't eat it.

*— Tim Allen*

There are certain tastes which those who have never experienced them as children can neither understand nor cure: who but an Englishman, for example, can know the delights of stone-cold leathery toast for breakfast, or the wonders of "Dead Man's Leg"?

*— W. H. Auden*

France . . . is a land of milk and honey, the best milk and the most perfumed honey, where all the good things of the earth overflow and are cooked to perfection.

*— William Bolitho*

Bad French cuisine is perhaps the most unfortunate on earth.

*— Craig Claiborne*

A French cook passes almost everything through a sieve, and according to the theory of evolution, he will himself one day pass through the sieve and become a purée.

*— E. S. Dallas*

Nobody has ever been able to find out why the English regard a glass of wine added to a soup or stew as a reckless foreign extravagance and at the same time spend pounds on bottled sauces, gravy powders, soup cubes, ketchups and artificial flavourings.

*– Elizabeth David*

One symptom of the decline of culture in Britain is indifference to the art of preparing food.

*– T. S. Eliot*

When the normal American, for instance, reads that Mexicans eat fried worms, that Indians eat dogs and monkeys, that Africans eat grasshoppers, and that the Chinese and many Europeans eat coagulated blood, he simply retches and thanks God for the good old U.S.A. where wholesome food comes in bright cans and crisp boxes.

*– Bergen Evans*

Porridge or Prunes . . . Breakfast had begun. It is an epitome — not, indeed, of English food, but of the forces which drag it into the dirt. It voices the true spirit of gastronomic joylessness. Porridge fills the Englishman up, prunes clear him out, so their functions are opposed. But their spirit is the same: they eschew pleasure and consider delicacy immoral.

*– E. M. Forster*

The French cook; we [the English] open tins.

*– John Galsworthy*

An Italian meal is a story told from nature, taking its rhythms, its humors, its bounty and turning them into episodes for the senses.

*– Marcella Hazan*

The real American pattern of feeding is the snack. It lasts from early morning to bedtime.

*– John Hess*

The French have an honest but somewhat misguided sense of transcendent superiority in every sphere of human activity, which has little basis in actual accomplishment and is perhaps best exemplified by the Western world's veneration of French haute cuisine, which has been accurately characterized as a creation of madmen for the delectation of fools.

*— Jay Jacobs*

Many things have struck me as prodigious in [England], none so much as the restraint that the ordinary Englishman practices towards the woman, wife or servant, who prepares his meals. Why he does not murder her is a great and insoluble mystery.

*— Odette Keun*

Japanese food is very pretty and undoubtedly a suitable cuisine in Japan, which is largely populated by people of below average size. Hostesses hell-bent on serving such food to occidentals would be well advised to supplement it with something more substantial and to keep in mind that almost everybody likes french fries.

*— Fran Lebowitz*

The trouble with eating Italian food is that five or six days later you're hungry again.

*— George Miller*

Because of their cuisine, Germans don't consider farting rude. They'd certainly be out of luck if they did.

*— P. J. O'Rourke*

I used to think . . . that the English cook the way they do because, through sheer technical deficiency, they had not been able to master the art of cooking. I have discovered to my stupefaction that the English cook that way because that is the way they like it.

*— Waverley Root*

He [Marie-Antoine Carême] knew exactly what he was doing—which was to conquer the world with French cooking, just as Napoleon had conquered it with the French army.

— *Raymond Sokolov*

There is no question that Rumanian-Jewish food is heavy. One meal is equal in heaviness, I would guess, to eight or nine years of steady mung-bean eating.

— *Calvin Trillin*

A man accustomed to American food and American domestic cookery would not starve to death suddenly in Europe, but I think he would gradually waste away, and eventually die.

— *Mark Twain*

There is here and there an American who will say he can remember rising from a European table d'hôte perfectly satisfied; but we must not overlook the fact that there is also here and there an American who will lie.

— *Mark Twain*

Hell is a place where all the cooks are British.

— *Anonymous*

*See also* BREAKFAST

# Exercise

I believe every human has a finite number of heartbeats. I don't intend to waste any of mine running around doing exercises.

— *Neil Armstrong*

The only reason I would take up jogging is so that I could hear heavy breathing again.

— *Erma Bombeck*

Exercise is the most awful illusion. The secret is a lot of aspirin and marrons glacés.

— *Noël Coward*

You know you've reached middle age when your weightlifting consists of merely standing up.

— *Bob Hope*

I'm Jewish. I don't work out. If God wanted us to bend over he'd put diamonds on the floor.

— *Joan Rivers*

*See also* DIETING AND DIETS

# Figs

*People are passionate about figs and there doesn't seem to be any middle ground — you either love them or hate them. I know a woman who deems herself extremely well bred who, after one too many glasses of wine in the Napa Valley, went into a fig frenzy, stealing pocketsful of ripe fruit from a winemaker's tree and showing no compunction at all when she got caught with the goods. Such is the passion that figs inspire. I grew up in the other camp. My first exposure to this honey-sweet fruit was in the form of Fig Newtons, probably the only detested food of my childhood. It was not until I was well into adulthood that I tasted the full glory of a fresh fig, and only then because I didn't recognize it — it wasn't after all dark brown, full of hard, yukky seeds, and stuck in the middle of a cakelike cookie.*

To eat figs off the tree in the very early morning, when they have been barely touched by the sun, is one of the exquisite pleasures of the Mediterranean.

— *Elizabeth David*

Shape is a good part of the fig's delight.

— *Jane Grigson*

## Fig Talk

DON'T GIVE A FIG: Couldn't care less about

FIG LEAF: Besides the leaf itself, a phrase that refers to insufficient covering or camouflage

IN FINE (OR FULL) FIG: In great physical shape; dressed to the nines

NOT WORTH A FIG: A trivial or contemptible amount

We bought figs for breakfast, immense thin-skinned ones. They broke in one's fingers and tasted of wine and honey.

– *Katherine Mansfield*

There were glossed sticky dates, cold rich figs, cramped belly to belly in small boxes. . . .

– *Thomas Wolfe*

# Finnan Haddie

*Finnan haddie (also called "finnan haddock") is partially boned, lightly salted, and smoked haddock. Its name is derived from the northeast Scotland fishing villages Findon and/or Findhorn.*

Give me a platter of choice finnan haddie, freshly cooked in its bath of water and milk, add melted butter, a slice or two of hot toast, a pot of steaming Darjeeling tea, and you may tell the butler to dispense with the caviar, truffles and nightingales' tongues.

– *Craig Claiborne*

*See also* FISH

# Fish

*Some people will go to great lengths to have a fish tale to tell. Why, they'll even risk their lives by eating the incredibly deadly fugu (FOO-goo), also known as "puffer fish" and "blowfish." This fish is so potentially lethal that entire books have been written on properly cleaning and preparing it. The Japanese train and license special chefs to handle fugu, whose skin, ovaries, liver, and intestines contain tetrodotoxin, a chemical hundreds of times more lethal than strychnine or cyanide. A minute amount of this potent neurotoxin produces dizziness, vomiting, numbness, dilated pupils, cramps, labored breathing, horrendous itching all over the body, and, finally, a neurological paralysis that induces a comalike state during which the victims are often aware of what's going on — until, that is, they die. They don't always die — some recover, only to relate the horror of being presumed dead and not being able to twitch a muscle to tell anyone otherwise. For thrillseekers, fugu — traditionally prepared as sashimi — has a sweet white flesh similar to that of pompano, only no one has been poisoned by pompano.*

Food is meant to tempt as well as nourish, and everything that lives in water is seductive.

— *Jean-Paul Aron*

It is better to be the head of a live sardine than the tail of a dead trout.

— *Francis Beeding*

Fish is held out to be one of the greatest luxuries of the table and not only necessary, but even indispensable at all dinners where there is any pretense to excellence or fashion.

— *Isabella Beeton*

# Sounds Fishy!

The old adage "cook fish until it flakes" produces dry, over-cooked fish, which has turned more people off to fish than almost anything else. Fish is at its best at the point when it turns opaque. A basic guideline: Cook fish for 10 minutes per inch of thickness. The timing will vary on the fish's density, fat content, and whether or not it's boned. To test fish for doneness, stick the tip of a knife into the thickest part of the flesh and check the opacity. Don't forget that residual heat will continue to cook the fish for a few minutes after it's removed from the heat source. Another way to test fish doneness is to insert an instant-read thermometer into the thickest part of the flesh—a reading of 145°F means it's cooked.

. . . I consider'd the taking of every fish as a kind of unprovoked murder, since none could do us any injury to justify the slaughter.

*— Benjamin Franklin*

Fish and visitors stink in three days.

*— Benjamin Franklin*

Ruling a big country is like cooking a small fish (too much handling will spoil it).

*— Lao-tzu, 550 B.C.*

Fish to taste right, must swim three times—in water, in butter and in wine in the stomach.

*— Polish proverb*

I must confess that fishing has never been a great passion of mine, as it seems to require more patience than I normally have on hand. But cooking and eating fish . . . well, that's a different story.

*— Wolfgang Puck*

# Fish Talk

A FINE KETTLE OF FISH: An unpleasant situation

BIG FISH: Someone important. It's definitely preferable to be a big fish in a small pond than a small fish in a big pond

BIGGER FISH TO FRY: To have something more important to do

COLD FISH: One who's impassive or hard-hearted

DEAD FISH: A cold and/or clammy, limp handshake

DRINK LIKE A FISH: To drink to excess (and not, like a fish, water)

FISH; FISHING EXPEDITION: To investigate (often covertly) information regarding a situation or person; also to ask indirectly for a compliment

FISHEYE: An unfriendly or suspicious look

FISH OUT OF WATER: Someone out of his or her element; one ill at ease

FISH STORY: One that's exaggerated or embellished

FISHY: Something suspicious

FOOD FOR THE FISHES: Movie mafioso lingo for a corpse

"The bigger the better" is, though a common, not a universal rule; it does not, for instance, apply to fish. . . .

– *George Saintsbury*

*See also* ABALONE; CATFISH; CAVIAR; CHILDREN AND FOOD; CLAMS; COD; CRAB; EELS; FINNAN HADDIE; HADDOCK; LOBSTER; MUSSELS; OCTOPUS; OYSTERS; SALMON; SHRIMP; SURIMI; SUSHI; TROUT

# Cracked Pepper Tuna Steaks

Fresh tuna has a distinctively rich-flavored flesh that's so firm it feels almost like meat in the mouth. Buy tuna steaks that are all about the same thickness so they cook evenly and get done at the same time. If you use a nonstick pan you won't need as much oil. Swordfish can be successfully substituted for the tuna, if you prefer.

about ⅓ cup cracked black pepper
6 tuna steaks
salt
2 to 4 tablespoons olive oil
¼ cup heavy whipping cream
2 tablespoons dry white wine
about 3 tablespoons chopped fresh chives for garnish

Generously sprinkle pepper on both sides of each tuna steak, pressing it into the surface. Salt to taste. In a large skillet over medium-high heat, heat oil until hot. Sauté tuna steaks until rare to medium-rare *(or done to your preference)*. Remove to a warm platter; cover and place in a 250°F oven. Add cream and wine to pan drippings. Cook over medium-high heat for 3 minutes, stirring constantly. Salt to taste. Drizzle sauce over tuna steaks; garnish with chives. **Serves 6.**

# Food, General

**A word to the wise:** *The word "victuals" (food) is not pronounced VIK-choo-uhlz, but VIT-ulz. According to Charles Harrington Elster in his intriguing book* There Is No Zoo in

*Z*oology, *"You can take your cue on this word from Jed Clampitt and the other Beverly Hillbillies: VIT-ulz is the only standard pronunciation. More often than you might think, the plain folk of the world are correct in their pronunciation of plain English words, for sometimes the result of a little education is a lot of overrefinement."* *T*o me, the variant spelling of vittles *actually* looks more like the word sounds than the standard victuals. *S*o, now that we've chewed that over sufficiently, just how did that *C* get in there? *E*tymologists tell us that the word is rooted in the *L*ate *L*atin vìctuâlia *(pertaining to nourishment)*, which was altered to the *M*iddle *E*nglish vitaille *(provisions)*. *N*o one knows why, but the *C* crept back into the word in the sixteenth century. *O*h, well, it seems to be there for good . . . just remember to forget that it is there and say VIT-ulz.

*A*ll food is the gift of the gods and has something of the miraculous, the egg no less than the truffle.

*– Sybille Bedford*

*T*here is no known navy-blue food. If there is navy-blue food in the refrigerator, it signifies death.

*– Erma Bombeck*

*I*n this uncertain world, the food is disposable. It is the wrappings that are permanent.

*– Irena Chalmers*

*T*here are conceivably those in Kalamazoo who think that a Philadelphia scrapple has to do with fisticuffs, and that hush puppies have to do with footgear.

*– Craig Claiborne*

*M*other Nature clearly intended for us to get our food from the "patty" group, which includes hamburgers, fish sticks and McNuggets. . . .

*– Dave Barry*

Man is the only animal that can remain on friendly terms with the victims he intends to eat until he eats them.

*— Samuel Butler*

Cuisine is when things taste like themselves.

*— Curnonsky*

The right food always comes at the right time. Reliance on out-of-season foods makes the gastronomic year an endlessly boring repetition.

*— Roy Andries de Groot*

The greatest dishes are very simple dishes.

*— Auguste Escoffier*

. . . the joy of living was wrapped up in the delights of food.

*— Laura Esquivel*

Reminds me of my safari in Africa. Somebody forgot the corkscrew and for several days we had to live on nothing but food and water.

*— W. C. Fields*

If Time, so fleeting, must like humans die, let it be filled with good food and good talk, and then embalmed in the perfumes of conviviality.

*— M. F. K. Fisher*

Food has a rare ability to carry you back. . . . [it] can be counted on to produce a sensation in time present that will duplicate a sensation from time past.

*— Michael Frank*

Food, like love, must never be a joyless experience.

*— Bert Greene*

. . . when from a long-distant past nothing subsists, after the people are dead, after the things are broken and scattered, still . . . the smell and taste of things remain. . . .

*— Bert Greene*

Satisfy your hearts with food and wine, for therein is courage and strength.

*— Homer*

Laughter is brightest where the food is plentiful and the company cordial.

*— Irish proverb*

Ingredients, whether individually or in combination with others, haven't much to say for themselves; they lie mute on the plate, imparting no information concerned with anything but their intrinsic properties, their contrast to, or harmonization with, their bedfellows and the proficiency of the cook.

*— Jay Jacobs*

I'm as much for health as the next one. However, I think that it's important to remember, in our harried search for vigor, that food should be a happy idea. The scare headlines have gotten out of control. Food will not kill you. Doing without is what does us in.

*— Barbara Kafka*

Food is an important part of a balanced diet.

*— Fran Lebowitz*

If food did not exist it would be well-nigh impossible to get certain types off the phone, as one would be unable to say "Look, I've got to run but let's have dinner sometime soon."

*— Fran Lebowitz*

When you get to fifty-two food becomes more important than sex.

*— Prue Leith*

All's well that ends with a good meal.

*— Arnold Lobel*

What is food to one may be fierce poison to others.

*— Lucretius*

How do they taste? They taste like more.

*— H. L. Mencken*

Food is a subject of conversation more spiritually refreshing even than the weather, for the number of possible remarks about the weather is limited, whereas of food you can talk on and on and on.

*– A. A. Milne*

. . . food and charity make a wonderful blend.

*– Paul Newman*

Food doesn't exist, but can only be invented. And reinvented.

*– Joyce Carol Oates*

. . . our relationship to food makes us human, and our repudiation of a relationship to food is a repudiation of our humanity as well.

*– Joyce Carol Oates*

No decent person ever starts a food fight he's not sure he can win.

*– P. J. O'Rourke*

All I ask of food is that it doesn't harm me.

*– Michael Palin*

I have always maintained that there is nothing wrong with nursery food now that we are grown up and can have a glass of wine with it.

*– Elizabeth Ray*

Food always means something beyond the fact of what we put into our mouths. Food, I found, is about loving and living and dying.

*– Paul Schmidt*

There is no love sincerer than the love of food.

*– George Bernard Shaw*

Sadness and good food are incompatible.

*– Charles Simic*

When our souls are happy, they talk about food.

*— Charles Simic*

That food has always been, and will continue to be, the basis for one of our greater snobbisms does not explain the fact that the attitude toward the food choice of others is becoming more and more heatedly exclusive until it may well turn into one of those forms of bigotry against which gallant little committees are constantly planning campaigns in the cause of justice and decency.

*— Cornelia Otis Skinner*

However humble it may be, a meal has a definite plot, the intention of which is to intrigue, stimulate, and satisfy.

*— Margaret Visser*

I hate people who are not serious about their meals.

*— Oscar Wilde*

If a man be sensible and one fine morning, while he is lying in bed, count at the tips of his fingers how many things in this life truly will give him enjoyment, invariably he will find food is the first one.

*— Lin Yutang*

# French Food

*See* ETHNIC FOODS

# Fruit

While forbidden fruit is said to taste sweeter, it usually spoils faster.

*— Abigail Van Buren*

This special feeling towards fruit, its glory and abundance, is I would say universal. . . . We respond to strawberry fields or cherry orchards with a delight that a cabbage patch or even an elegant vegetable garden cannot provoke.

*— Jane Grigson*

*See also* APPLES; APRICOTS; BLACKBERRIES; BLUEBERRIES; CHERRIES; CRANBERRIES; FIGS; GRAPES; LEMONS; MANGOES; MELONS; NECTARINES; ORANGES; PEACHES; PEARS; PRUNES; RASPBERRIES; RHUBARB; STRAWBERRIES

# Fruitcake

*See* CAKE

# Garlic

Down through the ages, garlic has been credited with miraculous healing abilities as well as some occult powers, such as warding off demons, not to mention vampires. Egyptians fed this potent bulb to their pyramid-building slaves because it was thought to increase physical strength. Modern-day research credits this member of the lily family with compounds that forestall numerous diseases, including cancer, asthma, arthritis, diabetes, cardiovascular disease, and infections. In fact, scientists tell us that garlic is an excellent antibiotic, often more effective than penicillin and tetracycline for some bacterial infections. Eating more garlic to improve overall health is great, but no one wants to become a social recluse because of dragon breath. And you don't have to suffer this fate if you chew on fennel seeds, a coffee bean, or chlorophyll-rich greens like parsley; or drink a tablespoon or two of lemon juice diluted with a little water and sugar; or take some chlorophyll tablets or a product like Breath Assure, which is based on parsley oil. So now you can enjoy the lusty pleasures of garlic while feeling at the same time downright upright about being good to your body.

The honest flavor of fresh garlic is something I can never have enough of.

— *James Beard*

It is not really an exaggeration to say that peace and happiness begin, geographically, where garlic is used in cooking.

— *X. Marcel Boulestin*

Tomatoes and oregano make it Italian; wine and tarragon make it French. Sour cream makes it Russian; lemon and cinnamon make it Greek. Soy sauce makes it Chinese; garlic makes it good.

— *Alice May Brock*

There are many miracles in the world to be celebrated and, for me, garlic is the most deserving.

— *Leo Buscaglia*

Garlic in everything is just as bad as garlic in nothing.

— *Minna Cohn*

The offensiveness of the breath of him that hath eaten garlick will lead you by the nose to the knowledge thereof.

— *Nicholas Culpeper*

## The Bitter Truth

Treat garlic roughly and it'll pay you back—the more it's crushed, chopped, pressed, or puréed the more bitter and assertive its flavor becomes. Garlic that is sliced or left whole is milder. Another caveat: Garlic will turn pungent and bitter if overbrowned. Minced garlic takes no more than a minute to cook over medium-high heat.

Garlic is the Fifth Element. As important to our existence as earth, air, fire and water. Without garlic I simply would not care to live.

*– Chef Louis Diat*

It has been said of garlic that everyone knows its odour save he who has eaten it, and who wonders why everyone flies at his approach.

*– George Ellwanger*

To dream that you are eating garlic denotes that you will discover hidden secrets and meet with some domestic jar. To dream that there is garlic in the house is lucky.

*– Richard Folkard*

Garlic is the "vanilla" of Provence.

*– French proverb*

The emotional content of garlic almost equals its culinary value.

*– Arthur E. Grosser*

## Some Like It Sweet

For sweeter, milder garlic, put unpeeled garlic cloves in a small saucepan; cover with cold water. Bring to a boil, then drain and rinse. Repeat two more times. Peel off skins and use as desired.

You are what you eat. For example, if you eat garlic you're apt to be a hermit.

*– Franklin P. Jones*

A nickel will get you on the subway, but garlic will get you a seat.

*– old New York proverb*

Garlic is the ketchup of intellectuals.

*– Anonymous*

There is no such thing as a "little" garlic.

*– Anonymous*

*See also* APHRODISIACS

## Roasted Garlic

When garlic is roasted it becomes buttery-soft and golden, its flavor slightly sweet and nutty. Squeeze the soft roasted-garlic pearls out of their skins (from the pointed end) and spread like butter on bread or crostini. Or mash roasted garlic and use in soups, sauces, and salad dressings or on vegetables and meats.

3 heads garlic
3 teaspoons olive oil

From the tip (pointed) end of each head of garlic, gently rub off the outer layers of papery skin. Separate the cloves, but leave their skins intact. *Or* leave the individual cloves connected with their skin intact. Preheat oven to 400°F. Place individual cloves (or garlic heads, root end down) in a medium baking dish or pan; drizzle with oil. Cover with foil; bake about 30 minutes, or until soft when pierced with the tip of a pointed knife. Baking time may vary, depending on the size of the cloves. Refrigerate leftover cloves in an airtight jar for up to 10 days.

# Garnishes

For everyone doing rustic food, there are others out there braiding chives.

*– Joyce Goldstein*

I hate tomato roses, parsley on plates where no one will ever eat it, and any food gotten up to look like something else.

*— Barbara Kafka*

# Gastronomes

*See* GOURMETS, GASTRONOMES, GOURMANDS, GLUTTONS, AND EPICURES

# Gingerbread

*Queen Elizabeth I so loved gingerbread that she employed a full-time baker to make it. Sixteenth-century gingerbread was not the simple preparation it is today, but was intricately shaped, then decorated and sometimes adorned with gold leaf.*

Had I but a penny in the world, thou shouldst have it for gingerbread.

*— William Shakespeare*

## Ginger Power

Ginger is a remarkable spice in many ways. Not only does it lend an exotic flavor to myriad sweet and savory dishes, but its medicinal qualities have been prized for eons. Modern-day science now confirms that ginger does, indeed, have many healing qualities—it's an antioxidant and an anti-inflammatory, relieves nausea, thins the blood, and destroys bacteria.

*See also* DESSERTS

# Gluttons; Gluttony

*See* GOURMETS, GASTRONOMES, GOURMANDS, GLUTTONS, AND EPICURES

# Gourmets, Gastronomes, Gourmands, Gluttons, and Epicures

**Epicuriosity** *is, with most food writers, an addiction. We just have to know all there is to know about food. In my case, it's even worse — I want to know what the words mean, which brings us to the heading of this section. It breaks down like this:* **Gourmets** *have discriminating palates and are considered connoisseurs of fine food and drink;* **gastronomes** *are the same as gourmets, only the word is harder to pronounce;* **gourmands** *are people who appreciate fine food, but often to excess;* **gluttons** *have a gargantuan appetite for both food and drink, often without regard to quality; and* **epicures** *not only have refined taste, but cultivate the knowledge and appreciation of fine food and wine. (I don't know about you, but I rather like the sound of that last one.) Oh, but we're not through. The word "epicure" is derived from the name of the Greek philosopher* **Epicurus,** *the founder of* **Epicureanism,** *which — among other things — declared that the highest good is pleasure. However, Epicurus was referring not to hedonistic indulgence, but to tranquillity, a truth that did not escape Thomas Jefferson, as you'll see in the quote on page 172.*

**A** daydream is a meal at which images are eaten. Some of us are gourmets, some gourmands, and a good many take their images precooked out of a can and swallow them down whole, absent-mindedly and with little relish.

*— W. H. Auden*

**I** am not a gourmet chick.

*— Pearl Bailey*

**F**oodies are all palate, with a vestigial person attached.

*— Ann Barr and Paul Levy*

A gourmet who thinks of calories is like a tart who looks at her watch.

— *James Beard*

To be a gourmet, you must start early. . . . You must live in France; your father must have been a gourmet. Nothing in life must interest you but your stomach. With hands trembling, you must approach the meal about which you have worried all day and risk dying of a stroke if it isn't perfect.

— *Ludwig Bemelmans*

Actually, the true gourmet, like the true artist, is one of the unhappiest creatures existent. His trouble comes from so seldom finding what he constantly seeks: perfection.

— *Ludwig Bemelmans*

Cannibal, *n.* A gastronome of the old school who preserves the simple tastes and adheres to the natural diet of the pre-pork period.

— *Ambrose Bierce*

Glutton, *n.* A person who escapes the evils of moderation by committing dyspepsia.

— *Ambrose Bierce*

I am not a glutton — I am an explorer of food.

— *Erma Bombeck*

Good living is far from being destructive to good health . . . all things being equal, gourmands live much longer than other folk.

— *Jean-Anthelme Brillat-Savarin*

Gourmandism is an impassioned, reasoned, and habitual preference for everything which gratifies the organ of taste . . . [it] is the common bond which unites the nations of the world.

— *Jean-Anthelme Brillat-Savarin*

I am a gourmet
YOU are a gourmand
HE is fat.

*– Craig Brown*

The gentle art of gastronomy is a friendly one. It hurdles the language barrier, makes friends among civilized people, and warms the heart. . . .

*– Samuel Chamberlain*

I have never been anything so refined as a *gourmet;* so I am happy to say that I am still quite capable of being a glutton. My ignorance of cookery is such that I can even eat the food in the most fashionable and expensive hotels in London.

*– G. K. Chesterton*

Life itself is the proper binge.

*– Julia Child*

Gluttony is an emotional escape, a sign something is eating us.

*– Peter de Vries*

A complete lack of caution is perhaps one of the true signs of a real gourmet: he has no need for it, being filled as he is with a God-given and intelligently self-cultivated sense of gastronomical freedom.

*– M. F. K. Fisher*

Once at least in the life of every human, whether he be brute or trembling daffodil, comes a moment of complete gastronomic satisfaction. It is, I am sure, as much a matter of spirit as of body. Everything is right; nothing jars. There is a kind of harmony, with every sensation and emotion melted into one chord of well-being.

*– M. F. K. Fisher*

It is a curious fact that no man likes to call himself a glutton, and yet each of us has in him a trace of gluttony, potential or actual. I cannot believe that there exists a single coherent human being who will not confess, at least to himself, that once or twice he has stuffed himself to bursting . . . for no other reason than the beastlike satisfaction of his belly.

*– M. F. K. Fisher*

Gourmets dig their graves with their teeth.

*– French proverb*

A gourmet is just a glutton with brains.

*– Philip W. Haberman Jr.*

An epicure is one who gets nothing better than the cream of everything but cheerfully makes the best of it.

*– Oliver Hereford*

I am an Epicurean. I consider the genuine (not the imputed) doctrines of Epicurus as containing everything rational in moral philosophy which Greece and Rome have left us.

*– Thomas Jefferson*

An epicure eats with his brain as well as his mouth.

*– Charles Lamb*

The art of being a gourmet has nothing to do with age, money, fame or country. It can be found in a thrifty French housewife with her *pot-au-feu* or in a white-capped chef in a skyscraper hotel.

*– Earle R. MacAusland*

A true gastronome should always be ready to eat, just as a soldier should always be ready to fight.

*– Charles Monselet*

A gourmet is a being pleasing to heaven.

*– Charles Monselet*

Gluttony is ranked with the deadly sins; it should be honored with the cardinal virtues. For the glutton, duty and amusement go hand in hand. Mind and body alike are satisfied. The good of a pleasantly planned dinner outbalances the evil of daily trials and tribulations.... Gluttony is a vice only when it leads to stupid, inartistic excess.

*– Elizabeth Robbins Pennell*

Certainly there are gourmets who would happily dine on monkey brains and Venezuelan human cube steak, but would flee in horror from the prospect of a white-bread-and-bologna sandwich.

*– Francine Prose*

It requires a voracious appetite to be a glutton. It demands exquisite judgment, a profound knowledge of every branch of the culinary art, a sensual and delicate palate, and a thousand other qualities very difficult to combine, in order to merit the title of gourmand.

*– Grimod de la Reynière*

The word "gourmet" has been run into the ground. Anybody's cousin who drinks wine with his meals, or who substitutes broccoli for potatoes considers himself a gourmet. It's become a dreaded word in the American language.

*– Will Rogers*

After eating, an epicure gives a thin smile of satisfaction; a gastronome, burping into his napkin, praises the food in a magazine; a gourmet, repressing his burp, criticizes the food in the same magazine; a gourmand belches happily and tells everybody where he ate.

*– William Safire*

Gourmand is the greedy fellow who does not mind very much about quality so long as he gets a lot.... Gourmet is the "choosey" eater, with definite likes and dislikes of his own, who prefers quality to quantity. Gastronome is the cultured and knowledgeable gourmet; his approach to all that is best to eat and drink is that of the epicurean philosopher who recognizes the ethical value of the amenities of a gracious way of living. . . . The greater number of gastronomes there will be in the world, the happier world it will be.

— *André Simon*

He who distinguishes the true savor of this food can never be a glutton; he who does not cannot be otherwise.

— *Henry David Thoreau*

Gluttony is not a secret vice.

— *Orson Welles*

# Grapes

*One of my favorite summertime treats as a kid was frozen grapes. Put them into the freezer for a couple of hours and those innocent little globes seemed to become (at least in my imagination) almost exotic. My friend Mary Beth and I would pop the icy green orbs into our mouths, one at a time, pretending that with each grape we would become more beautiful. I still eat frozen grapes — seedless red now — and find that my adult experience is different but even better, more sensuous. I still savor them one by one, rolling each grape around in my mouth and, just as it begins to soften, biting down through the frosty flesh, its juice in suspended animation.*

Always eat grapes downward—that is, always eat the best grapes first; in this way there will be none better left on the bunch, and each grape will seem good down to the last. If you eat the other way, you will not have a good grape in the lot.

— *Samuel Butler*

The word snob belongs to the sour-grape vocabulary.

— *Logan Pearsall Smith*

"Beulah, peel me a grape!"
> – *Mae West* (in the film *She Done Him Wrong*)

## Cool Grapes

Imagine my surprise when I discovered that my switching from green grapes—a childhood favorite—to red grapes was a very good thing. You see, scientific studies confirm that red grapes are rich in the powerful antioxidant quercetin, as well as the trace mineral boron, which is associated with brain power and bone strength. So my cool treat of frozen *red* grapes is also cool for my cells!

*See also* FRUIT

# Gravy

*In American slang, the word "gravy" means easy money or profit. The early 1920s saw the popularization of the term "gravy train" – a job or position that provides maximum advantage (in the form of fast or major money or other profit) with minimal or no effort. So, if someone says they're on a "gravy train," find out what track it's on and hop aboard!*

I come from a home where gravy is a beverage.
> – *Erma Bombeck*

Madam, I have been looking for a person who disliked gravy all my life: let us swear eternal friendship.
> – *Sydney Smith*

*See also* SAUCES

# Red-Eye Gravy with Ham Steaks

Red-eye gravy was allegedly so named because one of its integral ingredients is a healthy slug of strong coffee, which, of course, causes insomnia in some people. The number of servings this recipe makes depends on the heartiness of the appetites.

2 ($\frac{1}{2}$-inch thick) ham steaks
$\frac{3}{4}$ cup very strong coffee
3 tablespoons heavy whipping cream
salt and freshly ground black pepper

In a large skillet over medium-high heat, sauté ham steaks until well browned on both sides, 10 to 15 minutes. Transfer steaks to warm plates. Pour off any excess fat. Add coffee and cream to skillet. Cook over medium-high heat, stirring and scraping the bottom of the pan to loosen all the bits of browned ham. Cook until gravy is slightly reduced and nicely thickened. Pour over warm ham steaks; serve immediately. **Serves 2 to 4.**

# Grilling

**Where there's smoke there's flavor!** *No doubt about it, wood smoke adds fabulous flavor to grilled foods. Remember, however, to only use fruitwoods (apple, cherry, and peach) or hardwoods (alder, hickory, maple, mesquite, and oak) for cooking. Softwoods (pine and spruce) exude noxious resins and fumes that can ruin a food's flavor and possibly give you a stomachache. Both wood chips and chunks are available, but chips cook faster because they're smaller. They also take less soaking time, a necessary procedure to ensure that the wood doesn't go up in flames shortly after it hits the heat source.*

Grilling is like sunbathing. Everyone knows it's bad for you but no one ever stops doing it.
— *Laurie Colwin*

I'm a man. Men cook outside. . . . That outdoor grilling is a manly pursuit has long been beyond question. If this wasn't understood, you'd never get grown men to put on those aprons with pictures of dancing wienies and things on the front, and messages like "Come N' Get It." . . . Try putting that stuff on the family dog.
— *William Geist*

*See also* BARBECUE

# Haddock

[The haddock] was covered with a sort of hard yellow oilskin, as if it had been out in a lifeboat, and its insides gushed salt water when pricked.
— *E. M. Forster*

*See also* FINNAN HADDIE; FISH

# Ham

Carve a ham as if you were shaving the face of a friend.
— *Henri Charpentier*

I think food should be uncomplicated and undisguised. A ham is beautiful to behold, but it has no business being decorated to look like a violin.
— *Helen Corbitt*

A definition of eternity: A ham and two people.
— *Irma S. Rombauer and Marion Rombauer Becker*

Nothing helps scenery like ham and eggs.
— *Mark Twain*

*See also* BACON; MEAT; PORK; SAUSAGE

# Chutney Ham Rolls

These zingy rolls are perfect finger food for everything from cocktails to picnics. Use a chutney that's not too sweet, such as a ginger-mango or tomato chutney. You shouldn't need salt for the filling because the ham adds plenty of its own. Smoked or regular turkey slices may be substituted for the ham. If you use ham slices smaller than those called for in the recipe, the filling will go further.

6 hard-cooked eggs, finely chopped
1/4 cup chutney (finely chop any large pieces of fruit)
3 tablespoons mayonnaise (reduced-fat or fat-free is fine)
1 tablespoon Dijon mustard
1/3 cup minced toasted slivered almonds
black or cayenne pepper
10 (6 × 4-inch) very thin slices smoked ham

Turn chopped eggs into a medium bowl; use the back of a fork to smash finely. Add chutney, mayonnaise, mustard, and almonds; blend well. Add pepper to taste. Place one slice of ham, one of the long sides toward you, on a work surface. Spoon about 3 tablespoons of the egg mixture evenly along the ham edge nearest you, all the way to the ends. Starting with egg-covered side, roll up tightly. Use a knife to press any filling that squeezes out back into ham roll. Repeat with remaining egg mixture and ham slices. Place rolls, seam side down, on a plate. Cover and refrigerate until ready to serve. For cocktail-size rolls, cut in half crosswise. Serve chilled. **Makes 10 (6-inch) or 20 (3-inch) rolls.**

# Hamburgers

*Hamburgers rank right up there with hot dogs as one of the all-American foods. More than foods, really — edible institutions. The word "hamburger" derives from the port city of Hamburg, Germany, where the nineteenth-century people enjoyed pounded beefsteak in various forms. German immigrants undoubtedly brought the idea to American shores, where the first printed mention of "hamburger steak" appeared on an 1836 Delmonico restaurant menu.*

*There are myriad and varied legends of the Americanization of the hamburger — today's sandwich version. One of them credits a young 1885 Wisconsin county-fair concessionaire whose customers wanted his butter-fried ground beef in a walk-around form so they could eat and enjoy the fair simultaneously. Another says an 1892 Ohio county fair concessionaire invented the burger sandwich. Some say the hamburger was created in 1900 by the owner of a three-seat diner in New Haven, Connecticut, while others claim the hamburger made its first public appearance in 1904 at the St. Louis Exposition. So who knows, or cares really, when the end result is such down-to-earth-great-eating as the hamburger? The truth is that good ideas often occur to several people at the same time — it just depends on who acts on them first. Remember that the next time you have one.*

Hamburgers are not like pizza, climbing weirdly upscale. Hamburgers are down home.

*— Irena Chalmers*

It is the Americans who have managed to crown minced beef as hamburger, and to send it around the world so that even the fussy French have taken to *le boeuf haché, le hambourgaire.*

*— Julia Child*

Sacred cows make the tastiest hamburger.

*— Abbie Hoffman*

There's a lot more future in hamburgers than in baseball.

*— Ray Kroc*

It was not her sex appeal but the obvious relish with which she devoured the hamburger that made my pulse begin to hammer with excitement.

*— Ray Kroc*

You can find your way across this country using burger joints the way a navigator uses stars.

*— Charles Kuralt*

## Tips for Better Burgers

During cooking, higher-fat meats shrink more than lean meats. So when using ground chuck or regular ground beef, form the patties about a half inch larger than the diameter of the hamburger bun and the cooked burger will be just about the right size.

Overmixing the ingredients produces dense, heavy burgers, so mix and shape the meat mixture quickly.

Dipping your hands in cold water before shaping hamburger patties keeps the meat from sticking to your fingers as much.

For well-done burgers with a crusty, seared surface, make thin patties and cook them quickly over high heat. For succulent, juicy burgers, shape thick patties and cook them slowly.

Never press down on a hamburger patty during cooking — while it may speed the cooking slightly, it will most definitely squeeze out much of the meat's flavorful juices.

As a safeguard against bacterial infection, cook hamburgers until well done.

**A** hamburger is warm and fragrant and juicy . . . soft and nonthreatening. . . . A hamburger is companionable and faintly erotic.

*– Tom Robbins*

**A**nybody who doesn't think that the best hamburger place in the world is in his home town is a sissy.

*– Calvin Trillin*

*See also* BEEF; HOT DOGS; MEAT; SANDWICHES

# Hash

**H**ash, *x.* There is no definition for this word—nobody knows what hash is.

*– Ambrose Bierce*

**I**t may not be a dish for every occasion, but when it comes to those American foods that somehow always evoke casual warmth, wholesome relaxation, and goodwill, a toothsome hash served with green salad, fresh bread, and premium beer is still pretty hard to beat.

*– James Villas*

*See also* MEAT

# Healthy Eating; Health Foods

*As consumer advocate Debra Lynn Dadd once wrote, "We literally are what we eat. . . . Would you rather have a body built from pesticide-contaminated, processed, artificially flavored, and preserved fried potato chips, or luscious, vine-ripened, organically grown vegetables and fruits?" And we all know that "health food" is supposed to be good for you, right? Unfortunately, many think such vittles don't always (if ever) taste great, as noted by the following personalities.*

This stuff tastes awful; I could have made a fortune selling it in my health-food store.

*— Woody Allen*

Eatnik: Health-food buff who won't touch it if it isn't enriched with granular kelp and blackstrap molasses.

*— Peg Bracken*

I want nothing to do with natural foods. At my age I need all the preservatives I can get.

*— George Burns*

We are eating today as though we are out-patients suffering (or about to suffer) from a disease that no one yet understands. We are deathly afraid of eating the wrong thing, but do not know what is that one right thing that will guarantee us life everlasting and keep us regular at the same time!

*— Irena Chalmers*

Things that are supposed to be good for you should keep the secret of their good intentions strictly to themselves.

*— Minna Cohn*

Health nuts are going to feel stupid someday, lying in hospitals dying of nothing.

*— Redd Foxx*

Old people shouldn't eat health foods. They need all the preservatives they can get.

*— Robert Orben*

In our frenzy to avoid it, we have introduced cholesterol into every food conversation, we've tarnished the reputation of our formerly revered beef, eggs, and butter while we have grown to idolize corn, oats, and soybeans, and we have learned to worship the salad.

*— Phyllis Richman*

What good are vitamins? Eat four lobsters, eat a pound of caviar—live!

— *Arthur Rubinstein*

Health food makes me sick.

— *Calvin Trillin*

Be careful about reading health books. You may die of a misprint.

— *Mark Twain*

The first time I ate organic whole-grain bread I swear it tasted like roofing material.

— *Robin Williams*

*See also* VEGETARIANS

# Holidays

It has been an unchallengeable American doctrine that cranberry sauce, a pink goo with overtones of sugared tomatoes, is a delectable necessity of the Thanksgiving board and that turkey is uneatable without it. . . . There are some things in every country that you must be born to endure; and another hundred years of general satisfaction with Americans and America could not reconcile this expatriate to cranberry sauce, peanut butter, and drum majorettes.

— *Alistair Cooke*

A lovely thing about Christmas is that it's compulsory, like a thunderstorm, and we all go through it together.

— *Garrison Keillor*

In my experience, clever food is not appreciated at Christmas. It makes the little ones cry and the old ones nervous.

— *Jane Grigson*

On Thanksgiving Day all over America, families sit down to dinner at the same moment—halftime.

— *Anonymous*

# Honey

**You might be amazed!** *Did you know that honey has been used for medicinal purposes since ancient times? Over two thousand years ago Hippocrates, the father of medicine, prescribed it for sundry maladies including reducing fevers, coughs, sore throats, stomach pain, and gout. And almost two thirds of the nine hundred-plus medical remedies recorded in ancient Egypt were based on honey (the Egyptians also used honey as currency). Honey has long been known as an effective disinfectant, antiseptic, and antibiotic (but it should never be given to babies under a year old because it could cause botulism poisoning in very young systems). Modern scientific studies have used honey in preventing infections and speeding healing of topical wounds, burns, and bedsores, as well as in arresting the bacterium that causes gastric ulcers. Almost everyone has taken honey mixed with lemon and tea (or brandy) to help a sore throat. And the list goes on. Bottom line? Not only does this sweet elixir taste delicious, but it is also a healthy honey of a deal!*

> The pedigree of honey
> Does not concern the bee;
> A clover, any time, to him
> Is aristocracy.
>
> *— Emily Dickinson*

**H**oney is too good for a bear.

> *— Thomas Fuller*

## Tame That Garlic

Too much garlic in a dish? A teaspoon of honey will soften the harshness. Stir it into the mixture and taste before adding any more.

From his tongue flowed speech sweeter than honey.

— *Homer*

The Owl and the Pussycat went to sea
In a beautiful pea-green boat,
They took some honey, and plenty of money,
Wrapped up in a five-pound note.

— *Edward Lear*

The only reason for being a bee that I know of is making honey . . . and the only reason for making honey is so I can eat it [*said by* Winnie-the-Pooh].

— *A. A. Milne*

How doth the little busy bee
Improve each shining hour,
And gather honey all the day
From every opening flower!

— *Isaac Watts*

## Warm It Up!

When honey crystallizes and turns sugary, reliquefy it right in the glass jar or bottle by microwaving it (sans metal lid) at HIGH (100 percent power) for 15 to 60 seconds, depending on the amount. Or set the honey container in a pan or bowl of *very hot* water for 5 minutes, then stir. Leave honey in water, stirring every minute, until it reliquefies.

If God had not made brown honey, men would think figs much sweeter than they do.

— *Xenophanes*

# Honeyed Orange Scones

Overworking this dough—in fact, any quick-bread dough—will produce a dense, tough end result. For the most tender scones, the final size of the butter chunks should be about ³/₈ inch in diameter. The butter is the *only* ingredient that should be cold—everything else should be room temperature. If your honey is particularly thick or crystallized, heat it as in the tip on page 185. It's particularly important for the honey you brush on top of the hot-from-the-oven scones to be thin enough not to tear these delicate wedges.

2¼ cups all-purpose flour
coarsely grated zest of 2 large oranges
2 teaspoons baking powder
¼ teaspoon baking soda
½ teaspoon salt
¾ cup (1½ sticks) cold butter, cut into 12 pieces
½ cup orange juice
⅓ cup plus about 2 tablespoons orange blossom honey, divided
2 teaspoons pure vanilla extract

# Hors d'oeuvres

*The words "hors d'oeuvres" (pronounced or-DERV, not, as I once overheard a cowboy say, "horse doover") is properly used in both the singular and plural forms. Why? Because, literally translated, it's hors (outside) d'oeuvre (of the main work [meal]), and although composed of many dishes, there is only one "work."*

Grease a large baking sheet; set aside. Preheat oven to 400°F. By food processor: Place flour, orange zest, baking powder, baking soda, and salt in bowl fitted with the metal chopping blade; process 5 seconds. Add butter; process in quick ON/OFF pulses only until mixture resembles coarse chunks. In a 1-cup measuring cup, stir together orange juice, 1/3 cup of the honey, and vanilla. With machine off, add liquid mixture. Process in quick ON/OFF pulses only until dry ingredients are moistened. *Do not overprocess.* By hand: In a large bowl, combine the first 5 ingredients. Use a pastry cutter or 2 knives to cut in butter until mixture resembles *very* coarse crumbs. Combine liquid ingredients; add to flour mixture, stirring only until dry ingredients are moistened.

Turn out dough (which will be *very* moist) onto a generously floured work surface. Flour your hands and gently press dough together, patting into a circle 8 inches in diameter. Use a sharp knife to cut circle into 8 wedges, flouring knife edge between cuts. Place dough wedges 2 inches apart on prepared baking sheet. Bake 12 to 15 minutes, or until dark golden brown. Lightly brush hot scones with remaining 2 tablespoons honey. Cool scones 5 minutes before serving warm. **Makes 8 scones.**

*Modern parlance, however, has legitimized the usage of the plural "hors d'oeuvres" in both verbal and written forms.*

I regard cold hors d'oeuvres as quite unnecessary in a dinner; I even consider them counter to the dictates of common sense. . . .

— *Auguste Escoffier*

# Zara's Decadent Dip

My friend Zara Muren is a beautiful and talented documentary filmmaker who can also cook! There's a lot of talent in the family—her husband is Oscar-winning special-effects wizard Dennis Muren. Zara's recipe is incredibly rich and she's incredibly slender, which leads me to believe she doesn't eat it very often—or maybe she only eats the crudités. Note that to make the crème fraîche you have to start this recipe the day before. There may be more than one kind of white wine Worcestershire sauce, but I use the Lea & Perrins brand.

1 cup crème fraîche, page 224
1 tablespoon white wine Worcestershire sauce
¼ teaspoon salt
¼ teaspoon coarsely ground black pepper
1 cup (4 ounces) crumbled Gorgonzola cheese
1 small head cabbage, white or red
5 to 6 cups assorted crudités (raw carrots, celery,
   fennel, jícama, broccoli, etc.)

In a food processor fitted with the metal blade, combine crème fraîche, Worcestershire sauce, salt, and pepper; process until smooth. Add cheese; process just until combined yet still slightly chunky. Refrigerate until ready to serve.

Pull down outer leaves of cabbage for flower effect. Use a sharp, pointed knife to hollow out the cabbage, leaving walls 1 to 1½ inches thick. Place cabbage on a large plate; fill with dip. Surround with crudités. **Serves 10 to 12.**

Hors d'oeuvres have always a pathetic interest for me; they remind me of one's childhood that one goes through wondering what the next course is going to be like—and during the rest of the menu one wishes one had eaten more of the hors d'oeuvres.

*— Saki*

# Hosts; Hostesses

*See* ENTERTAINING

# Hot Dogs

*There are so many quotes in this book that make me chuckle or even giggle. This one, by English author George Orwell, reminded me of my maternal grandmother's description of her first "dog": "At this moment I bit into one of my frankfurters, and — Christ! I can't honestly say that I'd expected the thing to have a pleasant taste. I'd expected it to taste of nothing, like the roll. But this — well, it was quite an experience. . . . The frankfurter had a rubber skin. . . . I had to do a kind of sawing movement before I could get my teeth through the skin. And then suddenly — pop! The thing burst in my mouth like a rotten pear. A sort of horrible soft stuff was oozing over my tongue. But the taste! For a moment I just couldn't believe it! Then I rolled my tongue around it again and had another try. It was fish! A sausage, a thing calling itself a frankfurter, filled with fish! I got up and walked straight out without touching my coffee. God knows what that might have tasted of. "*

I watched the hot dog being built. First the bun was taken out of a large tin pot, mustard was splashed across it from stem to stern, then came the frankfurter itself, shining from the hot, greasy water. . . . He shook the sauerkraut before laying it lovingly over the shiny tube of meat.

*— June Havoc*

The noblest of all dogs is the hot-dog; it feeds the hand that bites it.

— *Laurence J. Peter*

[The hot dog] . . . a twin pillar of democracy along with Mom's apple pie. In fact, now that Mom's apple pie comes frozen and baked by somebody who isn't Mom, the hot dog stands alone.

— *William Zinsser*

*See also* HAMBURGERS; MEAT

# Hunger

No man can be wise on an empty stomach.

— *George Eliot*

Love and business and family and religion and art and patriotism are nothing but shadows of words when a man's starving.

— *O. Henry*

A meager dish served to someone who is famished may seem as subtly wrought as an Escoffier masterpiece. . . .

— *Evan Jones*

# Ice Cream

*One of the very first "poems" I learned as a child was "I scream, you scream, we all scream for ice cream." Indeed, my favorite time of a summer day was the arrival of the ice-cream man, his loud-speaker music box tinkling a siren call that set my mouth watering and feet running. As soon as he turned the corner, I'd race all the way up the street (I'm still not a patient woman) and stop breathlessly beside his truck, heart racing, mouth watering. Although I would earnestly peruse his offerings, I always ordered one of two things — a Fudgesicle or a Dreamsicle, the latter being a glorious alliance of orange and vanilla. On hot summer days, I sometimes find myself wondering just what I'd do if I heard an ice-cream truck coming down my suburban street today. I'd like to think that, as an adult, I wouldn't embarrass myself by running pell-mell down the street to buy a frozen treat. I'd like to think that I would have the willpower . . . to walk.*

I doubt the world holds for anyone a more soul-stirring surprise than the first adventure with ice cream.

*– Heywood Broun*

We dare not trust our wit for making our house pleasant to our friends, so we buy ice cream.

*– Ralph Waldo Emerson*

# A Lot of Cold Air!

Did you know that all commercial ice creams have air pumped into them? In the ice-cream industry, this is called "overrun," the percentage of which ranges from 0 (no air) to 200 (which would be invisible ice cream because it would be *all* air). Naturally, ice cream needs *some* air or it would be rock hard and absolutely unscoopable. Although the legal overrun limit for ice cream is 100 percent (half air), the mixture would be unappetizingly mushy; it would also melt like a spring thaw. More desirable would be 20 to 50 percent, which would produce a denser, creamier, and eminently more satisfying ice cream. The percentage of overrun isn't listed on an ice-cream carton, so the only way to calculate how much air you're paying for is to weigh the package. Ice cream with 50 percent overrun (25 percent air) will weigh about 18 ounces per pint (subtract about 1½ ounces for the container). Bottom line: The less overrun, the more a pint of ice cream will weigh.

# Fudged Ginger Ice Cream

Ellen Wagner, a student in one of my classes at LaVarenne at the Greenbrier (a West Virginia resort) gave me this idea. It's easy, sophisticated, and simply delicious. Crystallized (or candied) ginger is available in Asian markets and most supermarkets. Don't skimp on the ice cream—buy the best you can afford for this elegant dessert.

    ¼ cup minced crystallized ginger
    1 quart premium vanilla ice cream, slightly softened
    Black Satin Sauce, page 74, or store-bought fudge
        sauce

Use a rubber spatula to gently fold ginger into softened ice cream (*do not let ice cream become so soft that it liquefies around the edges*). Immediately return ice cream to freezer; freeze at least 1 hour before serving. Serve topped with slightly warm chocolate sauce. **Serves 4 to 6.**

Ice cream unleashes the uninhibited eight-year-old's sensual greed that lurks within the best of us.

— *Gael Greene*

She was a butterscotch sundae of a woman. . . .

— *A. J. Liebling*

That night for dessert we had a Singapore Ice Cream, which was studded with ginger and covered with whipped cream. Gertrude Stein looked very voluptuous as she licked at her spoon, which she did with half-closed eyes and a slow, stately rhythm. Her tongue suggested the bow of an expert fiddler who is playing a languid and delicious adagio.

— *Frederic Prokosch*

The only emperor is the emperor of ice-cream.

*– Wallace Stevens*

Enjoy your ice cream while it's on your plate—that's my philosophy.

*– Thornton Wilder*

*See also* DESSERTS; SWEETS

# Indigestion

*See* DIGESTION

# Italian Food

*See* ETHNIC FOODS

# Jam

"The rule is, jam tomorrow, and jam yesterday—but never jam today."

"It must come sometimes to 'jam today,'" Alice objected.

"No, it can't," said the Queen. "It's jam every other day: today isn't any other day, you know."

*– Lewis Carroll*

# Japanese Food

*See* ETHNIC FOODS

# Jewish Food

*See* ETHNIC FOODS

# Junk Food

*You've probably heard the old garage-sale slogan: One man's junk is another man's treasure. Well, that goes for food, too. I think most people would classify junk food as quick, usually prepackaged, calorie laden, and generally a fast fix for the munchies. Many connect the term with fast-food drive-in fare like burgers and fries or quick fixes like chips, pretzels, and candy. But flip the coin and you find purists who deem foie gras, caviar, and Godiva chocolates "junk" food because they respectively contain too much fat, salt, and sugar. Go figure.*

My respect for the glories of French cuisine is unsurpassed, but I am a fool for junk food.

— *Gael Greene*

# Ketchup

*Truth to tell, and whether you like it or not, one of the most popular, all-time condiments in America is bright red and gloppy — you've got it, ketchup. By the way, do you spell the word catsup or ketchup? You're on the right track if you said "ketchup," the preferred spelling in all the dictionaries I checked. The word originates from the Cantonese kê-tsiap, which became the Malay kêchap. This Asian condiment was a spicy, extraordinarily pungent (tomato-free) pickled-fish sauce. Early eighteenth-century British seamen brought this odoriferous condiment home, and throughout the years the formula began its gradual transformation. In the late 1700s, New Englanders added tomatoes to the blend, and that was the beginning of the ketchup we know today. Of course, that thick red stuff isn't the only ketchup available — gourmet markets carry versions that are based on everything from mushrooms to mangoes. By the way, the correct pronunciation is KECH-up or KACH-up, not CAT-sup or CATCH-up.*

Shake and shake
The catsup bottle.
None will come,
And then a lot'll.

*– Richard Armour*

*See also* CONDIMENTS

# Kitchens

*I'll never forget the first time I saw a New York apartment kitchen – it belonged to my dear friend Bert Greene and was the size of a small walk-in closet. Two people could barely stand side by side, much less back to back. But the wondrous thing is that Bert tested hundreds of recipes for his many cookbooks right there in that postage-stamp kitchen. Which brings home what Julia Child once said: "A good cook can cook anywhere."*

My kitchen is a mystical place, a kind of temple for me. It is a place where the surfaces seem to have significance, where the sounds and odors carry meaning that transfers from the past and bridges to the future.

*– Pearl Bailey*

I don't like to say that my kitchen is a religious place, but I would say that if I were a voodoo princess, I would conduct my rituals there.

*– Pearl Bailey*

The kitchen, reasonably enough, was the scene of my first gastronomic adventure. I was on all fours. I crawled into the vegetable bin, settled on a giant onion and ate it, skin and all. It must have marked me for life, for I have never ceased to love the hearty flavor of raw onions.

*– James Beard*

When I'm old and gray, I want to have a house by the sea. And paint. With a lot of wonderful chums, good music and booze around. And a damn good kitchen to cook in.

*— Ava Gardner*

When I was a little girl, I always wanted to be in the kitchen, because it was warm, and that's where my mother was. You never lose that feeling.

*— Dolly Parton*

The kitchen is a country in which there are always discoveries to be made.

*— Grimod de la Reynière*

If you can't stand the heat, get out of the kitchen.

*— Harry S. Truman*

On days when warmth is the most important need of the human heart, the kitchen is the place you can find it. . . .

*— E. B. White*

I said to my wife, "Where do you want to go for your anniversary?"

She said, "I want to go somewhere I've never been before."

I said, "Try the kitchen."

*— Henny Youngman*

*See also* COOKING; COOKS

# Lamb

*Confused by the different types of lamb in your market? Here's how it breaks down:* **Baby lamb** *is customarily slaughtered between 6 and 8 weeks old;* **spring lamb** *is usually 3 to 5 months old;* **regular lamb** *is slaughtered at under a year;* **yearling lamb** *is between 12 and 24 months old;* **mutton** *refers to lamb that is over 2 years old.*

. . . that wonderful little lamb stew I had the other night . . .
it was so wonderful you could cuddle it in your arms.

*– James Beard*

Hell was to him a thousand years of tough mutton. . . .

*– Philippa Pullar*

*See also* MEAT

# Leftovers

*I know people who'd rather throw out food than eat leftovers the next day. Poor deprived souls. I, on the other hand, have always held leftovers in the highest esteem, viewing them as an opportunity to create a wonderful encore. One of my favorites is mashed potatoes, which I form into patties, dip into beaten egg and then into panko (Japanese bread crumbs), and refrigerate for an hour. After being sautéed in a little butter, these mashed potato pancakes are brown and crispy and so utterly delicious that I wouldn't hesitate serving them to Julia Child herself. Leftover veggies can be frozen and puréed at a future date to use as a soup base or in sauces; leftover meat can be chopped and used to create salads, soups, omelet fillings, or stuffings for bell peppers or acorn squash. The creative possibilities are endless!*

The art of using up leftovers is not to be considered as the summit of culinary achievement.

—Larousse Gastronomique

Casserole: Just another word for "leftovers."

*– Vinnie Tonelli*

The most remarkable thing about my mother is that for thirty years she served the family nothing but leftovers. The original meal has never been found.

*– Calvin Trillin*

# Lemons

*Lemon zest (the colored, outer portion of the skin) adds flavor magic to countless foods. Using a citrus zester — a tool with five tiny cutting holes that create threadlike strips — is one way of removing the peel. But if tradition binds you to the box grater, for easier grating try running the lemon diagonally across the grater, rather than up and down. For easy cleanup, coat the grater's surface with nonstick vegetable spray before grating. And to prevent the zest from sticking between the grater's teeth, stretch a used plastic bag or good-quality plastic wrap taut over the grater surface. Grate the lemon (or any citrus fruit), remove the plastic, and shake off the zest. If you need both zest and juice, always zest the lemon first. For maximum juice, roll the fruit a couple of times firmly between your palm and the countertop. Or prick the skin in several places (don't penetrate the flesh) and microwave the fruit at HIGH for 10 to 20 seconds; let it stand for 1 minute before rolling it on the countertop and squeezing.*

I'll be with you in the squeezing of a lemon.

*— Oliver Goldsmith*

I love lemon. It's a kick. It's an intrusion. Whenever a dish needs a little something and I'm not sure what that little something is, I start off with a squirt of lemon juice. When I need more punch, I use little chunks of seeded lemon flesh. . . . You can be chewing away and suddenly that burst of sun in your mouth makes every other flavor shine.

*— Maggie Waldron*

When life gives you lemons, make lemonade!

*— Anonymous*

*See also* FRUIT; ORANGES

# Preserved Lemons

This recipe is by way of my friend Stephen Simmons, chef-owner of Bubba's, a San Anselmo, California, diner with great food. The salt entirely transforms the lemon rind, mellowing the flavor and softening the texture. Steve adds a teaspoon of red pepper flakes in his lemons for sass. There are dozens of ways to use preserved lemons— chopped in guacamole, seviche, salsa, rice, aioli, salads, soups, and stews, and sprinkled over vegetables and meat, particularly lamb. Or add strips of preserved lemon to martinis or Bloody Marys. Deee-licious!

4 medium lemons
²/₃ cup Kosher salt
1 tablespoon black peppercorns
¹/₂ cup fresh lemon juice
water

Cut lemons lengthwise in quarters. In a large bowl, combine lemons and salt, tossing to coat thoroughly. Layer the lemons, peppercorns, and salt in a 1¹/₂-quart glass or earthenware jar. As you add the lemons, use a large spoon to press them down lightly to release their juices. Add lemon juice and just enough water to cover the lemons. Seal the jar tightly and refrigerate for 2 to 3 weeks, shaking the jar daily. To use, rinse or scrape the salt off the lemon, scrape out and discard pulp and pith. Chop or slice the rind to use as desired. **Makes 4 preserved lemons.**

# Lettuce

*Hold on to your gourmet toques, folks — iceberg lettuce is back. Although more exotic greens like frisée, arugula, escarole, mâche, mizuna, and radicchio have taken the gourmet center stage in recent years, the unassuming iceberg is now making a strong comeback. Restaurants that wouldn't have been caught dead with it on their menus two years ago are now offering wedges of chilled iceberg, ofttimes topped with old-fashioned calorie-laden dressings like Roquefort or Thousand Island. Very retro. The truth is, people have enthusiastically rediscovered iceberg's juicy crispness (it's 90 percent water), something lacking in most "designer" greens, and the texture that it adds to sandwiches can't be beat. However, don't think the iceberg renaissance has diminished the popularity of more flavorful greens — fans of bitter or tangy arugula or mâche would never give them up. Peaceful coexistence is the byword here — why not enjoy the best of both worlds?*

To dream of lettuces is said to portend trouble. . . .

*— Richard Folkard*

It is said that the effect of eating too much lettuce is "soporific."

*— Beatrix Potter*

Lettuce is divine, although I'm not sure it's really a food.

*— Diana Vreeland*

Lettuce is like conversation: it must be fresh and crisp, and so sparkling that you scarcely notice the bitter in it.

*— Charles Dudley Warner*

Lettuce entertain you,
Lettuce make you smile.
Lettuce make a salad,
The calories are valid,
To put your bod in style.

*— Anonymous*

*See also* SALADS

# Liquor

*Julia Child once said, "Only cook with spirits you would happily drink." Truer words were never said. Never buy an inferior potable believing "it'll do for cooking." Think about how the flavor of the liquid will translate to the dish. For instance, even though you like to drink low-calorie beer, its light flavor simply won't stand up to cooking — particularly if the recipe calls for dark beer. And please, never (but never!) use "cooking wine," the deplorable flavor of which can ruin a dish. Remember that cooking a sauce reduces it because some of the liquid evaporates, which means the flavor intensifies. When you reduce a sauce based on low-quality liquor, the flavor can only get worse. Wine, beer, and liquor can add rich layers of flavor to food, but only if you use the good stuff.*

Often Daddy sat up very late working on a case of Scotch.
*— Robert Benchley*

Oh, Georgia booze is mighty fine booze,
The best yuh ever poured yuh,
But it eats the soles right offen yore shoes,
For Hell's broke loose in Georgia.

*— Stephen Vincent Benét*

The human intellect owes its superiority over that of the lower animals in great measure to the stimulus which alcohol has given to imagination.

— *Samuel Butler*

I'm a Christian, but that doesn't mean I'm a long-faced square. I like a little bourbon.

— *Lillian Carter*

Forget the cheap white wine; go to beef and gin!

— *Julia Child*

[Definition of "corn licker"] It smells like gangrene starting in a mildewed silo, it tastes like the wrath to come, and when you absorb a deep swig of it you have all the sensations of having swallowed a lighted kerosene lamp. A sudden, violent jolt of it has been known to stop the victim's watch, snap his suspenders and crack his glass eye right across.

— *Irvin Shrewsbury Cobb*

Apart from cheese and tulips, the main product of the country is advocaat, a drink made from lawyers.

— *Alan Coren*

There is only one really safe, mild, harmless beverage and you can drink as much of that as you like without running the slightest risk, and what you say when you want it is, "Garcon! Un Pernod!"

— *Aleister Crowley*

Absinthe makes the tart grow fonder.

— *Hugh Drummond*

Liquor is not a necessity. It is a means of momentarily sidestepping necessity.

— *Clifton Fadiman*

There's no such thing as bad whiskey. Some whiskeys just happen to be better than others. But a man shouldn't fool with booze until he's fifty, and then he's a damn fool if he doesn't.

*– William Faulkner*

Anybody who hates dogs and loves whiskey can't be all bad.

*– W. C. Fields*

## Think a Drink Is a Drink?

Everyone's read or heard something like: "Two drinks per day is considered moderate alcohol consumption." Well, just what does that mean, and what exactly is a "drink"? First of all, one drink has been standardized as $1/2$ ounce of pure (100 percent) alcohol; 1 ounce of pure alcohol equals two drinks. But all drinks are not created equal (for example, beer contains less alcohol than whiskey), which means the volume per serving is different. Like it or not, here's how "two drinks a day" breaks down: 1 ounce of 100-proof (50 percent alcohol) liquor; $1^{1}/4$ ounces of 80-proof (40 percent alcohol) liquor; 3 ounces of fortified wine like sherry or Port (about $16^{1}/2$ percent alcohol); 4 ounces of ($12^{1}/2$ percent alcohol) wine; or 12 ounces of (4 percent alcohol) beer. By the way, in the United States, "proof" is exactly twice the percentage of alcohol.

I never drink anything stronger than gin before breakfast.

*– W. C. Fields*

Maybe alcohol picks you up a little bit, but it sure lets you down in a hurry.

*– Betty Ford*

God invented liquor so the Irish wouldn't rule the world.

*– Irish saying*

. . . vodka (no color, no taste, no smell) . . . is the ideal intoxicant for the drinker who wants no reminder of how hurt Mother would be if she knew what he was doing.

— *A. J. Liebling*

And when you wanna loosen up rather than introspect or perceive like a sonofagun, booze has it over dope going away. Not just the way the Beach Boys have it over Tommy James, but the way God has it over an apartment house.

— *Richard Meltzer*

Gimme a whiskey—ginger ale on the side. And don't be stingy, baby.

— *Eugene O'Neill*

Bourbon does for me what the piece of cake did for Proust.

— *Walker Percy*

There are two things a Highlander likes naked, and one of them is malt whisky.

— *Scottish proverb*

Gin was mother's milk to her.

— *George Bernard Shaw*

> It is not brandy, it is not wine,
> It is Jameson's Irish Whiskey:
> It fills the heart with joy divine,
> And makes the fancy frisky.

— *James Thomson*

Scotch whisky to a Scotsman is as innocent as milk is to the rest of the human race.

— *Mark Twain*

## Commonsense Spirited Cooking

Have you always thought, as have millions of others, that alcohol evaporates when heated and therefore is "safe" for alcohol-sensitive people? Not so. According to a USDA (U.S. Department of Agriculture) study, it was found that from 5 to 85 percent of alcohol may remain in a cooked dish, depending on several factors including how the food is heated, on the length of cooking time, and the alcohol's source. This is an important finding, since even a small amount of alcohol is inadvisable for some alcoholics and those with alcohol-related illnesses.

On the subject of cooking with alcohol, know that pure alcohol boils at 173°F, water at 212°F, and a mixture of the two somewhere between. Also, when you add liquor to ice-cream mixtures and other frozen desserts, remember that alcohol freezes at a much lower temperature than water, milk, and other mixtures. Bottom line: Too much alcohol and the dessert won't freeze properly.

Give an Irishman lager for a month, and he's a dead man. An Irishman is lined with copper, and the beer corrodes it. But whiskey polishes the copper and is the saving of him.

– *Mark Twain*

I have made an important discovery . . . that alcohol, taken in sufficient quantities, produces all the effects of intoxication.

– *Oscar Wilde*

*See also* BEER; BEVERAGES; BRANDY; CHAMPAGNE; COCKTAILS; DRINKING; PORT; TOASTS; WINE

# Liver

*Liver lovers are generally avid in their enthusiasm. Most know that this organ meat is a nutritional powerhouse packed with iron and vitamins A, D, and B-complex; many know (and don't care) that it's also loaded with cholesterol, making it jeopardous for those at coronary risk. What most liver enthusiasts don't want to hear is that because the liver is the body's clearinghouse, it contains many chemicals that may compromise health — a minor point to the true liverophile. As my friend Tom once said, while rhapsodizing about a plateful of crisp-fried chicken livers smothered with browned onions and crumbled crisp bacon, "I'll happily take the risk."*

## Chicken Liver Paprikas (PAH-pree-kash)

**M**ild (or sweet) paprika is commonly available in supermarkets, while hot paprika is most generally found in ethnic markets and gourmet food stores. I like to use 1½ tablespoons mild and ½ tablespoon hot paprika in this dish to add a little bite—if you can't find hot paprika, simply add ¼ teaspoon cayenne pepper. Hungarian paprika has a fuller flavor than the others.

4 tablespoons bacon drippings or vegetable oil
1½ pounds chicken livers
1 large onion, finely chopped
2 tablespoons paprika
1 large clove garlic, minced
1 large green bell pepper, seeded and finely chopped

Liver, *n*. A large red organ thoughtfully provided by nature to be bilious with.

— *Ambrose Bierce*

The best thing about liver is how virtuous it makes you feel after you've eaten some.

— *Bruce Jay Friedman*

I remember the liver my mother prepared as being fully two inches thick and battleship gray—it looked not unlike an ink eraser hiding under a wreath of limply fried onions and I hated its texture even more than its taste.

— *Bert Greene*

1 large tomato, peeled, seeded, and finely chopped
1 cup heavy whipping cream
salt and freshly ground black pepper
½ pound bacon, cooked until crisp, cooled, and
    crumbled (optional garnish)

In a large skillet, heat 3 tablespoons bacon drippings or oil over medium-high heat. Add chicken livers; sauté until lightly browned, but still slightly pink in the center. Use a slotted spoon to transfer chicken livers to paper towel to drain; set aside. If necessary, add remaining tablespoon bacon drippings or oil to skillet. Sauté onions and paprika over medium-high heat just until onions are soft. Add garlic; sauté for 2 more minutes. Stir in green pepper, tomato, and cream. Cook, uncovered, over medium heat, stirring often, until slightly thickened, 5 to 10 minutes. Salt and pepper to taste. Add chicken livers; cook just until warmed through, 2 to 3 minutes. Serve with rice or noodles, garnished with crumbled bacon, if desired. **Serves 6.**

The only thing worse than liver is a really dirty diaper.

*— Donna Michaud*

[Liver is] doted upon by the French, assaulted by the Irish, disdained by the Americans and chopped up with egg, onion and chicken fat by the Jews.

*— Richard Selzer*

My idea of heaven is eating *pâtés de foie gras* to the sound of trumpets.

*— Sydney Smith*

*See also* MEAT

# Lobster

*The Latin* locusta *is thought by some to be the root for the word "lobster," as well as, oddly enough, for "locust." The Old English* loppestre *(spidery creature), believed to have been formed from* locusta *and the suffix* -estre, *is the predecessor of "lobster." All of which may explain why the lobsters are often called "insects of the sea." Though I've never tasted a locust (and never hope to do so), I'll wager its flavor bears no resemblance to the sweet, seductive succulence of lobster meat.*

I personally see no significant difference between a lobster and, say, a giant Madagascar hissing cockroach. . . . I do not eat lobsters, although I once had a close call.

*— Dave Barry*

. . . a woman should never be seen eating or drinking, unless it be a lobster salad and Champagne, the only truly feminine and becoming viands.

*— Lord Byron*

Ah! who has seen the mailèd lobster rise,
Clap her broad wings, and soaring claim the skies?

*— John Hookham Frère*

## Lobster Yields

🌿Per serving, count on: 1 (8-ounce) lobster tail, or 1 (1 to 1½ pound) whole lobster, or 4 ounces cooked lobster meat
🌿1 pound cooked lobster meat = about 2 cups pieces

I've never heard of anyone being tired of eating lobster.

— *Jane Grigson*

All the ingenious men, and all the scientific men, and all the imaginative men in the world could never invent, if all their wits were boiled into one, anything so curious and so ridiculous as the lobster.

— *Charles Kingsley*

Although [lobsters] are delicious, getting them out of their shells involves giving them quite a brutal going-over.

— *Miss Piggy*

*See also* FISH

# Love, Romance, Sex, and Lust (with Food and Drink)

*The first time I remember thinking that food and love or sex might be emotionally and even physically coupled was when I saw the film Tom Jones. At the time I was too naive to fully understand just what the oyster-slurping scene was all about, but I sure as heck knew Tom and his inamorata were excited about something. Precocious filly that I was, I caught on quickly. It wasn't long before I was baking cookies to entice my high-school sweetheart, and in later years, spending all day creating a killer paella to seduce a shy suitor. I can tell you firsthand that love and food are a romantic duo — that shy suitor is now my husband!*

After a perfect meal we are more susceptible to the ecstasy of love than at any other time.

– *Dr. Hans Bazli*

Good food is so sexy in its way.

– *James Beard*

In later years I learned that love and cooking are the most important, the most basic, natural, and essential, as well as the most entertaining pastimes in the world. . . . But don't think that because you can crack two eggs over a piece of bacon, you are a cook or that because you have a house full of children, you are a lover. Certainly not! because for love and cooking you must be born.

– *Edward G. Danziger*

The way to a man's heart is through his stomach.

– *Fanny Fern*

Without bread, without wine, love is nothing.

– *French proverb*

Talking about food arouses certain individuals the way talking about sex does others!

– *Bert Greene*

Great food is like great sex—the more you have the more you want.

– *Gael Greene*

Only one marriage I regret. I remember after I got that marriage license I went across from the license bureau to a bar for a drink. The bartender said, "What will you have, sir?" And I said, "A glass of hemlock."

– *Ernest Hemingway*

The intimate sharing of meals is universally accepted as an overture to at least unilaterally anticipated amatory grapplings. . . .

– *Jay Jacobs*

> Drink to me only with thine eyes,
> And I will pledge with mine;
> Or leave a kiss but in the cup
> And I'll not look for wine.
>
> *— Ben Jonson*

Food is about loving and giving and performance and applause. . . . It is essential and sensuous.

*— Barbara Kafka*

When it comes to women, modern men are idiots. They don't know what they want, and so they never want, permanently, what they get. They want a cream cake that is at the same time ham and eggs and at the same time porridge. They are fools.

*— D. H. Lawrence*

To as great a degree as sexuality, food is inseparable from imagination.

*— Jean-François Revel*

When he is late for dinner and I know he must be either having an affair or lying dead in the street, I always hope he's dead.

*— Judith Viorst*

Ideally, the body of a woman should feel like a hot water bottle filled with Devonshire cream.

*— Kurt Vonnegut Jr.*

Perhaps food *is* a substitute for love. . . . My capacity for the former makes me tingle at the possibilities of what might have occurred had I the aptitude for the latter. Had things been different, I might have been lean and lusty.

*— Alexander Woollcott*

*See also* APHRODISIACS

# Mai Tai

*For those who haven't experienced at least one, a mai tai is a potent blend of light and dark rums, orgeat syrup, curaçao, and orange and lime juices, blended and served over ice, garnished with a skewer of fresh fruit and, often, a touristy miniature parasol. Victor Bergeron, the original owner of Trader Vic's restaurant, created this fruity libation for a couple of Tahitian friends who on tasting it exclaimed, "Mai tai!" ("out of this world").*

. . . *mai tai,* a tarted-up cocktail usually garnished with a miniature paper parasol and served to egregious rubes in Sino-Polynesian restaurants.

— *Jay Jacobs*

*See also* COCKTAILS

# Mangoes

*I'm sorry that I was only able to find one quote about mangoes, for a mango is, in my estimation, one of the most heavenly fruits on earth. Its brilliant golden-orange flesh is exceedingly juicy and exotically sweet and tart. Just writing these words makes my mouth begin to water. No wonder the mango tree is considered sacred in India and thought to have magical and aphrodisiacal powers. One bite and you know that mangoes are truly a gift of the gods.*

When I have eaten mangoes, I have felt like Eve.

— *Rose Macaulay*

*See also* FRUIT

# Manners

Etiquette, *n.* A code of social rites, ceremonies and observances, constituting a vulgarian's claim to toleration. The fool's credentials.

*— Ambrose Bierce*

Good manners: The noise you don't make when you're eating soup.

*— Bennett Cerf*

Good manners can replace morals. It may be years before anyone knows if what you are doing is right. But if what you are doing is nice, it will be immediately evident.

*— P. J. O'Rourke*

I'd discovered, after a lot of extreme apprehension about what spoons to use, that if you do something incorrect at table with a certain arrogance, as if you knew perfectly well you were doing it properly, you can get away with it and nobody will think you are bad-mannered or poorly brought up. They will think you are original and very witty.

*— Sylvia Plath*

Good manners have much to do with the emotions. To make them ring true, one must feel them, not merely exhibit them.

*— Amy Vanderbilt*

Manners are especially the need of the plain. The pretty can get away with anything.

*— Evelyn Waugh*

*See also* DINNER PARTIES; ENTERTAINING

# Margarine

*A great many people agree with the following quote from Mr. Herter, but even less radical margarine haters disdain it because of the ersatz flavor. For years well-meaning souls have been eating margarine because — in spite of its off-putting flavor — they knew this vegetable-oil–based spread was good for them. Those people must have been distressed indeed when a 1993 study at the Harvard School of Public Health revealed that hydrogenated oils (from which margarine is made) can actually increase cholesterol readings. The problem is that during hydrogenation extra hydrogen atoms are pumped into a liquid unsaturated fat, a process that creates trans-fatty acids. Unfortunately, this trans-fat acts like saturated fat and creates an imbalance of HDL (the good cholesterol) and LDL (the bad guy). Good grief! Millions of margarine fans must have almost had a heart attack upon hearing the news. But in 1994, the American Heart Association came out with the placating statement that margarine (a soft one) is still slightly more favorable than butter — just as long as it contains no more than 2 grams of saturated fat per tablespoon. Oh, well . . . just wait a year or two and some new study will undoubtedly espouse the theory that butter is better, which anyone with active taste buds already knows.*

Don't use margarine—the only good use for margarine is for children's suppositories.

— *George Leonard Herter*

*See also* BUTTER

# Martini

*The martini is, hands down, the favored cocktail of fictional characters in novels and films, and for obvious reasons. A properly made martini, stunning in its simplicity (gin and vermouth), can*

*take your breath away with its icy fire while simultaneously sooth-*
*ing the stress of a savage day. The threefold secret to an exceptional*
*martini combines prechilled ingredients, energetic stirring with ice*
*(essential for a silky texture), and a frosty-cold glass. Whether you*
*prefer your martini served up (sans ice) or on the rocks, whether*
*you like an olive or a lemon-twist garnish (a cocktail onion makes*
*a martini a Gibson), from the looks of the following quotable no-*
*tables, you're in good company.*

Why don't you slip out of those wet clothes and into a dry
Martini?

— *Robert Benchley*

Happiness is finding two olives in your martini when
you're hungry.

— *Johnny Carson*

You can no more keep a martini in the refrigerator than
you can keep a kiss there. The proper union of gin and vermouth is a great and sudden glory; it is one of the happiest
marriages on earth and one of the shortest-lived.

— *Bernard De Voto*

I would like a medium Vodka dry Martini. . . . Shaken and
not stirred, please.

— *Ian Fleming*

A man must defend his wife, his home, his children and his
martini.

— *Jackie Gleason*

There is something about a Martini,
Ere the dining and dancing begin,
And to tell you the truth,
It is not the vermouth —
I think that perhaps it's the gin.

— *Ogden Nash*

Zen martini: A martini with no vermouth at all. And no gin, either.

— *P. J. O'Rourke*

I like a good martini,
One or two at the most.
After one I'm under the table,
After two, I'm under the host.

— *Dorothy Parker*

One martini is all right. Two are too many, and three are not enough.

— *James Thurber*

It's true love because
If he said quit drinking martinis but I kept on
drinking them
and the next morning I couldn't get out of bed,
He wouldn't tell me he told me.

— *Judith Viorst*

I am prepared to believe that a dry martini slightly impairs the palate, but think what it does for the soul.

— *Alec Waugh*

*See also* COCKTAILS

# Mayonnaise

*Scottish poet and author Robert Louis Stevenson, who moved to Samoa in 1889 because he suffered from tuberculosis, was purportedly in the process of making mayonnaise when he died. It might be said that he was a man of distinctive taste to the very end.*

Mayonnaise, *n.* One of the sauces which serve the French in place of a state religion.

— *Ambrose Bierce*

Aïoli intoxicates gently, fills the body with warmth, and the soul with enthusiasm. In its essence it concentrates the strength, the gaiety of the Provençal sunshine.

*– Frédéric Mistral*

*See also* CONDIMENTS

# Jalapeño Aíolí

**This aioli will definitely warm body and soul. Try a dollop atop grilled meat, fish, or vegetables (like the grilled okra on page 243), or stir a tablespoon or two into hot mashed potatoes, salad dressings, or other cold sauces.**

4 medium cloves garlic, peeled
½ teaspoon salt
2½ tablespoons white wine vinegar or lemon juice
2 large egg yolks
1½ to 2 tablespoons finely chopped jalapeño peppers, fresh or canned
1½ cups olive oil or ¾ cup each olive and vegetable oils
2 tablespoons very hot water (optional)

In a food processor fitted with the metal chopping blade, drop garlic cloves one by one into running machine; process until garlic is chopped and clinging to sides of bowl. Scrape down sides of food processor bowl. Add salt, vinegar or lemon juice, egg yolks, and jalapeño; process to combine. With machine running, gradually add oil in a very thin drizzle. Process until all oil is incorporated and mixture is thick. For a lighter aioli, gradually add hot water, processing until combined. Refrigerate in an airtight container for up to 1 week. **Makes about 2 cups.**

# Meat

*Have you ever wondered why many meat recipes call for letting the meat stand for a few minutes before serving? It's because when meat cooks, the juices shift to the center, leaving the exterior somewhat dry. Covering the meat with foil and letting it rest for a while before carving or serving allows the juices to redistribute throughout the flesh, making it evenly moist and easier to carve. How long the meat should stand depends on its weight — a one-pound roast should stand about 10 minutes, while a fifteen-pound turkey needs closer to 20 minutes.*

Chop, *n.* A piece of leather skillfully attached to a bone and administered to the patients at restaurants.

— *Ambrose Bierce*

The nearer the bone, the sweeter the meat.

— *British proverb*

Man is the only animal that can remain on friendly terms with the victims he intends to eat until he eats them.

— *Samuel Butler*

Heaven sends us good meat, but the Devil sends cooks.

— *David Garrick*

Men have traditionally viewed red meat as having more charisma than vegetables. They like to swagger about the yard with a beer and a spear. The gene that tells all men they are warriors and therefore must bring home the bacon renews itself with each generation. Hurrah!

— *William Geist*

At the end of a long, hard day, a young man's fancy turns to meat and potatoes.

— *Herself*

Meat is the thing if you want to be fat.

*– Martial*

## Meat Talk

DEAD MEAT: Someone doomed, either literally or figuratively

MEAT AND POTATOES: Something basic or essential

MEATBALL: Someone clumsy, awkward, or ineffectual

MEATHEAD: A stupid person

MEAT HOOKS: Big hands

MEAT MARKET: A pickup place, such as a cocktail lounge

MEAT WAGON: An ambulance

MEATY: Something of substance

PIECE OF MEAT: A sex object, male or female

Americans have gotten themselves a reputation as a carnivorous people.

*– Wolfgang Puck*

The smell of roasting meat together with that of burning fruit wood and dried herbs, as voluptuous as incense in a church, is enough to turn anyone into a budding gastronome.

*– Helen Rowland*

Greater eaters of meat are in general more cruel and ferocious than other men.

*– Jean-Jacques Rousseau*

She unloaded sides of meat with their keyboard of ribs swollen with energy and strength, and seaweeds of vegetables like dead octopuses and squids—the raw material of meals with a yet undefined taste, the vegetative and terrestrial ingredients of dinner, exuding a wild and rustic smell.

*– Bruno Schulz*

*See also* BEEF; BUTCHERS; CHICKEN; HAM;
HAMBURGERS; DUCK; HOT DOGS; LAMB; LIVER;
PORK; POULTRY; SAUSAGE

# Bourbon Flank Steak

Overcooking flank steak turns it to shoe leather, so grill it only until medium-rare. This marinade is also great for pork chops!

1/2 cup bourbon
1/2 cup V-8 juice or spicy tomato juice
1/4 cup dark corn syrup
2 medium cloves garlic, peeled and minced
1 teaspoon coarsely ground black pepper
1/4 teaspoon ground allspice
1 (1 1/2-pound) flank steak, about 1/2 inch thick,
    trimmed of excess fat
salt to taste

In a large shallow glass or ceramic pan, combine all ingredients except steak; stir well. Use a sharp knife to score steak in a diamond pattern on both sides, cutting about 1/8 inch deep. Dip meat in marinade to coat one side; flip steak onto uncoated side in marinade. Cover tightly with plastic wrap. Refrigerate 24 hours, spooning marinade over surface once or twice during that time.

One hour before grilling remove meat from refrigerator; soak 2 cups wood chips in water to cover. When ready, light fire in outdoor grill according to manufacturer's directions. Drain marinade into a small saucepan. Bring to a boil; cook 3 minutes. Salt to taste; cover and keep warm. Just before grilling, sprinkle soaked wood chips over heat source. Grill steak over high heat 3 to 5 minutes per side. Carve immediately, cutting diagonally across the grain into thin slices. Drizzle cooked marinade over steak slices; pass remaining sauce on side. **Serves 4.**

# Melons

## Anagramatically Yours

The word "melons" has several anagrams, two of which are "solemn" and "lemons"—which, when linked, make an oxymoronic phrase, since everyone knows all lemons are lively. I know of at least one more anagram for melons—can you figure it out?

> For he on honey-dew hath fed
> And drunk the milk of Paradise.
> — *Samuel Taylor Coleridge*

## Melonsense

Melons are an ancient fruit—Egyptians are depicted with them in hieroglyphics dating back to 2400 B.C. There are two broad categories of this gourd-family fruit: watermelon and muskmelon. **Watermelon,** with its watery texture and simple flavor, is considered the less sophisticated of the two, which couldn't matter less to watermelon fans on a hot summer day. Choose whole watermelons that have dull (not shiny) rinds that barely yield to pressure; cut watermelon should have a brightly colored flesh. **Muskmelons,** with their more exotic, complex flavors, can be broken down into two types—those with netted skins (cantaloupe, Persian melon, and Santa Claus melon) and smooth-skinned varieties (casaba, Crenshaw, and honeydew). When ripe, most muskmelons have a sweet, perfumy fragrance and are slightly soft at the blossom end. Melons picked before they're mature will never reach their full flavor potential. They will continue to ripen and soften, however, if left out at room temperature. Wrap ripe melons tightly in a plastic bag and refrigerate up to a week.

# Frosty Melon Frappé

For the best flavor, make sure the melon's ripe and ready to eat. An hour before making the frappés, pop two wineglasses in the freezer to get frosty.

⅔ cup plain, low-fat yogurt
2½ cups cold cantaloupe or honeydew melon chunks
    (about 1 medium melon)
2 tablespoons granulated sugar
¾ teaspoon pure vanilla extract
4 ice cubes
2 mint sprigs for garnish, if desired

In a blender, combine all ingredients; process until smooth. Pour into frosted glasses, garnish with mint sprigs, and serve immediately. **Serves 2.**

Men and melons are hard to know.

— *Benjamin Franklin*

Friends are like melons. Shall I tell you why?
To find one good you must a hundred try.

— *Claude Mermet*

Women, melons and cheese should be chosen by weight.

— *Spanish proverb*

Success to me is having ten honeydew melons and eating only the top half of each one.

— *Barbra Streisand*

When one has tasted watermelons one knows what angels eat. It was not a Southern watermelon that Eve took; we know it because she repented.

*– Mark Twain*

*See also* FRUIT

# Milk

**The Nonsensical Fable of Mr. M.:** *Once upon a time* in the land of milk and honey *there was a man named* Mr. Milktoast *who was widely referred to as a* milksop *because of his* milk-and-water *demeanor.* One day at lunch the meek Mr. M. *ordered a glass of* mother's milk, *which he promptly knocked over.* Now, *even* Mr. M. *knew there was* no use crying over spilt milk, *yet tears still welled up in his eyes as he asked this time for some* milk of human kindness. *The waitress, usually a patient woman, thought he was* milking *her for sympathy and, rolling her eyes toward a* buttermilk *sky, told him to go take a flying leap to the* Milky Way. *So he did.*

Condensed milk is wonderful. I don't see how they can get a cow to sit down on those little cans.

*– Fred Allen*

There are three reasons for breast-feeding: the milk is always at the right temperature; it comes in attractive containers; and the cat can't get it.

*– Irena Chalmers*

> Things are seldom what they seem,
> Skim milk masquerades as cream.
>
> *– W. S. Gilbert*

> The cow is of the bovine ilk;
> One end is moo, the other milk.
>
> *– Ogden Nash*

In North American culture nothing bathed in fresh milk can be threatening or bad.

*— Margaret Visser*

# Crème Fraîche

This velvety-rich, thickened cream (pronounced krehm fresh) is a specialty in France, where unpasteurized cream contains "friendly" bacteria that naturally thicken it. In the United States, milk products are pasteurized, which means we have to add fermenting agents to them to get a similar result. Crème fraîche has a slightly tangy, nutty flavor that's well worth the little effort it takes. It makes an ideal thickener for many sauces and soups because it doesn't curdle when boiled. Or add a dollop of it to vegetables (particularly potatoes), fresh fruit, cakes, cobblers, and puddings. You can use either buttermilk or sour cream to culture crème fraîche—the buttermilk creates a slightly tangier version than the sour cream.

1 cup heavy whipping cream (preferably non-ultrapasteurized), room temperature
1 tablespoon buttermilk *or* ½ cup dairy sour cream, well stirred, room temperature

Combine whipping cream and buttermilk *or* sour cream in a glass

Carnation Milk is the best in the land;
Here I sit with a can in my hand—
No tits to pull, no hay to pitch,
You just punch a hole in the son of a bitch.

*— Anonymous*

jar with a screw top. (Note: If ingredients are cold, combine and microwave at MEDIUM (50 percent power) 1 minute, or until lukewarm.) Seal tightly; shake 15 seconds. Set aside at room temperature 24 hours, or until very thick. Stir once or twice during that time. Cream will thicken faster if the room is warm. Stir thickened crème fraîche; refrigerate at least 6 hours before using. Cover and store in refrigerator up to 2 weeks. **Makes 1** (with buttermilk) **to 1⅓ cups** (with sour cream).

**Variations:**

**Sweetened Crème Fraîche:** Add 1 to 2 tablespoons powdered sugar to cultured cream.

**Chocolate Crème Fraîche:** In the bottom of a glass jar, combine 2 tablespoons each unsweetened cocoa and sugar. Add 2 tablespoons of the whipping cream; stir until smooth. Stir in the remaining cream and buttermilk or sour cream.

**Vanilla Crème Fraîche:** Stir 1 to 1½ teaspoons vanilla extract into crème fraîche just before refrigerating.

**Extra-Thick Crème Fraîche:** Spoon thickened cream into a strainer lined with a double layer of cheesecloth or a paper-filter–lined coffee cone. Set over a bowl so that the bottom of the strainer or coffee cone is 2 inches above the bottom of the bowl. Cover bowl and refrigerate 24 hours.

# Mint

*According to Greek mythology, the word "mint" comes by way of the beautiful nymph Mínthês. You see, Persephone, daughter of Zeus and Demeter, the goddess of fertility, thought Mínthês had designs on her husband, Pluto, and, in a jealous rage, turned the hapless nymph into a mint plant (but then nymphs were always being transformed into something or other). All of which seems rather odd, considering that Persephone wasn't particularly fond of Pluto, a rather grim, unattractive god, who abducted his bride-to-be and held her captive in the underworld Hades, home of the dead. It would have been a hopeless existence if her mother, Demeter, hadn't persuaded the gods to let Persephone return to her on earth each year for eight months. Persephone's story was celebrated by the principal religious cult of ancient Greece as a symbol of nature's annual cycle of death and rebirth, as well as of the immortality of the soul. It seems to me that if Persephone had been truly perspicacious she'd have let Mínthês seduce Pluto, hoping he'd become besotted and send Persephone back to earth forever. But then we might never have been able to enjoy the redolent pleasures of mint.*

Mint is an aggressive herb — no doubt about it. Outspoken in all its culinary collaborations, the aromatic plant is also hell on a garden — and the gardener!

— *Bert Greene*

It is the destiny of mint to be crushed.

— *Waverley Root*

# Minty Spiced Fruit

This fragrant fruity mélange is just as wonderful for breakfast as it is for a refreshing dessert. Don't even *think* about substituting dried mint leaves for the fresh—and if you do use dried mint, please don't tell anyone the recipe came from me. Why? Because both the flavor and appearance of desiccated mint leaves are remarkably lackluster, and the luscious fresh fruit that you've gone to the trouble to prepare deserves better. So do you!

3/4 cup chopped fresh mint leaves
3 (3-inch) cinnamon sticks, broken in half
15 each whole cloves and allspice berries
julienned zest of 1 large lemon
3 cups orange juice
1/2 cup granulated sugar
6 cups fresh fruit (raspberries, chopped peaches or
    strawberries, melon balls)

Combine mint leaves, spices, and lemon zest in the center of a three-layered, 6-inch circle of cheesecloth. Bring edges of cheesecloth up to the center; tie securely with string. Place bag in a medium saucepan; add orange juice and sugar. Bring to a boil. Reduce heat; simmer, uncovered, 40 minutes. Remove bag of spices. Turn marinade into a shallow 2-quart dish; refrigerate or freeze until cool. Add fruit, stirring to coat with marinade. Cover and refrigerate 12 to 24 hours, stirring occasionally. **Serves 8.**

# Miscellaneous

*The following quotes, although not necessarily related to food, appealed to me for various reasons. Actually, they could easily be correlated to food (but then I think that about most things), and I've appended my personal associations here and there.*

Lead me not into temptation; I can find the way myself.
> – *Rita Mae Brown* (*Almost any food one lusts after*)

Imagination is more important than knowledge.
> – *Albert Einstein* (*Without imagination,*
> *cooking is merely a mechanical act.*)

My idea of roughing it is staying in a hotel that doesn't have room service after midnight.
> – *Herself*

The beginning is the most important part of the work.
> – *Plato* (*Setting the scene with a stunning hors d'oeuvre*
> *or first course; also, you eat with your eyes first*)

Too much of a good thing can be wonderful.
> – *Mae West* (*This can apply to anything,*
> *from champagne to chocolate to mashed potatoes.*)

The only way to get rid of a temptation is to yield to it.
> – *Oscar Wilde*

# Mom's Cooking

*I happen to be one of those fortunate souls whose mother is, indeed, an excellent cook. Not that every meal when I was growing up was haute cuisine, but every meal was good. In fact, on a recent visit home I sat down to an absolutely delicious dinner – roasted pork with mango salsa, garlic mashed potatoes, rum-glazed carrots, and hot rolls with pesto spread. You'd think after all these years of cooking the last thing Mom would want to do was create such a great meal, but she did. I often think that, having been born at noon on Thanksgiving Day, it was only natural for me to have a career in the world of food. But secretly I know that I might as easily have become an accountant if I hadn't grown up in a house where food was treated with such loving care. Thanks, Mom!*

It is odd how all men develop the notion, as they grow older, that their mothers were wonderful cooks. I have yet to meet a man who will admit that his mother was a kitchen assassin and nearly poisoned him.

*– Robertson Davies*

My mother was a good recreational cook, but what she basically believed about cooking was that if you worked hard and prospered, someone else would do it for you.

*– Nora Ephron*

My mother . . . could boil water without noticeably diminishing its flavor, but that was about the extent of her culinary skills.

*– Jay Jacobs*

My mother didn't really cook. But she did make Key lime pie, until the day the top of an evaporated milk container accidentally ended up in the pie and she decided cooking took too much concentration.

*– William Norwich*

My mom was not a cook. Her china pattern was a skull and crossbones. . . . My sister and I always tried to be good. . . . Whenever we were bad, our punishment was being sent to bed with dinner.

*– Joan Rivers*

When a man talks to you about his mother's cooking, pay no attention, for between the ages of 12 and 21, a boy can eat large quantities of anything and never feel it.

*– Sarah Tyson Rorer*

*See also* COOKING; KIDS AND FOOD

# Muffins

*Until I found the quote from George Bernard Shaw (see page 231), I thought everyone loved muffins. They're so friendly, so comfortable — you can eat them walking around or in the car; you can spend hours eating a single muffin, pinching off tiny bites, and it'll stay moist and tender. Unless of course you're the virtuous sort and into nonfat muffins, which because they're fat-free (and baked goods need fat to be tender) have an unpleasantly dank texture with all the tenderness of foam rubber. And heaven help you if you wind*

## Making Muffins Easy

Preheat the oven for 10 to 15 minutes before beginning to mix the batter. If your oven runs hot, place a small pan with a cup of hot water on the bottom shelf to help prevent the muffin edges from overbrowning.

Grease a muffin tin without getting messy by using nonstick vegetable spray or by dipping a piece of crumpled paper towel into shortening. For perfectly rounded muffin tops, grease only the bottom and halfway up the sides of each cup. Don't grease unused compartments or the grease will burn onto the pan.

A partially filled muffin tin won't warp because of oven heat if you put 2 to 3 tablespoons of water in the unused cups.

When substituting buttermilk or yogurt for milk (for more tender muffins), be sure to add ½ teaspoon baking soda for each cup you use.

Any muffin can be lightened with beaten egg whites. Simply separate the eggs, mix the yolks with the other liquid ingredients, then beat the whites until stiff and fold in at the last minute.

*up with a fat-free, low-calorie muffin with reduced sugar and salt. I always say nothing can put you in a good mood as fast as starting your day with a tasteless wet rubber muffin!*

In L.A., everybody sends everybody muffins, as a little gesture of good will, like a thank-you muffin or a get-well muffin or a welcome-to-the-show muffin. . . .

*– Janeane Garofalo*

. . . at the end of a week you'll find no more inspiration in her than in a plate of muffins.

*– George Bernard Shaw*

🌿Only stir a muffin batter until all the dry ingredients are moistened; vigorous stirring produces tough muffins with pointed, peaked tops. Any lumps left in the batter will disappear during baking.

🌿Filling muffin cups over three quarters full could produce "flying saucer" tops (which isn't the worst thing that could happen).

🌿Check muffins for doneness by inserting a toothpick in the center—if it comes out clean, they're ready.

🌿To remove muffins from the pan, run a dinner knife around the edges of each cup, then under the muffin to tilt it out of the pan.

🌿Loosely wrap leftover muffins in foil and reheat in a 325°F oven for about 10 minutes. Or place muffins on a plate and microwave at HIGH (100 percent power) *only* for 15 to 30 seconds— if they stay too long in the microwave, muffins will turn into stones.

🌿Freeze muffins in heavy-duty foil or freezer-weight plastic bags for up to 3 months.

# Gingerbread Muffins

Gingerbread fans will love these spicy muffins, hot from the oven and slathered with Ginger-Orange Cream. Whenever you use both fat and a syrupy sweetener in a recipe, always measure the fat first, then use the same measuring cup for the sweetener. That way, the molasses or maple syrup will slip right out of the measuring cup without sticking to the sides. For the coffee in this recipe, I mix 1 tablespoon instant espresso with ½ cup hot water. Lastly, my muffin tin has cups that are 1½ inches deep. If your pan has shallow, ½-inch deep cups, this recipe yields about 16 muffins.

3 cups all-purpose flour
2 teaspoons baking powder
1 teaspoon baking soda
1½ teaspoons ground ginger
1 teaspoon ground cinnamon
1 teaspoon salt
2 eggs
½ cup vegetable oil
¾ cup dark, full-flavored molasses
½ cup packed dark brown sugar

When I am in trouble, eating is the only thing that consoles me. . . . At the present moment I am eating muffins because I am unhappy. Besides, I am particularly fond of muffins.

— *Oscar Wilde*

*See also* BREAD

½ cup strong coffee, room temperature
½ to ⅔ cup chopped walnuts

Grease 12 muffin cups. Preheat oven to 400°F. In a medium bowl, combine flour, baking powder, baking soda, ginger, cinnamon, and salt; set aside. In a medium bowl, lightly beat eggs. Stir in oil, molasses, brown sugar, and coffee. Add to flour mixture, stirring only until dry ingredients are moistened. Spoon batter into greased muffin cups until about two thirds to three quarters full. Sprinkle each muffin with about 2 teaspoons walnuts. Bake 15 minutes, or until a wooden pick inserted in center comes out clean. Serve hot with Ginger-Orange Cream, if desired. **Makes 12 muffins.**

## Ginger-Orange Cream

2 (3-ounce) packages cream cheese, softened
1½ tablespoons confectioners' sugar
1 tablespoon finely grated orange zest
2 to 3 teaspoons minced crystallized ginger
1 to 2 tablespoons orange juice

In a medium bowl, mix all ingredients until thoroughly combined and spread is creamy and light. **Makes about ¾ cup.**

# Murder and Food

*I've always found the combination of murder and food intensely intriguing. This is undoubtedly why my partially completed murder-mystery novel is still sitting impatiently in my desk drawer for me to get back to it (if I could only stop writing food books long enough!). I do plan to get back to it soon, though, and have come up with some appetizing ways to knock people off most deliciously. All books require thorough research, of course, but that doesn't mean you should be nervous about accepting a dinner invitation from me in the next year or so!*

It's frightening how easy it is to commit murder in America. Just a drink too much. I can see myself doing it. In England, one feels all the social restraints holding one back. But here, anything can happen.

*– W. H. Auden*

Food is high on the murderer's list of handy ways to dispose of a murderee. Strychnine in the soup, belladonna in the beef, arsenic in the apple tart and cyanide in the coffee—the opportunities are endless.

*– Kerry Greenwood and Jenny Pausacker*

Man doesn't only need murder, he also needs a good meal.
*– Alfred Hitchcock*

The carp was dead, killed, assassinated, murdered in the first, second and third degree. Limp, I fell into a chair, with my hands still unwashed reached for a cigarette, lighted it, and waited for the police to come take me into custody.

*– Alice B. Toklas*

Murder is always a mistake. One should never do anything that one cannot talk about after dinner.

*– Oscar Wilde*

# Mushrooms

*The early Greeks and Romans were among the first to cultivate mushrooms and enjoyed them in a wide array of dishes. According to Maggie Waldron in Cold Spaghetti at Midnight, "Fungi*

*were so highly prized in early Roman times that no mere servant
was allowed to cook them. Aristocrats prepared their own mushroom dishes in special silver vessels called boleteria. Guests could
tell where they stood in their host's esteem by the number and variety of mushroom dishes served them." The word "boleteria" is
undoubtedly a derivative of boletus, a genus of fungus, the most
well known of which is the porcini mushroom, also known as cèpe,
steinpilz, and king bolete.*

Life is too short to stuff a mushroom.

— *Shirley Conran*

Mushrooms are like men — the bad most closely counterfeit
the good.

— *George Ellwanger*

To dream of mushrooms denotes fleeting happiness, to dream
you are gathering them, fickleness in a lover or consort.

— *Richard Folkard*

The brief emergence [of morels] coincides with the season
of rebirth and beauty, when Nature springs awake with a
sweeping mandate for all her subjects to breed. Seeking
morels during this time puts lead in your pencil.

— *John Ratzloff*

*See also* VEGETABLES

# Mussels

Mussels have a bad reputation: something mysterious has
to be done to them before they can be eaten with safety and
no-one seems able to tell one exactly what it is.

— *James Laver*

*See also* FISH

# Mustard

*Did you know that many people – including the ancient Chinese and Frederick the Great – once considered mustard an aphrodisiac? Then there were those, like the Greeks, who used mustard as an antiaphrodisiac – which I suppose any food might become, depending on where one rubs it. The venerable mustard plant was*

## Mustard Manual

Prepared mustards come in a wide variety of textures, from smooth to grainy, and run the gamut of flavors from very mild to mouth-scorching hot. Following are some of the most popular types of mustard:

✒**American-style** is the smooth-textured, mild-flavored, bright yellow "hot dog" mustard. It's made from mild white mustard seeds, sugar, vinegar, and turmeric; the latter produces the mustard's characteristic color.

✒**Dijon mustard** hails from Dijon, France, is typically smooth in texture (though there are grainy Dijons), pale grayish-yellow in color, with a clean, sharp flavor that can range from mild to hot. It's made from brown mustard seeds, white wine, unfermented grape juice, and a blend of seasonings. Dijon mustards are usually spicier and more pungent than their American counterparts. Those labeled "Dijon-style" are made in the same way, but are not from Dijon.

✒**English mustard** is bright yellow, extremely hot, and made from both white and brown or black mustard seeds, flour, and turmeric.

*also known for its curative and restorative powers for myriad maladies, including digestive disorders, colds, muscle soreness, bronchitis, mental fatigue, and snake bites. The name itself is derived from the Roman mustum ardens (burning wine), a mixture of crushed mustard seed and must (unfermented grape juice). Likewise, the French word for mustard (moutarde) comes from a contraction of moust (must) and a form of ardent (hot or fiery).*

✌**German mustard** has a spicy, slightly sweet flavor that can range from mild to hot. Its color ranges from pale yellow to brown and its texture from smooth to coarse.

✌**Chinese mustard,** primarily used as a dipping sauce for Chinese dishes, can be created at home by making a paste from powdered mustard and a liquid such as water or wine. Make the paste at least 15 minutes before using in order for the flavor and "heat" to develop; use within an hour or so, as this mustard quickly loses its potency.

✌**Mustard seed** comes in three main types—white (also called yellow), brown, and black. White or yellow mustard seeds are larger than the darker varieties, but also less pungent. Brown seeds have a strong flavor; the slightly milder black seeds are most often used in Indian cooking. Whole white mustard seeds and powdered mustard are available in supermarkets. Black seeds can be found in Indian markets, and the brown seeds in some specialty gourmet markets.

✌**Powdered mustard** is made from mustard seeds that have been finely ground.

✌**Mustard oil** is a pale golden, aromatic, extremely hot, and pungent oil pressed from mustard seeds. You can find it in ethnic markets, gourmet shops, and in the ethnic sections of many supermarkets.

". . . flamingos and mustard both bite [said the Duchess]. And the moral of that is—'Birds of a feather flock together.'"

"Only mustard isn't a bird," Alice remarked.

"Right, as usual," said the Duchess. "What a clear way you have of putting things!"

"It's a mineral, I think," said Alice.

"Of course it is," said the Duchess, who seemed ready to agree to everything that Alice said. "There's a large mustard mine near here. And the moral of that is—'The more there is of mine, the less there is of yours.'"

— *Lewis Carroll*

A tale without love is like beef without mustard; an insipid dish.

— *Anatole France*

I am so helplessly addicted [to mustard] that I cannot manage to slip on an apron unless I know it is within easy reach.

— *Bert Greene*

Mustard's no good without roast beef.

— *Chico Marx*

*See also* CONDIMENTS

# Nectarines

## Anagramatically Yours

The anagram for "nectarines" is "transience," which seems perfectly logical, since the pleasure gained from biting into a ripe, drippingly decadent nectarine is achingly fleeting.

Talking of Pleasure, this moment I was writing with one hand, and with the other holding to my Mouth a Nectarine. . . . It went down all pulpy, slushy, oozy—all its delicious embonpoint melted down my throat like a large, beatified Strawberry.

*– John Keats*

*See also* FRUIT; PEACHES

# Nouvelle Cuisine

*For those too young to remember, nouvelle cuisine (French for "new cooking") was pioneered by numerous French culinary masters (including Michel Guérard and Paul Bocuse) in the seventies. This culinary craze favored small portions of fresh, light dishes over the heavier, richer, classic French cuisine. Nouvelle-cuisine sauces were based on reductions rather than on thickeners like roux or cream, and the vegetables were cooked quickly in order to retain their savor and freshness. But, as so often happens with good ideas, things ran amok, and it wasn't long before cooked vegetables were served almost raw, portions were lilliputian, and the plates themselves were artistically decorated with so many swirls, drips and drops of sauce, and other minutiae it was sometimes hard to find the food at all. Thankfully, reason finally reigned, and the nouvelle cuisine craze was pushed to the back burner. That's not to say that there aren't those waiting eagerly for the next culinary fad to whip us up into a frenzy over something wonderful and new. But then if you've been cooking over a long time, you'll agree that Anton Mosimann's quote on page 240 is right on the mark.*

The so-called nouvelle cuisine usually means not enough on your plate and too much on your bill.

*– Paul Bocuse*

It's so beautifully arranged, you know somebody's fingers have been all over it.

*– Julia Child*

Anyone who believes for one second that the nouvelle cuisine has had any impact on the way Americans eat in their homes is crazy. It has nothing to do with anyone except possibly ten people who have chefs and are silly enough to think raspberries go with meat and kiwi with shrimp.

*— Nora Ephron*

A plate doesn't have to be arranged like an abstract painting.

*— Larry Forgione*

To pretend that food is an art, or even a high art, is pretentious gluttony. La nouvelle cuisine is vegetables arranged to look like something other than vegetables on a side plate, small helpings, a big bill, and long boring descriptions of what you are going to eat from the menu, or worse, the proprietor.

*— Philip Howard*

There is really nothing new in [cooking]. I have four thousand cookbooks dating back to 1503 and everything that is in "nouvelle cuisine" was there two hundred years ago.

*— Anton Mosimann*

# Nutmeg

*See* SEASONINGS

# Nuts

*See* ALMONDS; PEANUTS

# Sassy-Sweet Nuts

The cayenne kick in these crowd-pleasers makes them perfect companions for cocktails and apéritifs. Chinese five-spice powder, available in most supermarkets, is a pungent mixture that commonly includes equal parts of cinnamon, cloves, fennel seed, star anise, and black pepper.

1 tablespoon Chinese five-spice powder
1/4 to 1/2 teaspoon cayenne pepper
1/2 teaspoon salt
finely grated zest from 1 large orange
1 large egg white
1/4 cup sugar
3 cups mixed nuts *(such as cashews, pecan halves, and whole blanched almonds)*

Adjust oven rack to center position; preheat oven to 275°F. Spray a large baking sheet with nonstick vegetable spray. In a large bowl, combine Chinese five-spice powder, cayenne pepper, salt, and orange zest. Beat egg white until frothy. Slowly add sugar, beating constantly until egg white forms soft mounds. Add to spice mixture, folding to combine. Add nuts, folding until well coated with spice mixture. Turn nuts out onto prepared baking sheet; use two forks to separate them into a single layer. Bake about 1 hour, using a metal spatula to turn halfway through; separate any nuts that are stuck together. Cool to room temperature. Store in an airtight container for up to 2 weeks. **Serves 4 to 6.**

# Oats

*In her book* Cold Spaghetti at Midnight *Maggie Waldron tells us that according to Greek legend, "Alexander the Great would allow nothing but the finest oats to be fed to his horse, Esepheus, because oats flourish where the wind blows, and he believed they imparted the swiftness of the wind to his animal." Could it be that Alexander, irrefutably one of the greatest generals of all time, ate oats himself, somehow intuiting their cholesterol-reducing prowess? No, it undoubtedly could not be, for oats were not a popular people food in ancient times. Odds are that even had Alexander's cholesterol count been lowered by eating oats, it wouldn't have mattered, for this powerful personality died of a fever at the tender age of thirty-three.*

Once we sowed wild oats, now we cook them in the microwave.

*— Irena Chalmers*

Oats — A grain, which in England is generally given to horses, but in Scotland supports the people.

*— Samuel Johnson*

The oat is the Horatio Alger of cereals, which progressed, if not from rags to riches, at least from weak to health food.

*— Waverley Root*

# Octopus

Some people like to eat octopus. Liberals, mostly.

*— Russell Baker*

*See also* FISH

# Okra

*According to Bert Greene's* Greene on Greens, *"Ancient Arab physicians called okra pods 'sun vessels.' They believed the ripening seeds contained therapeutic properties that, once consumed,*

# Garlic Grilled Okra

The perfect accompaniment for these garlicky, smoky pods is Jalapeño Aioli (page 217). If fresh okra is not in season, frozen okra can be used.

⅓ cup vegetable oil
2 tablespoons red wine vinegar
3 medium cloves garlic, minced
½ teaspoon salt
¼ teaspoon cayenne pepper
1 pound okra, stem ends trimmed, or 1 (16-ounce)
    bag whole, frozen okra, thawed

If using Jalapeño Aioli, make it several hours ahead or the day before and refrigerate. In a 13 × 9-inch baking pan, combine all ingredients, tossing thoroughly to coat okra. Cover and refrigerate at least 3 hours, preferably overnight.

At least 1 hour before grilling, soak 2 cups wood chips in water to cover. When ready, light fire in outdoor grill according to manufacturer's directions. Just before grilling, sprinkle soaked wood chips over heat source. Use tongs to arrange okra pods crosswise over grill grids. Cover and cook over medium-high heat about 3 minutes, or until lightly browned. Turn okra; grill an additional 2 to 3 minutes, or until lightly browned. Serve hot or at room temperature. **Serves 4 to 6.**

*floated through a man's body forever." I don't know if I want okra seeds floating around in my body, but I do love these little green pods. But they're so slimy!, you say. Not necessarily. It's lengthy cooking that brings out okra's viscous qualities — cook it quickly and you won't have that problem. There are dozens of ways to use okra deliciously, including raw, thin vinaigrette-marinated slices in salads; in a stir-fry with fresh corn, tomatoes, and onions; in soups and stews, where its viscosity can thicken the mixture; and the following grilled version, one of my favorite recipes.*

. . . the spoke-shaped flecks of green that floated on the surface like miniature life preservers. . . . Okra.

*– Bert Greene*

*See also* VEGETABLES

# Olives

**It's the pits!** *Hate the tedious job of pitting olives? Do it the easy way: Place several olives in a row on a work surface, hold the flat side of a French knife on top of them, and give the knife a gentle but firm whack with your other fist. Or roll over the olives with a rolling pin. Either way, the pits should slip right out.*

There was a time when olives were chiefly used as ballast and no one gave a fig about them until some entrepreneur decided to stuff them with pimientos.

*– Irena Chalmers*

. . . black olives between the teeth. A taste older than meat, older than wine. A taste as old as cold water.

*– Lawrence Durrell*

Good oil, like good wine, is a gift from the gods. The grape and the olive are among the priceless benefactions of the soil, and were destined, each in its way, to promote the welfare of man.

*– George Ellwanger*

To dream of olives portends concord, liberty and dignity. . . .

*– Richard Folkard*

The olive tree is surely the richest gift of Heaven. I can scarcely expect bread.

*— Thomas Jefferson*

# Onions

**Cry me a river.** *Why do onions make you cry? The tear-causing bad guys are sulfuric compounds, which vary in concentration depending on the variety of onion. Onions low in sulfuric compounds generally have higher amounts of sugar and water and are therefore sweeter and less caustic. Among the most popular of these sweet bulbs are Georgia's Vidalia onions, Hawaii's Maui onions, and Washington's Walla Wallas. But back to the tears. Here are some ways to keep them at bay: freeze an onion for 20 minutes before cutting it, or clench a wooden spoon between your teeth as you cut it, or bite down on two matches, their sulfur tips positioned beneath your nostrils, or place a cutting board atop the stove and chop onions with the exhaust fan on high, or — if all else fails — wear hardware-store safety goggles.*

The onion is the truffle of the poor.

*— Robert J. Courtine*

The onion tribe is prophylactic and highly invigorating, and even more necessary to cookery than parsley itself.

*— George Ellwanger*

Onion skins very thin,
Mild winter coming in.
Onion skins very tough,
Coming winter very rough.

*— old English rhyme*

Onions can make even heirs and widows weep.

*— Benjamin Franklin*

Though it be boyled, the onion causeth head ache, hurteth the eyes and make a man dim-sighted and . . . dull.

— *John Gerard*

I will not move my army without onions!

— *Ulysses S. Grant*

Life is like an onion; you peel off layer after layer and then you find there is nothing in it.

— *James Gibbons Huneker*

Banish [the onion] from the kitchen and the pleasure of eating flies with it. Its presence lends color and enchantment to the most modest dish; its absence reduces the rarest delicacy to hopeless insipidity, and the diner to despair.

— *Elizabeth Robbins Pennell*

Life is like an onion.
You peel it off one layer at a time;
and sometimes you weep.

— *Carl Sandburg*

Let onion atoms lurk within the bowl
And, scarce suspected, animate the whole.

— *Sydney Smith*

Let first the onion flourish there,
Rose among roots, the maiden-fair,
Wine-scented and poetic soul
Of the capacious salad bowl.

— *Robert Louis Stevenson*

For this is every cook's opinion,
No savoury dish without an onion;
But lest your kissing should be spoiled,
Your onions should be thoroughly boiled.

— *Jonathan Swift*

**I**t's probably illegal to make soups, stews, and casseroles without plenty of onions.

*– Maggie Waldron*

*See also* APHRODISIACS; CHIVES; GARLIC

## Onions Smunions

**These caramelized, mustard-scented onions are great with roasted or grilled meat, particularly pork. Leftovers are delicious on roast beef or ham sandwiches!**

2 tablespoons olive oil
1½ pounds yellow onions, peeled and thinly sliced
2 large cloves garlic, minced
2 tablespoons Dijon mustard
2 tablespoons packed brown sugar
¼ teaspoon ground allspice
½ cup dry sherry
½ cup heavy whipping cream
salt and freshly ground black pepper to taste

Heat oil in a large, heavy, shallow, ovenproof pan (I use a 12-inch Le Creuset gratin pan). Add onions; sauté over high heat, stirring often, until nicely browned, about 10 minutes. Meanwhile, heat oven to 375°F; in a small bowl, combine remaining ingredients, salting and peppering to taste. Pour mixture over browned onions, stirring to combine. Bake, uncovered, for 30 minutes, or until browned and bubbly. **Serves 6.**

# Oranges

*The origin of the word "orange" is thought to be the Tamil* naru, *Tamil being one of the large family of Dravidian languages spoken primarily in southern India and northern Sri Lanka. The word was ultimately incorporated into the Indo-European language of Sanskrit, transliterated as* naranga. *Surprisingly, today's Spanish word for orange has remained almost unaltered as* naranja.

California's a wonderful place to live — if you happen to be an orange.

*— Fred Allen*

. . . there is nothing more delicious than an orange. The very sound of the word, the dazzling exotic color that shimmers inside the word, is a poem of surpassing beauty, complete in this line:

Orange

*— Joyce Carol Oates*

After dinner we children would gather around Papa Andrea who, with his trusty pocket knife, would peel each of us an orange, magically fashioning the peel into eyeglasses, front and sides all in one piece.

*— Vincent Schiavelli*

*See also* FRUIT; LEMONS

# Oysters

**An old shell game.** *A popular food fable is that it's dangerous to eat oysters during months that don't have an "R" in their spelling. In fact, since refrigeration became the norm, oys-*

*ters can be safely eaten throughout the year. What is true is that oysters are at their best (particularly for serving raw) during fall and winter, because during the summer months when they spawn, oysters become soft and fatty.*

I will not eat oysters. I want my food dead — not sick, not wounded — dead.

*— Woody Allen*

In general, only mute things are eaten alive. . . . If oysters shrieked as they were pried open, or squealed when jabbed with a fork, I doubt whether they would be eaten alive. But as it is, thoughtful people quite callously look for the muscular twitch as they drop lemon juice on the poor oyster, to be sure that it is alive before they eat it.

*— Marston Bates*

What a flavor [oysters] have — mellow, coppery, with almost a creaminess when you chew and analyze. I drank some good beer with them and floated on a gastronomically sensual cloud.

*— James Beard*

Oyster, *n.* A slimy, gobby shellfish which civilization gives men the hardihood to eat without removing its entrails.

*— Ambrose Bierce*

Oysters are amatory food.

*— Lord Byron*

> "But wait a bit," the Oysters cried,
> "Before we have our chat.
> For some of us are out of breath,
> and all of us are fat."

*— Lewis Carroll*

It is true that I live almost entirely on bivalves. I prefer them as they are—and I think that oysters *au naturel* are as much a mental as a material enjoyment: you are eating the whole ocean.

*— Isak Dinesen*

The oyster is one of the most deprived mollusks in the kingdom of nature . . . it has neither an organ of sight, nor an organ of hearing, nor an organ of smell. . . . It also lacks an organ of locomotion. Its only exercise is sleep and its only pleasure is to eat.

*— Alexandre Dumas*

. . . oysters and champagne—the food of Aphrodite.

*— Isadora Duncan*

An oyster lives a dreadful but exciting life. Indeed, his chance to live at all is slim, and if he should survive the arrows of his own outrageous fortune and in the two weeks of his youth find a clean smooth place to fix on, the years afterwards are full of stress, passion and danger.

*— M. F. K. Fisher*

He was a very valiant man who first adventured on eating oysters.

*— Thomas Fuller*

He had often eaten oysters, but had never had enough.

*— W. S. Gilbert*

I ate the oysters with their strong taste of the sea and their faint metallic taste that the cold white wine washed away, leaving only the sea taste and the succulent texture. . . .

*— Ernest Hemingway*

# Pearls of (Oyster) Wisdom

❧Make sure live oysters are as fresh as possible by purchasing them from a store with a fast turnover. Reject any with broken shells, or that don't have tightly closed shells, or with shells that don't snap shut when tapped with your fingernail.

❧The smaller an oyster is for its species, the younger and more tender it will be.

❧Store live oysters in the refrigerator (larger shell down), covered with a damp towel, for up to 3 days. The sooner they're used, the better they'll taste. Tap any shells that open during storage and discard if they don't snap shut.

❧Scrub oysters under cold, running water before opening.

❧Opening will be easier if you freeze the oysters for 10 to 20 minutes; or place them, hinge outward, around the rim of a dinner plate and microwave at HIGH (100 percent power) for about 30 seconds, just until the shells open slightly.

❧One dozen shucked oysters = about 1 cup; 1 quart shucked = about 50.

I still eat raw, briny oysters and clams with ardor. That is an admission of gluttony, a certain point of view and the knowledge that cooking the seafood will not make any difference. You cannot cook clams and oysters long enough or to a hot enough temperature to kill pollutants unless you like to eat rubber bands.

— *Barbara Kafka*

The Oyster—the mere writing of the word creates sensations of succulence—gastronomical pleasures, nutritive fare, easy digestion, palatable indulgence—then go to sleep in peace.

— *Lucullus*

Why anybody would ever have taken an oyster seriously in matters related to sex is a mystery because the creature itself is incapable of making up its own mind about such things. A biological freak, it is a hermaphrodite, starting life sexless and then, as it matures, switching back and forth from male to female, a zigzag it continues throughout its lifetime.

— *Vernon Pizer*

Each of us is provided with an oyster knife for one hand and a large white glove for the other. The oysters open easily and we shuck them into our individual ramekins of melted butter and condiments. . . . We eat incredible dozens.

— *Marjorie Kinnan Rawlings*

It is proved by experience that, beyond five or six dozen, oysters certainly cease to be enjoyable.

— *Grimod de la Reynière*

You needn't tell me that a man who doesn't love oysters and asparagus and good wines has got a soul, or a stomach either. He's simply got the instinct for being unhappy highly developed.

— *Saki*

I think oysters are more beautiful than any religion. . . . They not only forgive our unkindness to them; they justify it, they incite us to go on being perfectly horrid to them. Once they arrive at the supper table they seems to enter into the spirit of the thing. There's nothing in Christianity or Buddhism that quite matches the sympathetic unselfishness of the oyster.

— *Saki*

Tolstoy's oysters are smelly, smirking signs of immorality. . . . The opened oyster is the mark of the adulterous affair, and it lies there looking at Tolstoy . . . winking lewdly at him from its bed of ice.

— *Paul Schmidt*

Oysters are not really food, but are relished to bully the sated stomach into further eating.

— *Seneca*

... I might eat some [oysters] too, provided they were roasted; I feel there is something barbarous in eating such a pretty little animal raw.

— *Voltaire*

*See also* FISH

# Pasta

*It has long been reputed that the great Venetian traveler Marco Polo brought the concept of noodles back with him when he returned to Italy from China. Archaeological studies have since proved otherwise: Noodles most likely originated in central Asia, possibly dating back to at least 1000 B.C. We now know, in fact, that this food form existed independently in both Asia and Europe well before Polo's expeditions. And, speaking of those expeditions, several distinguished sinologists now question whether the celebrated traveler ever really made it to China; their investigations suggest that his easternmost destination was in fact Persia. There, it is insinuated, he collected the lore of Kublai Khan and his empire from Persian merchants, the tales from which he purportedly wove the fabric of his acclaimed China travels. According to Paul Levy in the London Observer: "The text Marco Polo is supposed to have dictated to Rusticiano of Pisa, when they were both prisoners at Genoa after his capture in 1298, was not in Latin or the Venetian dialect, but in Provençal. The clincher is that the transliterations of Chinese terms used are always Persian." Oh-oh. Well, does it really matter whether Marco Polo actually visited China? The truth is, the account of his "travels" is colorful, immensely intriguing, and of great value to historians. He's certainly still a hero in my eyes!*

# Pasta Shape Primer

At last count, there were over six hundred pasta shapes and sizes. Needless to say, this can be very confusing, particularly since some manufacturers often use different names for the same shape (fusilli and rotini being two prime examples). The following list will hopefully ease your angst the next time you're shopping for pasta.

ACINI DI PEPE: Tiny peppercorn shapes

AGNOLOTTI: Small, crescent-shaped stuffed pastas

ANELLI: Ring-shape; ANELLINI: Tiny rings

ANGEL HAIR: *See* CAPELLI D'ANGELO

BAVETTINE: Narrow LINGUINE

BUCATINI: Hollow, spaghettilike strands

CANNARONI: Wide tubes; also called *zitoni*

CANNELLONI: Large, round tubes generally used for stuffing

CAPELLI D'ANGELO: Long, extremely fine strands, also called *angel hair*

CAPELLINI: Long, thin strands slightly thicker than CAPELLI D'ANGELO

CAPELVENERI: Very thin noodles

CAPPELLETTI: Hat-shaped stuffed pasta

CAVATAPPI: Short, thin, spiral MACARONI

CAVATELLI: Short, narrow, ripple-edged shells

CONCHIGLIE: Shell-shaped; CONCHIGLIONI: larger shells

CORALLI: Tiny tubes, generally used in soup

CRESTE DI GALLI: medium MACARONI with ruffled outer edge

DITALI: Small MACARONI about ½ inch long; DITALINI: the smallest ditali

FARFALLE: Bow or butterfly shapes; FARFALLINE: Small farfalle; FARFALLONE: Large farfalle

FEDELINI: Very fine SPAGHETTI

FETTUCCINE: Thin, flat egg noodles (¼ inch wide); FETTUCCE: The widest (½ inch) fettuccine; FETTUCCELLE: The narrowest (about ⅛ inch) fettuccine

FIDEO: Thin, coiled strands that resemble VERMICELLI when cooked

FISCHIETTI: Smallest of the tubular pastas

FUSILLI: Traditional fusilli comes in spaghetti-length spiral-shaped noodles; cut fusilli is about 1½ inches long

GEMELLI: Short, 1½-inch twists formed by two spaghettilike strands

GNOCCHI: Small, ripple-edged shells

LASAGNE: Long broad (2 to 3 inches wide) noodles, straight or ripple-edged

LINGUINE: Very narrow (⅛ inch wide or less) ribbons

LUMACHE: Large shells intended for stuffing

MACARONI: Tube shapes of various lengths; ELBOW MACARONI: Small to medium tubes

MACCHERONI: The Italian word for all macaronis (hollow tubes, shells, twists, etc.)

MAFALDE: Broad, flat, ripple-edged noodles

MAGLIETTE(A): Short, curved tubes

MALLOREDDUS: Small, ridged, and elongated

MANICOTTI: Very large tubes, used for stuffing

MARGHERITE: Narrow, flat noodles, rippled on one side

MARUZZE: Shell shapes of several sizes, from tiny to jumbo

MELONE: *See* SEMI DE MELONE

MEZZANI: Very short, curved tubes

MOSTACCIOLI: Tubes about 2 inches long

ORECCHIETTE: Tiny disk shapes

ORZO: Pasta "grains," the size and shape of rice

PAPPARDELLE: Wide (about ⅝ inch), ripple-edged noodles

PASTINA: Any of various tiny pastas (such as ACINI DI PEPE), generally used in soups

PENNE: Diagonally cut tubes with either smooth or ridged sides

PERCIATELLI: Thin, hollow strands about twice as thick as SPAGHETTI; similar to BUCATINI

PIZZOCCHERI: Thick buckwheat noodles

QUADRETTINI: Small, flat squares of pasta

RADIATORE: Short, chunky shapes (1 inch long and ½ inch in diameter) that resemble tiny radiators with rippled edges

RAVIOLI: Square-shaped stuffed pasta

RIGATONI: Large, grooved MACARONI about 1½ inches wide

RISO: Rice shapes; similiar to ORZO

ROSA MARINA: Pumpkin-seed–shaped pasta

ROTELLE: Small, spoked-wheel shapes

ROTINI: Short (1 to 2 inches long) spirals

RUOTE; RUOTE DE CARRO: Small, spoked-wheel shapes

. . . the only classical and true way to eat pasta is with gusto.

— *James Beard*

Italians say that only children, the infirm and the ill-mannered use soupspoons as props for their forks when picking up pasta. They stick the fork into the mass of pasta and twirl it around one or two times until they have a neat amount of pasta wrapped around the tines.

— *James Beard*

Pasta is always the same, yet different. It has a comforting familiarity, with its pale golden color and chewy, wheaten taste. And then there are all those amusing shapes and the thousands of ways to sauce them. . . .

— *James Beard*

SEMI DI MELONE: Tiny, flat melon-seed shapes

SPAGHETTI: Long, thin, round strands; SPAGHETTINI: Very thin spaghetti, but thicker than FETTUCCINE

STELLINE: Tiny star-shaped pastas

TAGLIARINI: Long, paper-thin ribbons, usually less than ⅛ inch wide

TAGLIATELLE: Long, thin, flat egg noodles about ¼ inch wide

TAGLIOLINI: Another name for TAGLIARINI

TORTELLINI: Small stuffed pasta, similar to CAPPELLETTI; TORTELLONI: Large tortellini

TRENETTE: A narrower, thicker version of TAGLIATELLE

TRIPOLINI: Small bow ties with rounded edges

TUBETTI: Tiny, hollow tubes

VERMICELLI: Very thin SPAGHETTI strands

ZITI: Slightly curved tubes, ranging in length from 2 to 12 inches

ZITONI: *See* CANNARONI

Macaroni, *n.* An Italian food made in the form of a hollow tube. It consists of two parts—the tubing and the hole, the latter being the part that digests.

*— Ambrose Bierce*

Life is a combination of magic and pasta.

*— Federico Fellini*

There is an inevitable ritual about serving and eating spaghetti . . . eaten as it should be, in varying degrees of longness and a fine uniformity of writhing limpness and buttery richness and accompanying noisy sounds.

*— M. F. K. Fisher*

Vermicelli: A Paste rolled and broken in the form of worms.

> — *Samuel Johnson*

I might as well confess an un-American loathing for pasta salad . . . most of the bastard, slimy, cooked, pseudo-Italian pastas dished up with bits of ends of vegetables and ham or shrimp swimming in oily vinaigrette or mayonnaise are inedible and tasteless. There is such a thing as adapting foods beyond their natural limitations.

> — *Barbara Kafka*

Everything you see I owe to spaghetti.

> — *Sophia Loren*

No man is alone while eating spaghetti—it requires so much attention.

> — *Christopher Morley*

For a plate of spaghetti, he'd leave home. For another woman? Never!

> — *Adua Pavarotti*

Marriage . . . is not merely sharing one's fettuccine but sharing the burden of finding the fettuccine restaurant in the first place.

> — *Calvin Trillin*

When I cook for myself and I'm not feeling so well, I make spaghetti. Not designer pasta. Spaghetti.

> — *Maggie Waldron*

Ah, yes, cold spaghetti eaten at midnight, eaten with your fingers, your body hanging on the open refrigerator door, your bare feet squishing around in whatever doesn't make it to your mouth.

> — *Maggie Waldron*

It's a comfort to always find pasta in the cupboard and garlic and parsley in the garden.

*– Alice Waters*

# Pastry

The fine arts are five in number, namely: painting, sculpture, poetry, music, and architecture, the principal branch of the latter being pastry.

*– Marie-Antoine (Antonin) Carême*

# Peaches

*The ancient appellation for peach was "Persian apple," undoubtedly because the route it took from its native China to Europe was through Persia. However it reached the New World, peach lovers are thankful, for there is nothing quite like the seduction of a plump, slightly soft, red-blushed peach in the height of summer. Oddly enough, although the phrase "Georgia Peach" suggests that state is the land of peaches, California is by far the largest grower in the United States. Incidentally, the quickest way to ripen peaches is to put them in a paper bag with an apple and set them aside at room temperature for a couple of days. The apple exudes ethylene gas, which speeds the ripening process.*

Rather one bite of peach than a basketful of apricots.

*– Chinese proverb*

An apple is an excellent thing—until you have tried a peach!

*– George Du Maurier*

I remember his showing me how to eat a peach by building a little white mountain of sugar and then dipping the peach into it.

*– Mary McCarthy*

# Ginger-Bourbon Peaches

These Southern-style peaches are wonderful plain, or driz-zled with cream, or topped with a dollop of whipped cream, or served over ice cream. When you're cutting the peaches, do so over the bowl so you don't lose any of their perfumy juice.

2 teaspoons minced crystallized ginger or fresh ginger
1/4 cup packed brown sugar
1/2 teaspoon ground allspice
1 tablespoon lemon juice
2 teaspoons pure vanilla extract
1/2 cup bourbon
4 large, ripe (but firm) peaches, peeled and cut into about 1/2-inch chunks

In a large bowl, combine ginger and sugar; use the back of a kitchen tablespoon to crush the sugar into the ginger to release its essence. Add remaining ingredients except peaches; mix well. Add peaches, fold to thoroughly coat with bourbon mix-ture. Cover tightly and refrigerate for at least 3 hours to let fla-vors permeate peaches. Let peaches stand at room temperature for 30 minutes before serving. **Serves 4 to 6.**

The ripest peach is highest on the tree.

— *James Whitcomb Riley*

She (my mother) could make Jell-O, for instance, with sliced peaches hanging in it, peaches just suspended there, in defiance of the law of gravity.

— *Philip Roth*

# It's the Pits!

Removing pits (stones) from peaches and nectarines is easier if you cut the fruit from stem to stem all the way to the stone. Twist the halves in opposite directions and lift out the pit!

Peach crisp is summertime — picnics at the river, casual dinners with friends.

— *Lindsey Shere*

If you don't like my peaches,
Daddy, don't you shake my tree.

— *Bessie Smith*

*See also* FRUIT; NECTARINES

# Peanuts; Peanut Butter

**Ever seen a peanut tree?** *No, of course not, because peanuts don't grow on trees like other nuts . . . in fact, they aren't really nuts at all. Peanuts are actually legumes (like beans), and at one stage of its growth, the peanut plant looks very much like the common-garden pea plant. The plant's seeds have a papery brown skin and are contained in a thin, netted, tan-colored pod. After flowering, the plant bends down to the earth and buries its pods in the ground, which is why peanuts are also called "groundnuts," "earth nuts," and, in the South, "goobers" or "goober peas." Here's an interesting fact you might want to consider the next time a flight attendant tosses you a bag of peanuts: Ancient Peruvians so venerated this common legume that they buried pots of peanuts with their dead for nourishment on the long journey to the hereafter. Knowing that, don't you think flight attendants ought to have more respect for those peanuts?*

If one begins eating peanuts one cannot stop.

— *H. L. Mencken*

Course, we don't get meat as often as our forefathers but we have our peanut butter and radio.

— *Will Rogers*

I hate television. I hate it as much as peanuts. But I can't stop eating peanuts.

— *Orson Welles*

*See also* ALMONDS

# Pears

*A pear isn't always simply a pear. For instance, did you know that a* **prickly pear** *is actually a pear-shaped and -sized cactus fruit? It has a prickly skin that can range in color from green to purplish red. Its flesh, which ranges in color from light yellow-green to gold, is soft and porous with a melonlike aroma and a lightly sweet flavor. On the other hand, an* **alligator pear** *is actually another name once often used for the avocado. Go figure.*

There are only ten minutes in the life of a pear when it is perfect to eat.

— *Ralph Waldo Emerson*

Two of life's mysteries—how does the ship get into the bottle, and how does the pear get into the bottle of pear *eau de vie.*

— *Jane Grigson*

*See also* FRUIT

# Peas

*No doubt about it, crisp green pods bulging with their payload of bright green peas are a sure sign that spring has sprung. Besides the obvious palate-pleasing pleasure, peas have other talents. In*

*his tome* Natural History, *Roman scholar* Pliny the Elder
*(c. A.D. 23–79) had a sure cure for warts: On the first day of the
new moon, touch each wart with a fresh green pea, then wrap the
peas in a cloth and throw them over your shoulder. Pliny doesn't
say whether it's the right or left shoulder – wonder if it makes a
difference?*

How luscious lies the pea within the pod.

*– Emily Dickinson*

In the vegetable world, there is nothing so innocent, so con-
fiding in its expression, as the small green face of the freshly
shelled spring pea.

*– William Wallace Irwin*

## Pea Greed

According to Bert Greene in his award-winning *Greene on
Greens*, King John of England so loved the flavor of green
peas that he "died from an attack of overindulgence at dinner—after consuming seven bowls of peas!"

*See also* VEGETABLES

# Pepper, Black

*Did you know that pepper was once extremely rare and considered
so valuable that it was used as currency? Indeed, it was covetous-
ness of the precious peppercorn that launched myriad fifteenth-
century sailing expeditions in search of alternate trade routes to its
primary source, the Far East. As Waverley Root wrote: "In
medieval times the habit arose of expressing a man's wealth, no
longer in terms of the amount of land in his estate, but of the
amount of pepper in his pantry. One way of saying that a man was*

*poor was to say that he lacked pepper. The wealthy kept large stores of pepper in their houses, and let it be known that it was there: it was a guarantee of solvency." Today, thankfully, there is a plentiful and inexpensive supply of this spice, and no amount of pepper makes one man better than another.*

Such epithets, like pepper,
Give zest to what you write;
And, if you strew them sparely,
They whet the appetite:
But if you lay them on too thick,
You spoil the matter quite!

*— Lewis Carroll*

Don't be too daring in the kitchen. For example, don't suddenly get involved with shallots. . . . Even with coriander you're on thin ice. . . . Stay with safe things, like pepper.

*— Bruce Jay Friedman*

Black pepper heate and comfort the brain.

*— John Gerard*

Pepper is small in quantity and great in virtue.

*— Plato*

*See also* SEASONINGS

# Pickles

*I have nothing particularly interesting or informative to say about pickles, but the sayings of my friend Irena Chalmers (one of the wittiest and erudite writers of today) so amused me that I was compelled to create a pickle section here so I could share them with you.*

In the last analysis, a pickle is nothing more than a cucumber with experience.

— *Irena Chalmers*

There was a young man named Perkins
Who was specially fond of small gherkins.
One fine day at tea he ate forty-three,
Which pickled his internal workin's.

— *Irena Chalmers*

# Picnics

*The French word for a picnic is* pique-nique *(peek-NEEK), with the verb form being* pique-niquer *(peek-nee-KAY). Somehow, at least to my ear,* pique-nique *just sounds more poetic, more romantic than "picnic." But then the French have always had a flair for such things, as is so beautifully exemplified in Jean-Anthelme Brillat-Savarin's lyrical words:*

Seating themselves on the green sward, they eat while the corks fly and there is talk, laughter and merriment, and perfect freedom, for the universe is their drawing room and the sun their lamp. Besides, they have appetite, Nature's special gift, which lends to such a meal a vivacity unknown indoors, however beautiful the surroundings.

— *Jean-Anthelme Brillat-Savarin*

There is a charm in improvised eating which a regular meal lacks, and there was a glamour never to be recaptured in secret picnics on long sunny mornings. . . .

— *Graham Greene*

Everything tastes better outdoors.

— *Claudia Roden*

Bread and butter, devoid of charm in the drawing-room, is ambrosia eaten under a tree.

*— Elizabeth Russell*

# Pies

*Etymologists are not at all certain about the origins of the word "pie." At first it was thought to have come from Medieval Latin picá or pia (pie or pasty), both of unknown origin. But to confuse matters further, the Middle English word "pie" was used in 1199, earlier than was the Medieval Latin pica (1310) or pia (1230). Some suggest that the root may be from the Latin pìca (magpie), equating a pie's varying ingredients with either the magpie's penchant for gathering miscellaneous items, or with its piebald (variegated black and white) coloration. Indeed, the first known pies contained assorted ingredients including game, fish, and vegetables. One thing we do know is that fruit pie (apple, of course) was first recorded in print in 1590 when English playwright Robert Greene wrote: "Thy breath is like the steame of apple-pyes." All of which makes no difference at all (not even to Simple Simon) when it comes to America's favorite dessert. Everyone has their favorite, but as far as I'm concerned Robert Greene can have his apple pies. Make mine pumpkin.*

Good apple pies are a considerable part of our domestic happiness.

*— Jane Austen*

Pie, *n.* An advance agent of the reaper whose name is Indigestion.

*— Ambrose Bierce*

An apple pie without some cheese
Is like a kiss without a squeeze.

*— English proverb*

# Humble Is as Humble Does

The term "humble pie" has long referred to words or deeds one had to recant. But did you know that there really was such a thing as humble pie? It was a popular seventeenth-century English dish in which deer innards—including heart, liver, and kidney—were mixed with apples, currants, sugar, and spices and baked as a pie. While the gentry dined on the venison, the servants supped on "numble" (deer innards) pie, which eventually was transliterated into humble pie.

> The best of all physicians
> Is apple pie and cheese!
>
> — *Eugene Field*

> But I, when I undress me
> Each night upon my knees
> Will ask the Lord to bless me
> With apple pie and cheese.
>
> — *Eugene Field*

A lot of people have never really had the chance to eat a decent apple pie, but after a minute's sensual reflection will know positively what they would expect if they did. They can taste it on their mind's tongue. . . .

— *M. F. K. Fisher*

For generations, it has been as American as apple pie to want a piece of the pie, even though getting it might not be as easy as pie. . . .

— *Jay Jacobs*

# Pie Talk

EASY AS PIE: Unbelievably simple

EAT HUMBLE PIE: Take back one's words; to apologize abjectly

NICE AS PIE: Extremely pleasant

PIE ALLEY: A term used by bowlers for a lane where strikes are easily made

PIEBALD: Having irregular patches or spots of colors, particularly black and white, as in a piebald cow (think Ben and Jerry's cows)

PIE BED: One that's short-sheeted; also called "apple-pie bed"

PIE-EYED: Having had one too many

PIE-FACED: Having a broad, flat face, ofttimes with a vacuous expression

PIE IN THE SKY: An illusory promise of future profits ("the good life") that never materializes

PIE PLANT: A nickname for rhubarb, because of its popularity for pies

SLICE OF THE PIE: A piece of the action; a portion of the profits

What is a roofless cathedral compared to a well-built pie?
— *William Maginn*

Pecan pie, with loads of cream, will be part of the American-built heaven.
— *Tom Stobart*

*See also* APPLES; PUMPKIN

# Piña Colada Impossipie

This recipe was inspired by an old recipe for "impossible pie"—a crustless milk-butter-egg-flour-coconut concoction of which there are myriad versions. So I began testing to create a new recipe, omitting everything from the original but the eggs and flour—I was out to create an instant piña colada pie. A cinch, I thought. Seven pies later, I finally had the recipe I wanted. Cream of coconut (don't substitute unsweetened coconut "milk") is a sweetened product that can be found in most supermarkets. It separates during storage, so must be stirred thoroughly before being used. Leftover cream of coconut may be frozen for future use.

2 (8-ounce) cans crushed pineapple packed in
   unsweetened juice (*do not drain*)
¾ cup cream of coconut
½ cup flour
4 eggs
1 teaspoon rum extract
½ teaspoon salt
⅓ cup shredded coconut
sweetened, rum-flavored whipped cream (optional)

With oven shelf in center position, preheat oven to 350°F. Grease a 9½- or 10-inch pie pan; set aside. In a blender jar, place all ingredients except shredded coconut and cream. Cover and process 2 minutes, starting on low speed and gradually increasing to high. Pour into prepared pie pan; sprinkle top with coconut. Bake 55 to 60 minutes, or until a knife inserted in the center comes out *almost* clean and top is golden brown.Cool on a rack to room temperature. Cover and refrigerate at least 4 hours before serving. Serve with rum-flavored whipped cream, if desired. **Serves 8.**

# Pizza

*Has it ever occurred to you that the addition of two Zs would turn pizza into pizzazz? No, I didn't think so. Only the odd vagaries of a writer's mind would come up with such trivia. But the truth is that there's plenty of pizzazz in pizza, and this pie of Italian origin (dating back to A.D. 1000) comes in so many styles it's hard to keep track. There are thin-crust, medium-crust, and deep-dish pizzas; pizzas with red (tomato) sauce, with white (clam) sauce, and with no sauce; pizzas with traditional toppings like mozzarella, Italian sausage, and garlicky tomato sauce, and with not-so-traditional toppings like pineapple or caviar or fruit; breakfast pizzas topped with bacon and eggs; dessert pizzas topped with chocolate and whipped cream; gourmet pizzas with goat cheese and sun-dried tomatoes; ethnic pizzas including Mexican, Thai, and Greek . . . well, you get the idea. But back to pizzazz, the definition of which is "style; flair; excitement" — that sounds like pizza to me!*

You better cut the pizza in four pieces because I'm not hungry enough to eat six.

— *Yogi Berra*

If you have few standards and no patience for details, better send out for pizza.

— *Tom Wicker*

# Politics and Food

An empty stomach is not a good political advisor.

— *Albert Einstein*

I tell you folks, all politics is applesauce.

— *Will Rogers*

We are the first nation to starve to death in a storehouse that's overfilled with everything we want.

— *Will Rogers*

I have always claimed Americans didn't want a drink as bad as they wanted the right to take a drink if they did happen to want one.

— *Will Rogers*

Undoubtedly the desire for food has been and still is one of the main causes of political events.

— *Bertrand Russell*

You tell me whar a man gits his corn pone, en I'll tell you what his 'pinions is.

— *Mark Twain*

Carving up a whole animal, whether a chicken or an ox, has from time immemorial expressed not only family feeling and cohesion among people sharing that animal, but also hierarchy and difference. . . . Many traditions have assigned status to various cuts; it mattered deeply which piece you got, and it usually fell to the head man to be the carver, who "did the honours" and assigned to each person his "portion," which could be broadly representative of his kinship or friendship status, and of his lot in life.

— *Margaret Visser*

What is patriotism but the love of the good things we ate in our childhood?

— *Lin Yutang*

# Pork

*How did pig, cow, and sheep become pork, beef, and lamb? Though such semantic changes are often hard to trace, it appears that the transition began with the Norman Conquest in the eleventh century, with the French derivatives gradually becoming part of the native Saxon language. Such is the privilege of conquerors.*

He has lived only to eat, he eats only to die. . . . The pig is simply a vast dish walking around until it is time to be served up at table . . . his firm and well-padded rump is already the shape of a ham.

— *Xavier Aubryet*

The pig is nothing but an enormous dish which walks while waiting to be served.

— *Charles Monselet*

Everything in a pig is good. What ingratitude has permitted his name to become a term of opprobrium?

— *Grimod de la Reynière*

## Piggy Talk

BLIND PIG: A speakeasy or any place alcoholic beverages are served illegally

IN A PIG'S EYE: It'll never happen!

PIG: Disparaging slang for someone like a police officer, sexist, or racist

PIGHEADED: Obstinate or stubborn

PIG IN A POKE: A shot in the dark; something uncertain or undefined

PIG LATIN: Jargon formed by moving the first consonant to the end of the word and adding the sound "ay," as in *illysay alktay*

PIG OUT: To overindulge; stuff oneself

PORKER: Someone who's pigged out once too often

*See also* BACON; HAM; MEAT; SAUSAGE

# Port

*As I write these words, the window's open and I can feel and smell the crispness of the autumn afternoon. It occurs to me how completely Pavlovian I am, for the fall chill brings with it yearnings for soups, stews, pumpkin pie, and port. There are few things more luscious and soul-satisfying than a postprandial port — silky smooth, slightly sweet, and as toe-curling as an intimate caress. The majority of the following quotes seem to view port as a rather philosophical, serious wine. I, on the other hand, see only its sensuous nature, which can — depending on with whom one is sharing it — be utterly seductive.*

Port is essentially the wine of philosophical contemplation.
                                                — *H. Warner Allen*

To taste port is to taste a tiny atom of England and her past.
                                                — *Clifton Fadiman*

Never have a small glass of port. . . . It just goes wambling around looking for damage to do. Have a large glass. It settles down and does you good.
                                                — *Lord Goddard*

The Gentleman did like a drop too much . . . more Port than was exactly portable.
                                                — *Thomas Hood*

Port speaks the sentences of wisdom. . . .
                                                — *George Meredith*

All wine would be port if it could.
                                                — *Portuguese proverb*

For Port, red Port, is incomparable when good. . . . It has not the almost feminine grace of Claret; the transcendental qualities of Burgundy and Madeira; the immediate inspiration of Champagne. But it strengthens while it gladdens as no other wine can do.
                                                — *George Saintsbury*

*See also* BEER; BRANDY; CHAMPAGNE; COCKTAILS; DRINKING; LIQUOR; TOASTS; WINE

# Potatoes

*Potatoes were being cultivated thousands of years ago by the ancient Incas, who were at the vanguard of civilization in myriad ways. Europeans, however, were slow to accept this humble tuber. First*

*of all, clerics condemned the potato on two grounds: It isn't mentioned in the Bible and it was thought to be an aphrodisiac. Then there were those who declared that, since it was a member of the nightshade family, the potato was undoubtedly poisonous. In fact, potatoes were pretty much vegetable outcasts until the sixteenth century when Sir Walter Raleigh, ever the adventurous trailblazer, helped debunk the poison-potato myth by planting them on his Irish property. A hundred years later, the canny Irish were growing potatoes prodigiously. But it wasn't until the eighteenth century that potatoes really came into vogue, all because French agriculturalist and ardent potato advocate Antoine-Augustin Parmentier sent King Louis XVI a birthday bouquet of potato blossoms, which so enchanted Marie Antoinette that she began using the flowers as a fashion statement. And potatoes have been "in" ever since!*

Zee always went naked in the house, except for the brassiere she wore when it was her turn to get dinner. Once, cooking French-fried potatoes in a kettle of boiling fat, she had come within an inch of crisping her most striking features.

— *G. S. Albee*

Peace of mind and a comfortable income are predicted by a dream of eating potatoes in any form.

— *Ned Ballantyne and Stella Coeli*

I appreciate the potato only as a protection against famine, except for that I know nothing more eminently tasteless.

— *Jean-Anthelme Brillat-Savarin*

He [Spencer Tracy] was solid and dependable, like a baked potato.

— *Katharine Hepburn*

'Tis the potato that's the queen of the garden.

— *Irish proverb*

## Potato Pet Names

Potato nicknames abound throughout the spud-eating world. Here are a few of the most popular: *croker*, *mickey*, and *murphy* from Ireland; *spud* from England; *tater* from Wales; *earth apple* *(pomme de terre)* from France.

One of the most whimsical names for a potato dish is *bubble-and-squeak*, an English dish of equal parts mashed potatoes, chopped cooked cabbage, and sometimes onions—so named for the sounds it makes while cooking.

Show me a person who doesn't like french fries and we'll swap lies.

— *Joan Lunden*

What I say is that, if a fellow really likes potatoes, he must be a pretty decent sort of fellow.

— *A. A. Milne*

A diet which consists predominantly of potatoes leads to the use of liquor.

— *Friedrich Nietzsche*

Just give me a potato, any kind of potato, and I'm happy.

— *Dolly Parton*

## Quick Thickener

Although I don't recommend them for general consumption, instant mashed potatoes *are* good as a last-minute thickener for soups and some sauces. Start by stirring in a tablespoon or two, then wait a minute to check the thickening action before adding more.

In my family, mashed potatoes *are* the main dish.

— *Cindy Pawlcyn*

Mashed potato is the gentile's chicken noodle soup. It's nature's tranquilizer, I take it instead of Valium.

— *Andrew Payne*

Pray for peace and grace and spiritual food,
For wisdom and guidance, for all these are good,
But don't forget the potatoes.

— *John Tyler Pettee*

Potatoes, like wives, should never be taken for granted.

— *Peter Pirbright*

Let the sky rain potatoes.

— *William Shakespeare*

There is no species of human food that can be consumed in a greater variety of modes than the potato.

— *Sir John Sinclair*

No-one has feared developing leprosy from eating French fries, or any potato, but we all do know that fries make us fat (or fatter), cause blemishes, induce indigestion, nourish ulcers, and make havoc of cholesterol counts. Yet everybody keeps on stuffing them down . . . the odd thing is that for most people the greasier and more awful the French fry the better.

— *James Villas*

Throughout my life, friends and fortune have come and gone, but I've always been able to count on a baked potato to see me through.

— *Maggie Waldron*

# Potato Power

The humble potato is a powerhouse of nutrition, easily digestible, and both fat- and cholesterol-free. Naturally, some preparation methods deliver more of its nutritional dividends than others. For example, a potato's skin (and the flesh just beneath it) is particularly nutrient-rich, so it is smart to cook potatoes unpeeled. Cooked in water, potatoes lose much of their vitamins to the liquid, which is a mighty good reason to save and use the cooking water. And—the worst news—the calorie count of a potato can triple with frying.

The nutritional stats for a medium (5.5-ounce) russet potato break down like this: 120 calories, 27 grams of carbohydrates (mostly complex), 3 grams of protein, a trace of sodium, 40 percent of the daily requirement of vitamin C, plus vitamin B-6, niacin (B-3), pantothenic acid, riboflavin (B-2), thiamin (B-1), and the minerals copper, iron, magnesium, potassium, phosphorus, and zinc. A small (5-ounce) sweet potato has around 160 calories and less protein, phosphorus, potassium, and niacin than a regular potato. It is, however, a good source of vitamin E and packs a nutritional wallop with a vitamin-A content that is almost 70 percent of the recommended daily allowance. One cup of cooked sweet potato contains more vitamin A than 23 cups of broccoli!

Excellent potatoes, smoking hot, and accompanied by melted butter of the first quality, would alone stamp merit on any dinner. . . .

— *Thomas Walker*

## Top It Off Right

You've heard it hundreds of times—it's not the potato that's fattening, but what you put *on* it (butter, sour cream, or bacon). For a delicious baked potato topping without the guilt, try a tablespoon or two of low-fat cream cheese for decadent flavor, creamy texture, and a lot fewer calories than sour cream. Stir in a couple of tablespoons of low- or nonfat cottage cheese to add a little moisture, if you like. Or try quark—a soft, unripened cheese with the texture and flavor of sour cream. Although the calorie count for low-fat quark is the same as for low-fat sour cream (35 calories per ounce), the texture is much richer. *See also* CHEESE *for more information on quark.*

What small potatoes we all are, compared with what we might be. We don't plow deep enough, any of us, for one thing.

— *Charles Dudley Warner*

Potatoes are to food what sensible shoes are to fashion.

— *Linda Wells*

My idea of heaven is a great big baked potato and someone to share it with.

— *Oprah Winfrey*

. . . potatoes, thin as coins but not so hard. . . .

— *Virginia Woolf*

*See also* VEGETABLES

# Prickly Potato Sticks

These super-satisfying potatoes look like funny french fries, but they're missing one thing—three times the calories! *Panko* is Japanese-style bread crumbs, coarser than the fine crumbs sold commercially. You can find panko in the ethnic section of many supermarkets, as well as in Asian markets. I like using these coarse bread crumbs because they contribute a rough-textured, light crunch to potatoes. If you can't find panko, simply use unseasoned fine bread crumbs.

    3 large (12-ounce) baking potatoes
    1 to 1½ cups panko (Japanese-style bread crumbs)
    1 large egg
    3 tablespoons olive or vegetable oil
    ½ teaspoon salt
    ¼ teaspoon ground nutmeg
    ¼ teaspoon cayenne pepper

Arrange oven shelves so one is at the bottom, the other at the top. Preheat oven to 450°F. Generously coat 2 large baking sheets with nonstick vegetable spray; set aside. Cut potatoes lengthwise into long ½-inch thick sticks. Sprinkle about 1 cup bread crumbs over the bottom of a large, shallow bowl or a dish. In a large bowl, combine egg, olive oil, salt, and cayenne pepper. Dip potato sticks, a few at a time, into the egg mixture, coating evenly, then roll in bread crumbs, turning to coat all sides. Arrange potatoes about ½ inch apart on prepared baking sheets. Bake 15 minutes. Remove from oven; use a metal spatula to flip potatoes. Return to oven, switching position of baking sheets so that the one that was on the top shelf is now on the bottom shelf. Bake 15 to 20 minutes more, or until golden brown. Serve hot. **Serves 4.**

# Poultry

. . . poultry is for the cook what canvas is for the painter.
— *Jean-Anthelme Brillat-Savarin*

*See also* CHICKEN; DUCK; MEAT; TURKEY

# Prunes

*A relatively new product on the market today is prune purée, which can be used in baked goods as a fat substitute. The California Prune Board tells us that using prune purée can eliminate the cholesterol in baked goods, reduce their fat by up to 90 percent, and calories by as much as 30 percent. The result is a baked good that's slightly moist and chewy, with a prune flavor that can range from mild to assertive, depending on the other flavors with which the purée is combined. All of which gives the phrase "prune power" an entirely new slant.*

Papa, potatoes, poultry, prunes, and prism, are all very good words for the lips: especially prunes and prism.
— *Charles Dickens*

. . . the prunes swam in grey juice like the wrinkled skulls of old men. . . .

— *E. M. Forster*

While it is undeniably true that people love a surprise, it is equally true that they are seldom pleased to suddenly and without warning happen upon a series of prunes in what they took to be a normal loin of pork.

— *Fran Lebowitz*

*See also* FRUIT

# Pudding

*When is a pudding not a pudding? When it's sausage, that's when. I refer, of course, to the popular British Isles comestible known as "blood pudding" or, in Ireland, "black pudding." This so-called pudding is actually a large, precooked, almost black link sausage made of bread crumbs, oatmeal, suet, and pig's blood. M-m-m-m, can we say "yummy"?*

There is for me a special lure in the names of English puddings: the Steamed Spotted Dog . . . and the Chocolate Mud. They have a realistic ugliness about them which sums up my whole finicky adult approach to something inseparable from the unquestioning, lusty appetite of childhood.

*– M. F. K. Fisher*

In moments of considerable strain I tend to take to bread-and-butter pudding. There is something about the blandness of soggy bread, the crispness of the golden outer crust and the unadulterated pleasure of a lightly set custard that makes the world seem a better place to live.

*– Clement Freud*

Blessed be he that invented pudding, for it is a Manna that hits the Palates of all Sorts of People; a Manna better than that of the Wilderness, because the People are never weary of it. . . .

*– Françoise Maximilien Mission*

*See also* CUSTARD; DESSERTS; SWEETS

# Peanut-Butterscotch Pudding

The placement for this recipe was a dilemma for me—should I put it under "pudding" or "comfort food"? I confess—its old-fashioned flavor and satiny texture makes me feel snuggly (and just a little naughty) all the way down to my toes. But because one's response to a particular food is so intensely personal, I opted for the literal placement and I'll let you decide whether or not it comforts you. The cautionary note with any egg-based mixture is to take it slow (never cook over high heat) and stir constantly. Keep those parameters in mind and it'll be easy pudding.

4 cups (1 quart) half-and-half
6 egg yolks
1 cup packed *dark* brown sugar
½ teaspoon salt
½ cup all-purpose flour
⅓ cup smooth peanut butter
2 tablespoons unsalted butter

# Pumpkins

*As a child I remember singing a song that went something like this:*

> *Peter, Peter, pumpkin eater,*
> *Had a wife and couldn't keep her.*
> *He put her in a pumpkin shell,*
> *And there he kept her very well.*

*The thing about such childhood fancies is that we repeat them mindlessly without a flicker of an idea of what they mean. It was a catchy ditty, and my friends and I would often sing it while*

1 tablespoon pure vanilla extract
heavy cream, whipped (optional)

In the top of a double boiler over medium heat, bring half-and-half to a simmer. While cream is heating, combine egg yolks, brown sugar, and salt in a blender container; cover and process until well combined. Add flour; blend until smooth, scraping down sides of blender as necessary. Remove center of blender lid (or entire lid). With machine running at low speed, slowly add 2 cups of the hot cream. Replace center of lid (or entire lid); blend at high speed for 1 minute. Whisking constantly, slowly add the egg mixture back into the hot cream in the pan. Place top of double boiler over simmering water. Stirring constantly, cook pudding over medium-low heat for 5 minutes. Remove from heat. Add peanut butter and butter, whisking until smooth. Strain through a fine sieve into a large bowl. Refrigerate, stirring often the first hour to release steam and prevent skin from forming on surface. Stir in vanilla. Cover and refrigerate for at least 4 hours. To serve, spoon pudding into individual stemmed glasses; top with whipped cream, if desired. **Serves 6.**

*jumping rope. Now I find myself thinking, just what the heck does that rhyme mean? Oh, I'm sure I can cogitate several dark, philosophical analyses, but — ever the optimist — I prefer to think it was simply nursery-rhyme nonsense. However, as long as we're on the subject of pumpkin shells, here's a little tip: Halloween pumpkins will keep longer if you coat them thoroughly inside and out with a spray-on antiseptic. I wouldn't suggest eating them afterward.*

To dream of pumpkins is a very bad omen.

— *Richard Folkard*

**M**y favorite word is "pumpkin." . . . You can't take it seriously. But you can't ignore it either. It takes ahold of your head and that's it. You are a pumpkin. Or you are not. I am.
*– Harrison Salisbury*

What moistens the lip and what brightens the eye?
What calls back the past, like the rich Pumpkin pie?
*– John Greenleaf Whittier*

*See also* VEGETABLES

# Raspberries

*My favorite berry by far is the raspberry, with its insouciant fusion of sweet and tart. And I am not alone in my ardor for this most ravishing berry, for legend tells us that from the start, it was food for the gods. And not just any god, but Greek mythology's ultimate god – Zeus. As the fable goes, raspberries were once all white. Then one day, when a nymph was picking raspberries to soothe the crying baby Zeus, she pricked her finger on one of the bush's many thorns. The sweet nymph's blood stained the berries a brilliant red, and they've been that way ever since. However, not all raspberries are red. They come in a variety of hues, from almost black to golden. No matter what the color, the only adornment for perfectly ripe raspberries is – at least for me – a kiss of cream.*

**N**obody can be insulted by raspberries and cream.
*– Barbara Kafka*

**T**he flavor of the raspberry stamps it "Made in Asia." It breathes of the Orient—rich, exotic, spice-laden and with a hint of musk.

*– Waverley Root*

*See also* BERRIES

# Recipes

## Anagramatically Yours

One anagram for the word "recipes" is "precise," which is exactly what a well-written recipe should be. In case you're wondering, two other, less recipe-symbolic anagrams are "pierces" and "piecers," the latter being textile workers who join together threads or fabric pieces. Back to the question of just what a recipe is: The tongue-in-cheek answer is that it is what causes trouble when you don't follow it. Some recipes can be played with, some can't. For instance, recipes for basic meat-and-potato foods generally can be altered without distressing consequences. On the other hand, recipes for baked goods such as breads and cakes have a delicate and precise balance of flour, fat, leavening, sweeteners, and liquid, the adjustments of which could mean disaster. Remember that the next time you blithely decide to substitute honey for sugar in your favorite muffins and wind up instead with honey-flavored hockey pucks.

A recipe is only a theme, which an intelligent cook can play each time with a variation.

— *Madame Benoit*

Don't take any recipe on faith. There are some hostile recipes in this world.

— *Peg Bracken*

In most recipes there are encouragingly few pitfalls. One mustn't go berserk with the thought, but a quarter cup of liquid, a tablespoon more or less of butter, five minutes or so of cooking time are all variable and the sooner the beginning cook learns it the better the food will be.

— *Craig Claiborne*

If six cooks followed the same recipe, the finished dish would vary six times.

— *Theodora Fitzgibbon*

No food writer confers the title "classic" on a recipe without inviting vituperative dissent from the world's culinary arbiters.

— *Bert Greene*

If a recipe cannot be written on the face of a 3 × 5 card, off with its head.

— *Helen Nearing*

Recipe cooking is to real cooking as painting by number is to real painting: just pretend.

— *John Thorne*

*See also* COOKBOOKS

# Restaurants

*Restaurant lingo:* **Restaurateur,** *a person who owns or manages a restaurant, is pronounced rehs-tuhr-uh-TOOR — there is no "n" in either the word or the enunciation.* **Front of the house** *refers to the dining room, bar, and waiting area, while* **back of the house** *designates the kitchen and preparation areas.*

The Paris restaurant is a phenomenon that the tourist comes upon for the first time with stunned surprise. To the end of his traveling days he will never get over that agreeable shock.

— *James Beard and Alexander Watt*

The murals in restaurants are on a par with the food in museums.

— *Peter de Vries*

The food here is so tasteless you could eat a meal of it and belch and it wouldn't remind you of anything.

*— Redd Foxx*

"Dinner theater," a way of positively guaranteeing that both food and theater will be amateur and mediocre, which means unthreatening and therefore desirable.

*— Paul Fussell*

In a restaurant choose a table near a waiter.

*— Jewish proverb*

Epitaph for a waiter: "God finally caught his eye."

*— George S. Kaufman*

A restaurant is a fantasy—a kind of living fantasy in which diners are the most important members of the cast.

*— Warner LeRoy*

If a waiter in a restaurant has a grudge against one, he will spit into one's food.

*— H. L. Mencken*

Avoid any restaurant where a waiter arrives with a handful of knives and forks just as you reach the punchline of your best story and says, "Which of you is having the fish?"

*— John Mortimer*

## Tips on Tipping

*In a quandary about tipping?* You're not alone. Modern etiquette suggests that an appropriate tip range is 15 to 20 percent of the total bill before tax has been added. If the food or service is outstanding, however, you may want to tip more. But give some thought before you leave a small tip or none at all. If the food was inferior or slow in coming, the fault most likely lies in the kitchen and may be out of the waitperson's hands.

Never trust the food in a restaurant on top of the tallest building in town that spends a lot of time folding napkins.

*— Andy Rooney*

When those waiters ask me if I want some fresh ground pepper, I ask if they have any aged pepper.

*— Andy Rooney*

Restaurants want to be judged on their intentions—not the results.

*— Mimi Sheraton*

When you find a waiter who is a waiter and not an actor, musician or poet, you've found a jewel.

*— André Soltner*

*See also* AIRLINE FOOD; DINING

# Rhubarb

*A nickname for rhubarb is "pieplant," because of its popularity in pies. However, although rhubarb is most often served in pies and other desserts, it isn't, as many assume, a fruit, but rather a member of the buckwheat family. There are two kinds of rhubarb:* **Hot-house rhubarb** *has pink to pale red stalks and yellow-green leaves;* **field-grown rhubarb,** *with its cherry-red stalks and bright greens, has the more pronounced flavor of the two. A rhubarb's thick, celerylike stalks are the only edible portions — the leaves contain oxalic acid and can therefore be toxic.*

Rhubarb, *n.* Vegetable essence of stomach ache.

*— Ambrose Bierce*

The first rhubarb of the season is to the digestive tract of winter-logged inner man what a good hot bath with plenty of healing soap is to the outer after a bout with plough and harrow. Even the tongue and teeth have a scrubbed feeling after a dish of early rhubarb.

*— Della Lutes*

# Rice

*When is rice not rice at all? When it's wild rice, that's when. History tells us that when the early explorers of America's Great Lakes region saw the Native American Ojibway (also known as Chippewa) harvesting the grain, the pioneers called it "wild rice" (also "Indian rice") because it resembled the grain they knew as rice. So important was this Native American crop that in 1750, the Ojibway warred with the Sioux (at the Battle of Kathio) for possession of the northern Minnesota lakes' wild rice stands. This "rice" for which battles were fought is actually a long-grain marsh grass. Although native to the northern Great Lakes area, it's also cultivated in California as well as several midwestern states. Wild rice has a luxurious nutty flavor and chewy texture that's prized by many. Nutritionally, it's high in dietary fiber and rich in iron, protein, and niacin.*

Risotto is the ultimate comfort food.

*— Joyce Goldstein*

Brown rice is ponderous, overly chewy, and possessed of unpleasant religious overtones.

*— Fran Lebowitz*

A diet that consists predominantly of rice leads to the use of opium. . . .

*— Friedrich Nietzsche*

## Puffed Wild Rice

I love these crunchy, nutty little niblets for snacking, but only when I'm feeling particularly extravagant. They make a great garnish for everything from soup to salad to vegetables, or you can toss them into a holiday dressing—wonderful!

2/3 cup wild rice
1 tablespoon olive oil
salt and freshly ground black pepper

Place rice in a strainer and rinse well with running water. Drain well, then turn out onto several layers of paper towel; spread rice in a single layer. Blot with additional paper towels to dry thoroughly. Heat oil in a large skillet over medium heat. Add rice, stirring well. Sauté, stirring often, until most of the grains have cracked open and puffed slightly. Salt and pepper to taste. Turn out onto dry paper towels. Serve warm or at room temperature. **Makes about 1 cup.**

# Rosemary

As for rosemary, I let it run all over my garden walls, not only because my bees love it but because it is the herb sacred to remembrance and friendship, whence a sprig of it hath a dumb language.

– *Thomas Moore*

*See also* SEASONINGS

# Saffron

*See* SEASONINGS

# Salads

*The term "salad days" refers to a time of youthful innocence and inexperience — we all had them, whether or not we remember them fondly. But now, salad days are becoming more and more frequent, and gone are the times when salad played a minor role in a meal. Today it's not at all uncommon for salad to take center stage in myriad guises and all shapes and sizes. The neat part about salads is that they're so friendly, not to mention versatile. They can be light and fruity or hearty and earthy; they can be hot, cold, or in between. The very best salads combine textures and flavors that contrast yet complement each other. As you can tell, I'm a fan of salads — mainly because of their infinite possibilities for flavor excitement. About the only kinds I avoid are those at salad bars, with their off-putting array of limp greens, canned beans and corn, rancid croutons, and flavorless processed cheese. One look at such a spread and I definitely go into a salad daze.*

He who has the best recipe for egg salad shall rule heaven and earth.

*— Woody Allen*

Salad bars aren't cheap. They aren't particularly healthy. They certainly aren't satisfying. So why are they sprouting up everywhere? It's because they're fast, clean, safe, and convenient — as is indoor plumbing.

*— Irena Chalmers*

You need to have the soul of a rabbit to eat lettuce as it is usually served — green leaves slightly lubricated with oil and flavored with vinegar. A salad is only a background; it needs embroidering.

*— Paul Reboux*

# Snappy Lime Cream Dressing

This spicy-hot dressing is great for everything from slaws to mixed greens to potato salads. I've even been known to drizzle it over baked potatoes . . . well, one can't be good *all* the time.

1 large clove garlic, peeled
2/3 cup olive oil
1/3 cup sour cream
1/4 cup fresh lime juice
2 teaspoons Dijon mustard
3/4 teaspoon chili powder
1/2 to 3/4 teaspoon cayenne pepper
1/2 teaspoon salt

In a food processor fitted with the metal chopping blade, drop garlic into running machine; process until garlic is chopped and clinging to sides of bowl. Scrape down sides of food-processor bowl. Or mince garlic and turn into a blender jar. Add remaining dressing ingredients; process 20 seconds, or until creamy. Cover and refrigerate until ready to use. Whisk before dressing salads. **Makes about 1 1/4 cups.**

My salad days, when I was green in judgment.
— *William Shakespeare*

What is more refreshing than salads when your appetite seems to have deserted you, or even after a capacious dinner—the nice, fresh, green, and crisp salad, full of life and health, which seems to invigorate the palate. . . .
— *Alexis Soyer*

You can put everything, and the more things the better, into a salad, as into a conversation; but everything depends on the skill of mixing.

*– Charles Dudley Warner*

To make a good salad is to be a brilliant diplomatist—the problem is entirely the same in both cases. To know how much oil one must mix with one's vinegar.

*– Oscar Wilde*

*See also* LETTUCE

# Salmon

Salmon are like men: too soft a life is not good for them.

*–James de Coquet*

*See also* FISH

# Salsa

*The number of salsas on the shelves today are enough to make one's head spin. The word "salsa" is Mexican for "sauce," but it's not that simple. Fresh salsa (salsa cruda) is uncooked, green salsa (salsa verde) typically refers to a mixture of tomatillos, green chiles, and cilantro. The tomato- and tomatillo-based fusions are the most common, but there are salsas based on everything from avocado to papaya; their heat quotients range from mild to mouth-searing. The common denominator is some kind of chile and lots and lots of flavor. As Reed Hearon has already so lyrically said:*

Feel that happy, mouthfilling wow? Taste that gimme-some-more-of-that, *boy*-that's-great flavor? That's salsa! That's musica for your mouth!

*– Reed Hearon*

# Ginger-Mango Salsa

Paper-thin slices of pale pink seasoned ginger can be found in Asian markets and many supermarkets. Two tablespoons of minced fresh ginger may be substituted, if desired. If you can't find fresh mango, look for jars of mango slices or frozen mango. This sassy salsa is terrific with grilled pork or chicken, on sandwiches, or even mixed into a salad dressing.

- 1 medium mango, peeled, seeded, and diced (about 1 heaping cup)
- 1 large ripe tomato, seeded and diced (about 1 heaping cup)
- 1 jalapeño chile, seeded and minced
- 2 tablespoons seasoned ginger, drained and finely chopped
- 2 tablespoons finely chopped fresh mint
- 1 tablespoon fresh lime juice
- salt to taste

In a medium bowl, combine mango, tomato, jalapeño, ginger, mint, and lime juice. Cover and refrigerate at least 1 hour for flavors to blend. Taste before serving and salt if necessary. Let stand at room temperature for 30 minutes before serving. Cover and refrigerate leftovers. **Makes about 2 cups.**

*See also* CONDIMENTS

# Salt

*Salt helps balance and brighten the flavors of a dish. Simply put, most food tastes bland without it, as several of the following quotes attest. The different kinds of salt available in markets today can sometimes be confusing. Here's a quick description:* **Table salt** *is a fine-grained, refined salt with additives to make it free-flowing;* **iodized salt** *is table salt with added iodine;* **kosher salt** *is a coarse-grained salt that's usually additive-free;* **sea salt,** *with its fresh, distinct flavor, comes from the ocean;* **pickling salt** *is additive-free and fine-grained, and is used to make brines for pickles, sauerkraut, and so on;* **rock salt** *has chunky crystals with a grayish cast because it's not highly refined and is used predominantly as a bed for oysters and clams, and with ice for crank-style ice-cream makers.*

Salt is what makes things taste bad when it isn't in them.

— *Irena Chalmers*

Salt is the policeman of taste: it keeps the various flavors of a dish in order and restrains the stronger from tyrannizing over the weaker.

— *Malcolm de Chazal*

Salt is white and pure—there is something holy in salt.

— *Nathaniel Hawthorne*

Salt is born of the purest of parents: the sun and the sea.

— *Pythagoras*

. . . undersalting shows either a political extremism in the kitchen or a lack of taste.

— *Patricia Unterman*

## The Arrogant Cook

Not putting salt and pepper on the table for guests to season their food as they wish is the height of culinary arrogance. At the very least, it indicates a thoughtless host. That goes for restaurants, too. Chefs who are imperious enough to think their palate is superior to anyone else's aren't worth their salt. If your table hasn't been provided with salt, and you want it, don't be shy about asking the waiter.

Salt is the only rock directly consumed by man. It corrodes but preserves, desiccates but is wrested from the water. It has fascinated man for thousands of years not only as a substance he prized . . . but also as a generator of poetic and of mythic meaning. The contradictions it embodies only intensify its power and its links with experience of the sacred.

*– Margaret Visser*

*See also* SEASONINGS

# Sandwiches

*There's something intrinsically comforting about a sandwich. Maybe it's because it's such a comfortable size, just right for two hands. My Irish grandmother used to call it a "handwich." Also, you can get familiar with a sandwich without getting slapped or sued – the very act of eating one necessitates holding, fondling, and squeezing it, albeit unconsciously. All of which means you might want to consider the familiarity with which you handle your sandwich the next time you eat one in public.*

Blandwich: Hamburger without any onions.

*– Peg Bracken*

We need to keep America what a child once called "the nearest thing to heaven." And lots of sunshine, places to swim and peanut butter sandwiches.

*– George Bush*

My objections to the sandwich are two: (i) the amount of bread is out of all proportion to the amount of meat; (ii) the fact that it is disguised by bread enables the preparer of the sandwich to use in it inferior meat . . . if I had my way I would make the provision of sandwiches a penal offense.

*– C. E. M. Joad*

## Sandwich Savoir-Faire

The newest craze in sandwiching is to keep it under wraps. Instead of the filling being enclosed between two slices of bread, it's contained in a wrapper like a flour tortilla, pita bread pocket, eggroll skins, or even large lettuce leaves. Anything soft, pliable, and edible will work as a sandwich wrapper. When I'm feeling particularly pious, I season nonfat cottage cheese with curry powder, add some fresh chopped tomatoes and cilantro, and roll it in a red lettuce leaf. It only takes a little imagination to convince myself that I'm eating a "real" sandwich!

I like the philosophy of the sandwich, as it were. It typifies my attitude to life, really. It's all there, it's fun, it looks good, and you don't have to wash up afterwards.

*– Molly Parkin*

Do not make a stingy sandwich;
Pile the cold cuts high.
Customers should see salami
Coming through the rye.

*– Allan Sherman*

I've got brown sandwiches and green sandwiches . . . it's either very new cheese or very old meat.

*— Neil Simon*

# Sauces

*As with so many culinary mainstays, the refinement of the art of saucemaking is credited to the French, specifically nineteenth-century chef Antonin Carême. This prolific food writer developed and recorded an intricate methodology by which hundreds of sauces were classified under one of the five mères (mother sauces): espagnole (based on brown stock), velouté (based on veal, chicken, or other light stock), béchamel (milk based), hollandaise and mayonnaise (emulsion sauces), and vinaigrette (oil and vinegar fusions). Although it's true that today's sensitivity to health consciousness equates with lighter-textured sauces, the classics are still the foundation of the sauce world, and any serious student chef masters the basics before taking wing.*

Sauce, *n.* The one infallible sign of civilization and enlightenment. A people with no sauces has one thousand vices; a people with one sauce has only nine hundred and ninety-nine. For every sauce invented and accepted a vice is renounced and forgiven.

*— Ambrose Bierce*

It [béarnaise sauce] frightens me! With it one might never stop eating. Merely reading the recipe arouses my hunger.

*— Baron Brisse*

Appetite is the best sauce.

*— French proverb*

Hollandaise sauce is indubitably asparagus' finest upholstery, and you won't go wrong with a spoonful of it on broccoli, either.

*— Bert Greene*

# Ooey-Gooey Caramel Sauce

The title says it all—this is a *serious* caramel sauce. It's an obvious choice on ice cream, but also does wonders for fruit, like the **Baked Caramel Apples** (page 111), or drizzled over broiled banana halves, and it makes a great fondue for dipping fresh fruit. For a more butterscotchy flavor, substitute dark brown sugar for the light.

3 cups packed light brown sugar
¾ cup heavy whipping cream
¾ cup dark corn syrup
⅓ cup butter
⅛ teaspoon salt
1½ tablespoons pure vanilla extract

In a medium, heavy saucepan, combine all ingredients except vanilla. Cook over medium-high heat, stirring occasionally, until mixture reaches 230°F on a candy thermometer (or until a spoon coated with boiling syrup forms a 2-inch thread when dipped in a cup of cold water). Remove from heat; cool 30 minutes before stirring in vanilla. Stir before serving warm or room temperature. Cover and refrigerate leftovers for up to 2 weeks. To reheat: Stir over low heat until consistency desired. Or microwave at MEDIUM (50 percent power) for about 1 minute. **Makes about 2 cups.**

Don't be a fuddy-duddy with your hollandaise; be bold, dunk your pretzels in it!

— *Miss Piggy*

I would eat my own father with such a sauce.

— *Grimod de la Reynière*

Sauces in cookery are like the first rudiments of grammar
. . . the foundation of all languages.

– *Alexis Soyer*

What is sauce for the goose may be sauce for the gander,
but is not necessarily sauce for the chicken, the duck, or the
guinea hen.

– *Alice B. Toklas*

The English have forty-two religions, but only two sauces.

– *Voltaire*

*See also* CONDIMENTS; GRAVY; SALSA

# Sauerkraut

*I'll never forget the first time I met my husband's relatives at a
family picnic where his grandmother had prepared her famous
"krautburgers." Imagine my budding epicurean dismay when I
discovered that the name came from the secret ingredient—canned
sauerkraut (horrors!). I've since lost (or perhaps tossed) the recipe
for krautburgers, but if I made those juicy burgers today I'd definitely use fresh sauerkraut, which was hard to find twenty years
ago. Today it's available in delis or in Cryovac packages in a supermarket's refrigerated section. Fresh sauerkraut is eminently better tasting than its canned counterpart; its flavor is milder, its
texture crisper. Keep fresh sauerkraut in the refrigerator and use it
within a week after opening. Try adding a cup of it to lean ground
beef and create your own "krautburgers"!*

It's really disagreeable to eat a lot of sauerkraut for lunch
and supper every day, but you do it if you're hungry.

– *Anne Frank*

*See also* CABBAGE

# Sausage

Walk into any supermarket today and you'll probably see more sausages than you can shake a stick at. Sausages in all shapes, sizes, and flavors, in links, patties, and in bulk, and in or out of casings. Sausages that weren't easy to find six or eight years ago are now generally available. Three of my personal favorites are andouille, linguiça, and lop chong. Andouille (an-DOO-ee or ahn-DWEE), a Cajun specialty, is spicy and heavily smoked – perfect for hearty dishes like jambalaya and gumbo. Linguiça (lin-GWEE-suh) is a garlicky but not particularly spicy Portuguese sausage – it's wonderful served in soups and stews. Lop chong (pronounced just like it looks) is a slightly sweet, highly seasoned Chinese specialty that's texturally similar to pepperoni – great in stir-fries. It's true that most sausages are calorie-laden because of their fat content, but you don't have to eat a plateful – just use a bit of it to give your dishes flavor excitement. One caveat: Before adding sausage to soups, stir-fries, or other dishes, sauté it well to render out much of the fat. That way, you'll have the flavor without so many calories.

Lawsuit, *n.* A machine which you go into as a pig and come out as a sausage.

— *Ambrose Bierce*

Before I knew its meaning, I thought [the word] *saucisson* so exquisite that it seemed the perfect name to give a child — until I learned it meant "sausage"!

— *Olivia de Havilland*

See also MEAT; PORK

# Rum Bums

This is an adaptation (food writers can never leave recipes alone) of one from self-described bon vivant and raconteur **Mick Cummins.** He and his lovely wife, **Jane,** say these rummy bites are always the first hors d'oeuvres to go at parties. The name is my concoction, inspired by a British friend who declared, "Yum, yum, pig's bum!" whenever she ate pork. The sausages can be skinless or in casings. I like skinless (such as **Jimmy Dean** skinless links) because they absorb more of the sauce. Definitely don't use **Brown 'N Serve** sausages! Make and refrigerate these saucy bites a day ahead so any fat can congeal and be removed before serving them.

24 pork link sausages, each cut into thirds
1½ cups dark rum

# Seasonings

*Healers throughout the ages have used herbs and spices for medicinal purposes, and modern science is finally confirming that some — basil, black pepper, cardamom, cilantro, cumin, ginger, nutmeg, oregano, rosemary, saffron, sage, tarragon, thyme, and turmeric — are known to have antioxidant activity that can protect cell damage from many diseases, including cancer. So now you can spice up your life and possibly live longer while you're at it!*

A man who is stingy with the saffron is capable of seducing his own grandmother.

— *Norman Douglas*

½ cup dark brown sugar
¼ teaspoon *each* ground cloves and cayenne pepper

In a very large skillet over medium-high heat, cook sausages until nicely browned, pouring off grease halfway through and thoroughly draining fat at the end. Use a paper towel to blot up excess fat in skillet and on sausages after final grease has been drained. While sausages are cooking, combine remaining ingredients in a 2-cup glass measure. With the burner off, pour over drained and blotted sausages. Over medium heat, bring mixture to a bubbling simmer. *Caution:* If the mixture gets too hot before the alcohol burns off, it can flare up, so heat it slowly. Reduce heat to medium-low; cover and cook for 30 minutes, stirring every 10 minutes to coat sausages with sauce. Transfer sausages to a dish; cover and refrigerate for up to 2 days. Before serving, scoop off congealed fat. Serve at room temperature or slightly warm, accompanied by toothpicks for spearing. If the sauce becomes too thick, thin it slightly with a little water or more rum. **Serves about 10.**

In the beginning there was James Beard and there was curry and that was about all.

— *Nora Ephron*

Nature was indeed at her artistic best when she created the nutmeg, a delight to the eye in all its avatars, from the completely garbed to nudity.

— *Waverley Root*

*See also* PEPPER, BLACK; SALT

# Shellfish

*See* CLAMS; CRAB; FISH; LOBSTER; MUSSELS;
OYSTERS

# Shortbread

*See* COOKIES

# Shrimp

The sort of shrimp hidden under a pound and a half of batter on what Midwestern menus call "French-fried butterfly
shrimp" could as easily be turnips.

*– Calvin Trillin*

# Soups, Stews, and Chowders

*I love soups, stews, and chowders. In fact, I can't think of a sin-
gle soul who doesn't. How could one not love something so versatile, so emotionally and physically satisfying? One of my very
favorite soups is gumbo, so beautifully characterized by William
Coleman's evocative quote: "There is no dish which at the same
time so tickles the palate, satisfies the appetite, furnishes the body
with nutriment sufficient to carry on the physical requirements, and
costs so little, as a Creole gumbo. It is a dinner in itself, being
soup, pièce de résistance and vegetable in one." Those lyrical
words elicit memories of a chilly New Orleans day in a backstreet
French Quarter bistro where Ron and I lustily consumed steaming bowls of rice topped with a thick, rich, spicy gumbo, chock-
full of shrimp and andouille sausage. The fragrance alone was
enough to make one swoon. That cozy little bistro is now gone,
but – thanks to the gumbo – it will never be forgotten.*

Eating stew in a dream portends a reunion with old friends.
— *Ned Ballantyne and Stella Coeli*

I would like to find a stew that will give me heartburn immediately, instead of at three o'clock in the morning.
— *John Barrymore*

Only the pure of heart can make a good soup.
— *Ludwig van Beethoven*

Beautiful soup, so rich and green
Waiting in a hot tureen!
Who for such dainties would not stoop?
Soup of the evening, beautiful soup!
Beautiful soup! Who cares for fish,
Game, or any other dish?
Who would not give all else for two
Pennyworth only of beautiful soup!
— *Lewis Carroll*

Bouillabaisse is one of those classic dishes whose glory has encircled the world, and the miracle consists of this: there are as many Bouillabaisses as there are good chefs or *cordons bleus.* Each brings to his own version his special touch.
— *Curnonsky*

It was a struggle not to accept second or even third helpings of soup and so risk having no appetite left for the dishes to follow. This is one of the dangers of good soup.
— *Elizabeth David*

I was always eager to salt a good stew. The trouble was that I was expected to supply the meat and potatoes as well.
— *Bette Davis*

There is nothing like a bowl of hot soup, its wisp of aromatic steam teasing the nostrils into quivering anticipation.

— *Louis P. de Gouy*

Bouillabaisse is only good because cooked by the French, who, if they cared to try, could produce an excellent and nutritious substitute out of cigar stumps and empty match boxes.

— *Norman Douglas*

Of all the items on the menu, soup is that which exacts the most delicate perfection and the strictest attention.

— *Auguste Escoffier*

## Stew Pot Pointers

Make stew a day ahead and refrigerate overnight—the flavors will mingle and heighten and any fat will solidify for easy removal.

Vegetables will be tender-crisp instead of mushy if you sauté them, then remove and refrigerate, adding them to the stew toward the end of the cooking time.

Cooking stew, covered, in a 350°F oven means less pot watching.

If the flavor of your finished stew is lackluster, enrich it with a teaspoon or two of chicken or beef extract or of bouillon, instant coffee powder, or unsweetened cocoa powder.

Last-minute stew thickeners include cooked potato, rice, vegetable purées, or a cornstarch slurry (2 to 3 tablespoons of broth, milk, or sherry stirred into 1/4 cup cornstarch). Stirring constantly, gradually add the thickening agent to the hot stew a little at a time until the desired thickness is reached.

For real comfort food, serve stew in a mashed-potato nest in a bowl or stretch a stew by serving it over rice.

This is not that, and that is certainly not this, and at the same time an oyster stew is not stewed, and although they are made of the same things and even cooked almost the same way, an oyster soup should never be called a stew, nor stew soup.

*– M. F. K. Fisher*

To make a good soup, the pot must only simmer or "smile."

*– French proverb*

I would often ask the butcher, in those days, for a few bones "for my dog." Then I would make the most exquisite soup of those bones. . . . It was several years before my butcher realized that I didn't have a dog.

*– Edward Giobbi*

Soup, as a category, is virtually disappearing from restaurant menus; and I feel that I am being deprived of my birthright, the steaming bowl that comforts and sustains.

*– Barbara Kafka*

. . . Hungarian housewives and cooks are either born with or develop a keen *soup sense.*

*– George Lang*

Cold soup is a very tricky thing and it is the rare hostess who can carry it off. More often than not the dinner guest is left with the impression that had he only come a little earlier he could have gotten it while it was still hot.

*– Fran Lebowitz*

So you have a kinder, more adaptable friend in the food world than soup? Who soothes you when you are ill? . . . Who warms you in the winter and cools you in the summer? . . . Soup does its loyal best. . . . You don't catch steak hanging around when you're poor and sick, do you?

*– Judith Martin (Miss Manners)*

. . . the pots were always boiling chowders. . . . Chowder for breakfast, and chowder for dinner, and chowder for supper, till you began to look for fish-bones coming through your clothes.

*— Herman Melville*

## It's Okay to Be a Chowderhead

If someone calls you a "chowderhead," they're not saying you love chowder—they're calling you thickheaded and not very bright! This particular pejorative undoubtedly derives from the fact that most chowders are indeed quite thick. But just how does chowder differ from soup or stew? While true that a chowder's texture is typically thicker than soup and thinner than stew, the definition for chowder is a chunky fish soup. The name comes from the French *chaudière*, a caldron in which fishermen cooked their fish stews. As with many things culinary, however, that definition has broadened to include all manner of thick, rich potages based on everything from corn to potatoes. Clam chowder is one of the most popular of the genre and comes in two basic styles: Manhattan clam chowder, made with tomatoes, and New England clam chowder, made with milk. Zealots in both camps decry the other as counterfeit.

An idealist is one who, on noticing that a rose smells better than a cabbage, concludes that it will also make better soup.

*— H. L. Mencken*

I live on good soup, not fine words.

*— Molière*

Isn't there any other part of the matzo you can eat?

> – *Marilyn Monroe*
> *(on being served matzo-ball soup three days in a row)*

As the days grow short, some faces grow long. But not mine. Every autumn, when the wind turns cold and darkness comes early, I am suddenly happy. It's time to start making soup again.

> – *Leslie Newman*

Chowder breathes reassurance. It steams consolation.

> – *Clementine Paddleford*

I believe I once considerably scandalized her by declaring that clear soup was a more important factor in life than a clear conscience.

> – *Saki*

Soup and fish explain half the emotions of life.

> – *Sydney Smith*

Of soup and love, the first is best.

> – *Spanish proverb*

A lusty stew brings out the primitive in all of us. . . .

> – *James Villas*

Worries go down better with soup.

> – *Yiddish proverb*

Eating stew in a dream portends a reunion with old friends. . . .

> –Your Horoscope and Dreams

*See also* CHILI

# Dark Beer Stew

This secret to this stew's husky flavor and rich, dark color is the coffee and sugar in it, the latter of which richly caramelizes the meat and onions. A bold red wine like Cabernet Sauvignon or Zinfandel can be substituted for the beer. Tailor this dish to your personal taste by adding your favorite vegetables (I might add potatoes, carrots, fennel, red bell pepper, mushrooms, celery . . . you name it). If you want to gild the lily, brown the vegetables in 2 tablespoons each oil and sugar, then add them to the hot stew to complete the cooking.

3 tablespoons olive or canola oil

2 tablespoons sugar

3 pounds boneless chuck or pork shoulder, well
   trimmed and cut into 1-inch chunks

1 large onion, finely chopped

¼ cup flour

½ teaspoon ground allspice

½ teaspoon freshly ground black pepper

2 medium cloves garlic, minced

# Special Occasions

My grandfather had a wonderful funeral. . . . It was held in a big hall with accordion players. On the buffet table there was a replica of the deceased in potato salad.

*– Woody Allen*

2 (12-ounce) bottles (3 cups) dark beer, room
   temperature
2 cups beef broth
3 tablespoons red wine vinegar
1 tablespoon instant coffee
5 cups chopped vegetables
finely chopped watercress or parsley for garnish
   (optional)

Preheat oven to 350°F. In a Dutch oven or other large, heavy pot, stir together oil and sugar; heat until hot over medium heat. Add meat and onion; cook, stirring occasionally, until all the liquid has evaporated and the ingredients are *darkly browned* (the time can vary greatly—meat that has had water pumped into it to make it weigh more will take much longer to brown). Sprinkle meat and onion with flour, allspice, and pepper; cook, stirring often, for 1 to 2 minutes. Stir in garlic, beer, beef broth, vinegar, and instant coffee. Bring mixture to a boil; scrape sides and bottom of pan to loosen all the clinging brown bits. Cover and transfer to oven; bake 1 hour. Remove pot from oven; stir in vegetables. Cover and continue to cook for about 1/2 hour, or until meat and vegetables are tender. Salt to taste. Garnish with finely chopped watercress or parsley, if desired. **Serves 6.**

Life is a banquet and most poor suckers are starving!
   *— Rosalind Russell (in the film* Auntie Mame)

# Spinach

*Don't tell Popeye, but all that spinach he eats has little to do with making his "mus-kuls" stronger when defending Olive Oyl's honor against big, bad Bluto. It's true that spinach is packed with iron (as well as carotenoids, folic acid, and vitamin C), but it also contains oxalic acid, which inhibits the body's absorption of both iron and calcium. That's not to say spinach isn't good for you. It is one of the healthiest greens we can eat, and it's known to be a preventative for everything from cancer to cataracts. Just don't count on it helping you conquer the Blutos that life throws your way.*

One man's poison ivy is another man's spinach.

*— George Ade*

On the subject of spinach: divide into little piles. Rearrange again into new piles. After five or six maneuvers, sit back and say you are full.

*— Delia Ephron*

Spinach is the broom of the stomach.

*— French proverb*

If I were faced with the onerous chore of selecting a last meal on earth . . . I'd choose a salad of tender [spinach] greens with a healthy tinge of grit between the leaves to remind me of the transitory retribution mortality imposes.

*— Bert Greene*

This would be a better place for children if parents had to eat the spinach.

*— Groucho Marx*

Spinach is not worth much essentially. It is susceptible of receiving all imprints; it is the virgin wax of the kitchen.

*— Grimod de la Reynière*

I say it's spinach, and I say the hell with it.

*– E. B. White*

*See* VEGETABLES

# Stews

*See* SOUPS, STEWS, AND CHOWDERS

# Strawberries

*I'll never forget testing recipes for one of my first cooking classes years ago. The subject was chocolate, and one of the dishes I planned to make was chocolate-dipped, long-stemmed strawberries. Now, the only trick to dipping strawberries in chocolate is to be sure the berries are scrupulously dry (any moisture will seize the chocolate); it's really pretty easy. But I wanted to inject them with Grand Marnier, a procedure that must be done after the chocolate has hardened on the berry. The secret, which I discovered after trial-and-error, is to inject just the right amount of liqueur – too little and there's no flavor, too much and the berry swells like a balloon and cracks the chocolate. Since it's my nature to push the culinary envelope, I began injecting berry after berry to just below the bursting point. I mastered the technique but not before the countertop was littered with cracked chocolate-covered strawberries, which – now that I think of it – made a decadent dinner.*

Doubtless God could have made a berry, but doubtless God never did.

*– William Butler (on the strawberry)*

On a sheep-cropped knoll under a clump of elms we ate the strawberries and drank the wine—as Sebastian promised, they were delicious together.

*– Evelyn Waugh*

*See also* BERRIES

# Surimi

**Just what is surimi?** *Pronounced soo-REE-mee and mean-ing "formed fish," surimi is boneless fish pulp that has been molded into various shapes — such as crab legs, shrimp, and scal-lops — and colored to complete its look-alike transformation. Most surimi found in North America is made from pollock, which has a lean, firm flesh and a sweet, delicate flavor. Surimi is often simply labeled imitation crabmeat, lobster, etc., and is available in most supermarkets. Bottom line? Well, it certainly doesn't taste as good as the real thing, but then the price doesn't hurt as bad, either.*

Surimi is the people-fodder of the future, a seafood with a thousand false identities but none of its own.

— *Irena Chalmers*

*See also* FISH

# Sushi

*For the uninitiated, sushi (SOO-shee) is a Japanese specialty in which sushi meshi (boiled rice flavored with sweetened rice vinegar) is typically formed in a roll around raw fish, chopped vegetables, pickles, and tofu, then wrapped in thin sheets of* nori *(seaweed). The rolls, which range from thin (hosomaki) to thick (futomaki), are then often cut into slices. It's the raw-fish part that's off-putting to many, including restaurateur José Simon, who described it so succinctly:*

In Mexico we have a word for sushi: bait.

— *José Simon*

*See also* FISH

# Sweets

**How sweet it is!** *Did you know that sugar was once so rare and expensive that only the exceedingly wealthy could afford it, which is why it was appropriately referred to as "white gold"? However, the first sugar wasn't white at all — it came in large, solid, light brown to cream-colored loaves and was commonly used medicinally. Even though sugarcane was cultivated in Persia and ancient Arabia in the fourth century B.C., sugar wasn't introduced to the Western world until the year 711, when the Moors conquered the Iberian peninsula — that was definitely the start of sweet things to come. Today, sugar is easy to come by, which is sweet news to those with a sweet tooth or to a sweet-tempered sweetheart who likes to be sweet-talked with sweetmeats.*

Do you think that God made good things only for fools?

*— René Descartes (on his propensity for sweets)*

Every sweet has its sour.

*— Ralph Waldo Emerson*

The sweets I remember best were white and tubular, much thinner than any cigarette, filled with a dark chocolate filling. If I found one now I am sure it would have the taste of hope.

*— Graham Greene*

Once in a young lifetime one should be allowed to have as much sweetness as one can possibly want and hold.

*— Judith Olney*

A fool likes sweet things.

*— Yiddish proverb*

Sweets for the sweet create big business for dentists.

*— Anonymous*

*See also* CAKES; CANDY; CHOCOLATE; COOKIES; CUSTARDS; DESSERTS; GINGERBREAD; ICE CREAM; PASTRY; PIES; PUDDING

# Tea

*When contemplating things terribly, terribly British, tea is one of the first thoughts that come to mind. However, tea wasn't always a British predilection. It might surprise you to know that Britons much preferred coffee until about 1850. The gradual conversion to tea happened because it was simply more affordable, with a pound of tea producing many more servings than the same amount of coffee. By the end of the nineteenth century, U.K. residents were consuming an average of 10 pounds per capita and never looked back. The trailblazing Americans were the first to drink tea iced, a beverage that many pundits claim was first served at the 1904 St. Louis Exposition. But, as with so many things, it ain't necessarily so. For in his 1860 book* How to Live, *Solon Robinson, a New York* Tribune *writer, wrote: "Last summer we got in the habit of taking the tea iced, and really thought it better than hot." However, to those of us who relish its refreshing salvation on a sweltering day, it really matters not when iced tea was first invented, but simply that it* was.

Tea in Russia and tea in England are as different as peppermint-water and senna. With us [the British] it is a dull, flavorless dose; in Russia it is a fresh invigorating draught.

*– Robert Brenner*

"Take some more tea," the March Hare said to Alice, very earnestly.

"I've had nothing yet," Alice replied in an offended tone: "so I can't take more."

"You mean you can't take less," said the Hatter: "it's very easy to take more than nothing."

*– Lewis Carroll*

Whether it's served from a silver teapot at Buckingham Palace or a samovar in St. Petersburg, whether it's foamed with a bamboo whisk in Kyoto or sipped from a paper cup in Chicago, tea is a drink on which the sun never sets.

*—Consumer Reports*

Tea, though ridiculed by those who are naturally coarse in their nervous sensibilities ... will always be the favourite beverage of the intellectual.

*— Thomas De Quincey*

I wish the English still possessed a shred of the old sense of humour which Puritanism, and dyspepsia, and newspaper reading, and tea-drinking have nearly extinguished.

*— Norman Douglas*

## Tea Talk

CUP OF TEA: Something particularly appealing or suitable to someone

HIGH TEA: A small late-afternoon or early-evening meal

NOT FOR ALL THE TEA IN CHINA: Not for any price

TEA AND SYMPATHY: Consolation

TEA PARTY: A social gathering or party, potentially with tea and refreshments

TEMPEST IN A TEACUP (OR TEAPOT): Much ado about nothing

THAT'S ANOTHER CUP OF TEA: A different matter entirely

Love and scandal are the best sweeteners of tea.

*— Henry Fielding*

... it took her a long time to prepare her tea; but when ready, it was set forth with as much grace as if she had been a veritable guest to her own self.    *— Mary Wilkins Freeman*

If you are cold, tea will warm you — if you are too heated, it will cool you — if you are depressed, it will cheer you — if you are excited, it will calm you.

— *William Gladstone*

"Oh, for a good cup of tea!" A truly British cry that I echo so often in my travels around four o'clock in the afternoon. Tea is my panacea, my consolation — if you will, my "fix."

— *Diana Kennedy*

> We had a kettle: we let it leak:
> Our not repairing it made it worse.
> We haven't had any tea for a week . . .
> The bottom is out of the Universe!

— *Rudyard Kipling*

The trouble with tea is that originally it was quite a good drink. So a group of the most eminent British scientists put their heads together, and made complicated biological experiments to find a way of spoiling it. To the eternal glory of British science their labour bore fruit.

— *George Mikes*

Our trouble is that we drink too much tea. I see in this the slow revenge of the Orient, which has diverted the Yellow River down our throats.

— *J. B. Priestley*

A woman is like a teabag — only in hot water do you realize how strong she is.

— *Nancy Reagan*

It has been well said that tea is suggestive of a thousand wants, from which spring the decencies and luxuries of civilization.

— *Agnes Repplier*

# Tea-ophyte Terminology

Although all tea plants belong to the same species, varying climates, soils, and processing techniques combine to create a multitude of distinctive tea leaves. Here's a breakdown of some of the basic terms:

**Black tea** comes from leaves that have been fermented before being heated and dried, resulting in a dark reddish-brown brew. Black teas—which include Darjeeling, English breakfast, and Lapsang souchong—have more assertive flavors than green or oolong teas. **Orange pekoe** refers not to a flavor or color, but to a black tea leaf's size, which is smaller than that of the medium pekoe leaf.

**Green tea** is made from unfermented, steamed, and dried leaves that produce a greenish-yellow, slightly bitter brew. Two of the more well-known green teas are Gunpowder and Tencha.

**Oolong tea,** the best known of which is Taiwan's Formosa oolong, is made from leaves that have been partially fermented, which creates teas with a flavor, color, and aroma somewhere between black and green teas.

**Herb tea** (also called a *tisane*) is not a true tea, because it is not based on tea-plant leaves, but rather on various herbs, flowers, and spices.

Thank God for tea! What would the world do without tea! How did it exist? I am glad I was not born before tea!

*– Sydney Smith*

The best quality tea must have creases like the leather boot of Tartar horsemen, curl like the dewlap of a mighty bullock, unfold like a mist rising out of a ravine, gleam like a lake touched by a zephyr, and be wet and soft like a fine earth newly swept by rain.

*– Lu Yu*

*See also* COFFEE

# Frost-Tea Cooler

This refreshingly cool sipper is perfect for those long, hot days of summer. For a double orange whammy, substitute orange sherbet for the ice cream.

2 cups cold water
4 bags black currant tea, or 4 dinner teaspoons loose
    tea of your choice
1/4 teaspoon ground cinnamon
1/4 teaspoon ground allspice
1/8 teaspoon ground cloves
1 cup very cold milk
6 ounces frozen orange juice concentrate
1 pint vanilla ice cream
6 orange slices, cut halfway through

In a small saucepan, bring water to a boil. Remove from heat; add tea, cinnamon, allspice, and cloves. Cover and let steep 5 minutes. Strain into a blender jar, pressing tea bags or loose tea to extract as much liquid as possible. Refrigerate about 3 hours (or freeze 1 1/2 hours), uncovered, until very cold. May be covered and refrigerated overnight. When ready to serve, add milk and orange juice concentrate to tea; blend until smooth. Spoon in half the ice cream; process until smooth. Divide remaining ice cream evenly between 4 tall glasses; top with tea mixture. Garnish each serving with an orange slice, hooking it over the glass rim. **Serves 4.**

# Thanksgiving

*See* HOLIDAYS

# Toasts; Toasting

*Just why do we call a verbal salute before drinking a "toast"? Historians tell us that the practice began — as did so many things — in Rome, where a piece of charred bread was placed in a goblet to mellow the wine's flavor. Indeed, today the interior of wine barrels are charred (as they have been for centuries) to add character to wine. In seventeenth-century England, spiced toast was floated in wine to flavor it. Then the toast was consumed when glasses were raised in honor of some event or person. If the glass was a communal goblet, the guest of honor had the privilege (or duty) of eating the toasted bread. Thankfully, the custom of "toasting" eventually became sans toast.*

Here's lookin' at you, kid.
> *— Humphrey Bogart (in the film* Casablanca)

Let us have wine and women, mirth and laughter,
Sermons and soda-water the day after.
> *— Lord Byron*

A toast is all at once a poem, a public prayer, a proverb, a secret sentiment, a roast, a bit of wit, and a veritable verbal badge of social facility . . . a good toast is hard to find.
> *— Dave Fulmer*

This wine is too good for toast-drinking, my dear. You don't want to mix emotions up with a wine like that. You lose the taste.
> *— Ernest Hemingway*

May the road rise to meet you,
May the wind be always at your back,
The sun shine warm upon your face,
The rain fall soft upon your fields,
And Until we meet again
May God hold you in the hollow of his hand.

*— Irish traditional toast*

To long lives and short wars.

*— Colonel Potter (on TV's Mash)*

Wedding: the point at which a man stops toasting a woman and begins roasting her.

*— Helen Rowland*

Here's hoping that you live forever and mine is the last voice you hear.

*— Willard Scott*

May you live all the days of your life.

*— Jonathan Swift*

To men: You can't live with 'em, and you can't shoot 'em.

*— Anonymous*

May you live as long as you want, and never want as long as you live.

*— Anonymous*

*See also* BEER; BRANDY; CHAMPAGNE; COCKTAILS; DRINKING; LIQUOR; PORT; WINE

# Toasts Around the World

Most of the following toasts roughly translate as "good health."

Austria — *Prosit*

Belgium — *Op uw gezonheid*

China — *Kan bei; Wen lie*

Czechoslovakia — *Na Zdravi; Nazdar*

Denmark — *Skål*

England — Cheers

Finland — *Kippis; Maljanne*

France — *Santé; A votre santé*

Germany — *Prosit*

Greece — *Eis Igian*

Hebrew — *L'chaim; Mazel tov*

Iceland — *Santanka nu*

Ireland — *Sláinte*

Italy — *Salute; Cin cin*

Japan — *Kampai; Banzai*

Netherlands — *Proost; Geluch*

Norway — *Skål*

Poland — *Na zdrowie; Vivat*

Portugal — *A sua saúde; Eviva*

Russia — *Na zdorovia*

Scotland — *Hoot mon*

Spain — *Salud*

Sweden — *Skål*

United States — Cheers

Yugoslavia — *Zivio*

# Tomatoes

*Although typically thought of as a vegetable, the tomato is really a fruit. Along with potatoes, red peppers, and eggplant, tomatoes belong to the nightshade family, as do some poisonous plants like the deadly nightshade. Although Spanish conquistadors brought tomato plants back to Spain from Mexico in the sixteenth century, the tomatoes' poison-relation calumny prevented them from being readily accepted by Europeans. Even by the nineteenth century, tomatoes were not clearly understood or accepted. According to James Trager's* The Food Chronology, *in 1861 Godey's Lady's Book advised that, although the tomato was delicious and wholesome, it required at least three hours' cooking time to prevent "a sour porridge." Today we know tomatoes are perfectly delicious raw and not only are they not poisonous, but they pack a nutritional bonus of vitamins A, B, and C, along with potassium, magnesium, phosphorus, and fiber; plus they're low in sodium. Tomatoes are also culinary chameleons: They taste entirely different when eaten raw than after slow, lengthy cooking. No wonder there are now thousands of tomato varieties, ranging in size from ½ inch to 5 inches in diameter and in colors from red to orange to purple. The world LOVES tomatoes!*

The idea of eating out-of-season tasteless tomatoes is a peculiarly American custom, though we keep being baffled and bewildered when we discover that each new one is just as awful as the last.

— *Irena Chalmers*

I grow my own tomatoes every summer for the same reason I diet: it makes me feel righteous!

— *Bert Greene*

**I**f I live to be a hundred, I will never forget the bliss of smelling a tomato as it first appears, dwarf-green, pale, and slightly fuzzy, from its petallike cocoon.

*— Bert Greene*

## Frozen Assets

My friend Lee Janvrin taught me a neat trick for those times when one has an abundance of fresh tomatoes and not enough time to eat them all. Lee freezes them whole. That way, when he is attacked with a yearning for vine-ripened tomatoes in the middle of winter, he simply strolls to his freezer and . . . voilà! Yes, it's true that chilling tomatoes reduces their flavor, but Lee's frozen, vine-picked fruit are better by far than wintertime hothouse tomatoes. Here's his technique: Place fresh-picked, ripe but firm tomatoes in a freezer-weight plastic bag and freeze until solid. If you want the tomatoes cored, do so before freezing, but *don't wash them*. When ready to use, briefly run the frozen tomato under lukewarm (not hot!) water, which not only washes the tomato but loosens the skin. Use your fingers or a paring knife to pull off the skin, then add the frozen tomato to a sauce, soup, or any other dish where you would normally use puréed tomatoes (freezing breaks down tomato cells so that they don't hold their shape). One caveat: Thawing tomatoes before using them allows much of their juice to escape. By the way, frozen tomatoes make a killer Bloody Mary!

**T**he low point in the life of America's tomato must have been reached when the government, in its wisdom, decided that ketchup was a vegetable from the point of view of school lunch.

*— Barbara Kafka*

# Tomato "Gin"ger Slush

This is a great little starter for a summer meal. The pink, thinly sliced ginger for this recipe has been pickled in a sweet vinegar marinade and is called *amazu shoga*. You can find it either in the ethnic section of some supermarkets or in Asian markets.

1 pound tomatoes, cored, seeded, and finely chopped
1½ tablespoons pink pickled ginger, finely chopped
2 tablespoons dry gin
salt and pepper
6 to 8 watercress or cilantro sprigs (optional)

In a large bowl, combine tomatoes, ginger, and gin; salt and pepper to taste. Cover and freeze, stirring occasionally, until solid, about 2 hours. Ten minutes before serving, remove tomato mixture from freezer and let stand at room temperature. Use a large spoon to break mixture into chunks; turn into a food processor fitted with the metal blade. Using quick ON/OFF pulses, process until mixture is slushy. Do not overprocess or it will begin to liquefy. Spoon into 6 to 8 tiny liqueur glasses or demitasse cups; garnish with watercress if desired. Serve immediately. **Serves 6 to 8.**

Life is too short to bother with tasteless tomatoes.

— *Cindy Pawlcyn*

Tomatoes are lusty enough, yet there runs through tomatoes an undercurrent of frivolity.

— *Tom Robbins*

A cooked tomato is like a cooked oyster: ruined.

— *André Simon*

In a world riven by hate, greed, and envy, everyone loves tomatoes. . . . Real (as I will call vine-ripened, soft-walled, acid-flavored, summer-grown) tomatoes are an article of faith, a rallying point for the morally serious, a grail.

— *Raymond Sokolov*

*See also* APHRODISIACS; VEGETABLES

# Trout

Some circumstantial evidence is very strong, as when you find a trout in the milk.

— *Henry David Thoreau*

*See also* FISH

# Truffles

**Pig power.** *Truffles, which sell for between $800 and $1,600 a pound, are one of the most expensive foods in the world. They're also one of the rarest, and are located by specially trained pigs (dogs, too, but our focus here is pigs), particularly in France's Périgord region. And we're not talking cute little "Babe-like" piggies, we're talking hogs!*

*Here's how truffle hunting works. Truffles grow 3 to 12 inches underground near tree roots (usually oak, but also chestnut, hazel, and beech), but never beyond the tree's canopy. The truffle hunter (trufficulteur) walks around with his prized keen-snouted pig who, when she detects a truffle, becomes extremely excited and begins to dig. This is where the trufficulteur takes over, gently scraping back the earth, being careful not to touch the truffle with his hands, which would cause the truffle to rot. If the truffle isn't ripe, he carefully reburies it for future harvesting. It's this painstakingly slow, labor-intensive process that makes truffles so expensive.*

*But back to poor Miss Pig, who's undoubtedly emotionally distraught by this time because she thought the pig of her dreams had just been found. You see, scientists have proven that truffles and male pigs have a rather important common denominator — they both contain androsterone, a sex hormone. The difference is that truffles contain almost twice as much of this pheromone as a male pig. So, here's Miss Pig, strolling nonchalantly along when she gets a whiff of what can only be a boar of massive proportions — a major stud with colossal sex appeal. Naturally, she becomes excited, and begins snorting and digging like crazy only to be yanked rudely away before she can reach the pig of her dreams. Is it any wonder, then, that Miss Pig considers the trufficulteur a pigheaded swine for selling her a pig in a poke when she thought she was headed for hog heaven?*

The truffle is the diamond of cookery.

*— Jean-Anthelme Brillat-Savarin*

The truffle is not a positive aphrodisiac, but it can upon occasion make women tenderer and men more apt to love.

*— Jean-Anthelme Brillat-Savarin*

Whoever says "truffles" utters a great word which arouses erotic and gastronomic memories among the skirted sex and memories gastronomic and erotic among the bearded sex.

*— Jean-Anthelme Brillat-Savarin*

If I can't have too many truffles, I'll do without truffles.

*— Colette*

Away with all this slicing, this dicing, this grating, this peeling of truffles! . . . eat it on its own, scented and grainy-skinned, eat it like the vegetable it is, hot and served in munificent quantities.

*— Colette*

# Anagramatically Yours

One anagram for "truffle" is "fretful," which must be the state Miss Pig is in when she finds that that sexy smell she's after isn't Mr. Right after all.

The truffle is not an outright aphrodisiac, but it may in certain circumstances make women more affectionate and men more amiable.

*– Alexandre Dumas*

. . . the man who first put truffles into his paste of fat goose livers and spice and brandy . . . who first consummated this celestial wedding of high flavour should be rendered some special gastronomical salute. . . . There is nothing much better in the Western world than a fine, unctuous, truffled pâté.

*– M. F. K. Fisher*

Truffles, of course, are not a vegetable; they are a miracle.

*– André Simon*

Presently we were aware of an odour gradually coming towards us, something musky, fiery, savoury, mysterious — a hot, drowsy smell, that lulls the senses and yet enflames them — the truffles were coming.

*– William Thackeray*

*See also* APHRODISIACS

# Turkey

*Long before colonists arrived in the New World, wild turkeys populated the United States, Mexico, and Central America. The conquistadors returned to Spain with crates of turkeys, which soon became quite popular. James Trager's* The Food Chronology *tells us that the name most likely derives from the English having* confused turkeys with guinea fowl (originally from Africa) that had been imported by "turkey merchants," meaning Turks. Europeans began breeding these turkeys into a much plumper bird, which settlers brought back to the New World in the 1600s.

Most turkeys raised in the United States today are of the White Holland variety and are bred to produce a maximum of white meat (America's favorite). As a matter of fact, turkeys today have breasts that are so massive they can't get close enough to mate and have to rely on artificial insemination. And therein lies a turkey tale.

Turkey: This bird has various meanings depending on the action in your dream. If you saw one strutting and/or heard it gobbling, it portends a period of confusion due to instability of your friends or associates. . . . However, if you ate it, you are likely to make a serious error in judgment. . . .

–The Dreamer's Dictionary

Turkey takes so much time to chew. The only thing I ever give thanks for [at Thanksgiving] is that I've swallowed it.

– Sam Greene

See also CHICKEN; DUCK; MEAT; POULTRY

# Turnips

Contrary to what some people think, the so-called yellow turnip is not a turnip at all, but a close relative, the rutabaga. The real turnip has a white flesh and skin with a purple-tinged top. The rutabaga, thought to be a cabbage-turnip cross, has a yellow flesh and skin (there is a white rutabaga that isn't commercially available). The name comes from the Swedish rotabagge, which is why this vegetable is also called a "Swedish turnip." The turnip, when small and young, has a delicate, slightly sweet flavor. The older the turnip, the stronger the flavor and coarser the texture. Your best bet is to purchase turnips that are about 2 inches in diameter and heavy for their size. One pound of turnips yields about 2½ cups chopped turnips.

A degenerate nobleman, or one that is proud of his birth, is like a turnip. There is nothing good of him but what is underground.

*— Samuel Butler*

*See also* VEGETABLES

# Vanilla

*We've all heard the term "plain vanilla" used in a denigrating way to describe something simple, ordinary, without embellishment. Well, let me tell you, nothing could be further from the truth, for vanilla's allure is intensely exotic. In the first place, vanilla is derived from a luminous celedon-colored orchid that's the only one of over 20,000 orchid varieties that bears anything edible. Then there's the labor-intensive pollination process, which must be done either by two tiny, overworked creatures — the Melipone bee and the hummingbird — or by human hands.*

*The Aztecs were cultivating and processing vanilla hundreds of years ago, and Europe was introduced to it by Spanish conquistadors, who called the long, thin pod vainilla (little scabbard). Vanilla took Europe by storm because of its reputedly wide-ranging medicinal and aphrodisiacal powers. By the second half of the sixteenth century, vanilla was extremely popular but so rare that only the extremely prosperous upper class could afford it. Indeed, Queen Elizabeth I was so fond of vanilla that in her declining years she demanded that all her food be flavored with it. Americans can thank esteemed statesman and connoisseur Thomas Jefferson for bringing this aromatic pod back from France. Today, vanilla is used in infinite ways — in perfumes, cosmetics, room deodorizers, envelope glue, and of course in cooking. So let's not hear any more "plain vanilla" talk, for nothing about this tropical orchid fruit is ordinary.*

When a vanilla bean lies like a Hindu rope on the counter, or sits in a cup of coffee, its aroma gives the room a kind of stature, the smell of an exotic crossroads where outlandish foods aren't the only mysteries.

— *Diane Ackerman*

The truth about vanilla is that it's as much a smell as a taste. Saturate your nose with glistening, soulful vanilla, and you can *taste* it. It's not like walking through a sweetshop, but more subterranean and wild. Surely this is the unruly beast itself, the raw vanilla that's clawing your senses.

— *Diane Ackerman*

And when we add the delicious perfume of vanilla to this mixture of sugar, cacao and cinnamon, we achieve the *ne plus ultra* of perfection, to which such a concoction may be carried.

— *Jean-Anthelme Brillat-Savarin*

I prefer vanilla in tradition-bound formulas that maximize my sense of emotional comfort when I lick the spoon.

— *Bert Greene*

The sweet promise of vanilla's seductive aroma and complex flavor is at once comforting and intensely sensual.

— *Herself*

Like a host at a good party, vanilla encourages all the elements present to rise to the occasion and make their own contributions to the whole, without calling undue attention to itself.

— *Richard Sax*

Ah, you flavor everything; you are the vanilla of society.

— *Sydney Smith*

# Vegetables

**Eat your veggies!** *For eons we've been told that vegetables are good for us, but now we know that's particularly true for some, specifically broccoli, Brussels sprouts, cabbage, cauliflower, chard, kale, mustard greens, rutabagas, and turnips. Why? Because these earthy edibles are all cruciferous (krew-SIH-fer-uhs) vegetables, which research has proven may provide protection against certain cancers. Not only are they all high in fiber, vitamins, and minerals, but they contain a healthy dose of antioxidants in the form of beta-carotene and the compound sulforaphane. So, what do you say, how about a little respect for these often maligned nine?*

No vegetable exists which is not better slightly under-cooked.

*– James Beard*

My vegetables don't speak to me in words, but we are in communication. Before I harvest them to take them to the market, I always say, "Thank you so much, you sweeties."

*– Elizabeth Berry*

Shipping is a terrible thing to do to vegetables. They probably get jet-lagged, just like people.

*– Elizabeth Berry*

There are many ways to love a vegetable. The most sensible way is to love it well-treated. Then you can eat it with the comfortable knowledge that you will be a better man for it, in your spirit and your body too.

*– M. F. K. Fisher*

What was paradise but a garden full of vegetables and herbs and pleasures. Nothing there but delights.

*– William Lawson*

Vegetables are interesting but lack a sense of purpose when unaccompanied by a good cut of meat.

— *Fran Lebowitz*

## Alphabet Soup

Don't let anyone tell you that the word "vegetable" has four syllables and is pronounced VEJ-eh-tuh-buhl. According to Charles Harrington Elster in *There Is No Zoo in Zoology*, such enunciation is "... pedantic ... an archaism ... rarely heard in educated speech...." So, stick with VEJ-tuh-buhl and avoid sounding passé.

The seminal signs of spring are fragile, tender and easily bruised. Cooks beware: the less done, the better. The impressionability of a life not yet weathered is the essential charm of spring ingredients. Sparing the rigors of long cooking and heavy or complicated seasoning will not spoil this sort of child.

— *Molly O'Neill*

*See also* ARTICHOKES; BEETS; BROCCOFLOWER; BROCCOLI; CABBAGE; CARROTS; CAULIFLOWER; CORN; CUCUMBERS; EGGPLANT; LETTUCE; MUSHROOMS; OKRA; ONIONS; PEAS; POTATOES; PUMPKINS; SAUERKRAUT; SPINACH; TOMATOES; TRUFFLES; TURNIPS

# Greeked Green Beans

The Greeks have created an art of using spices—particularly nutmeg and cinnamon—in savory dishes. Here nutmeg, allspice, and cinnamon are combined in a tomato-cream sauce that will set your mouth to singing.

1 tablespoon olive oil
1 large onion, finely chopped
2 cloves garlic, minced
1¼ cups chicken broth
¼ cup tomato paste
½ teaspoon *each* ground nutmeg, allspice, and
    cinnamon
1 pound green beans, trimmed and cut into 1-inch
    lengths
⅓ cup heavy whipping cream
salt and freshly ground black pepper to taste

In a large, nonstick skillet, heat oil over medium-high heat. Add onion and sauté, stirring often, until nicely browned, about 10 minutes. Add garlic, chicken broth, tomato paste, and spices, stirring to combine. Stir in beans, coating them thoroughly with the sauce; bring mixture to a boil. Reduce to a simmer; cover and cook about 20 minutes, or until fork-tender. Stir in cream; heat 1 minute. Salt and pepper to taste. **Serves 4.**

# Vegetarians

**Just what is a vegetarian?** *I'm glad you asked, for there is some confusion on this ancient, multifaceted practice. Very simply, a* **vegetarian** *is someone who abstains from eating meat or other animal foods. But the wide-ranging custom of vegetarianism may be based on a variety of personal principles. In ancient Greece a religious cult known as the Orphics (ascribed to Orpheus), who believed that the soul could be freed from evil and achieve eternal bliss through reincarnation, were vegetarians on moral grounds. Certain Hindu and Buddhist sects are vegetarians for religious reasons, while for others it's the ethical aspect (animal cruelty and more efficient use of world food resources) that is important. Some people look to the nutritional benefits of a meatless diet; others are vegetarians for economic reasons (non-meat products are, on the average, less expensive).* **Vegans** *refuse to eat all animal-derivated foods, including butter, cheese, eggs, and milk; they're the purists of the vegetarian world and have the most limited diet.* **Ovo-lacto vegetarians** *will eat some animal-derived foods but refuse meat. Then there are those "vegetarians" who eat fish and/or poultry but no other meat, which, according to the dictionary, means they aren't really vegetarians, but don't tell them that.*

If you become a vegetarian, you separate from your ancestors and cut off posterity.

— *G. K. Chesterton*

You will find me drinking gin
In the lowest kind of inn,
Because I am a rigid vegetarian.

— *G. K. Chesterton*

Vegetarians always say, "I never eat flesh" in a way that puts you right off your nice little beefsteak.

*– Agatha Christie*

Never would it occur to a child that a sheep, a pig, a cow or a chicken was good to eat, while, like Milton's Adam, he would eagerly make a meal off fruits, nuts, thyme, mint, peas and broad beans which penetrate further and stimulate not only the appetite but other vague and deep nostalgias.

*– Cyril Connolly*

Most vegetarians I ever see looked enough like their food to be classed as cannibals.

*– Finley Peter Dunne*

I won't eat anything that has intelligent life, but I'd gladly eat a network executive or a politician.

*– Marty Feldman*

And God said: Behold I have given you every herb-bearing seed upon the earth, and all trees that have in themselves seed of their own kind, to be your meat.

*– Genesis 1:29*

Leprechauns, I know, are vegetarian. They prefer to nibble the soft under-leaves of plants, or so an old Irish nurse once told me, because they are clever little people and know that whatever blooms directly over the root is the sweetest part of the flowering.

*– Bert Greene*

I eat everything that nature voluntarily gives: fruits, vegetables, and the products of plants. But I ask you to spare me what animals are forced to surrender: meat, milk, and cheese.

*– Adolf Hitler*

Vegetarian: A person who eats only side dishes.

*– Gerald Lieberman*

Don't eat anything that has a face. Don't eat anything that has sexual urges, that has a mother and father or that tries to run away from you.

*– John Robbins*

A man of my spiritual intensity does not eat corpses.

*– George Bernard Shaw*

Vegetarians claim to be immune from most diseases but they have been known to die from time to time. . . . You do not obtain eminence so cheaply as by eating macaroni instead of mutton chops.

*– George Bernard Shaw*

My hearse will be followed not by mourning coaches but by herds of oxen, sheep, swine, flocks of poultry and a small travelling aquarium of live fish, all wearing white scarves in honor of the man who perished rather than eat his fellow creatures.

*– George Bernard Shaw*

I have no doubt that it is part of the destiny of the human race, in its gradual improvement, to leave off eating animals, as surely as the savage tribes have left off eating each other when they came in contact with the more civilized.

*– Henry David Thoreau*

Vegetarianism serves as a criterion by which we know that the pursuit of moral perfection on the part of man is genuine and sincere.

*– Count Leo Tolstoy*

I never go without my dinner. No one ever does, except vegetarians and people like that. . . .

*– Oscar Wilde*

*See also* HEALTH FOODS

# Vinegar

*See* CONDIMENTS

# Vitamins

*See* HEALTH FOODS

# Water

**Water, water everywhere** . . . *No*, *Dorothy*, *water isn't simply water, and with well over six hundred different kinds of bottled water available throughout the world today, the subject can be confusing. Here's a brief rundown of different drinking waters:*

**Club soda** *(also called* **soda water, carbonated water,** *or* **seltzer water***) has been highly charged with carbon dioxide and contains a small amount of sodium bicarbonate, which, because it's alkaline, can help neutralize an acidic stomach. (See following natural Seltzer water.)*

**Mineral water** *comes from an underground source and contains various minerals, which may either be natural or added. It can be still or effervescent, and is generally named after its source.*

**Seltzer water,** *named for the German town of Nieder Selters, is flavorless, naturally effervescent, and has a high mineral content. Carbon-dioxide–injected soda water is also sometimes referred to as "seltzer water."*

**Sparkling water** *has become a generic term for any water with effervescence, either man-made or natural.*

**Spring water** *comes from underground springs that surface naturally. Only water which is bottled without processing may be labeled "natural."*

**Tonic water** *(also called* **quinine water***) has been charged with carbon dioxide and flavored with fruit extracts, sugar or a low-calorie sweetener, and a small amount of quinine (a bitter alkaloid).*

Once, during Prohibition, I was forced to live for days on nothing but food and water.

*– W. C. Fields*

I hate water — fish fuck in it.

*– W. C. Fields*

No poems can please for long or live that are written by water drinkers.

*– Horace*

In the world there is nothing more submissive and weak than water. Yet for attacking that which is hard and strong nothing can surpass it.

*– Lao-tzu*

Water is the only drink for a wise man.

*– Henry David Thoreau*

Water taken in moderation cannot hurt anybody.

*– Mark Twain*

# Wine

*It's clear by the following quotes that the world has been having a love affair with wine since the moment the first grape was stomped. And why not, for what other potable has the ability to inspire, exhilarate, and nurture body, intellect, soul, and spirit — all at the same time? Whether you say vino, vin, Wein, or wine, the word translates to pure pleasure, inspiration, comfort, joy, relaxation, poetry . . . in short, to all things pleasing. And wine and food? Well, they go together like Bogie and Bacall, like Astaire and Rogers, like chocolate and vanilla. They're naturals . . . they belong together. Or, in the words of André Simon: "Food without wine is a corpse; wine without food is a ghost; united and well matched they are as body and soul, living partners."*

Great wine is a work of art. It . . . sharpens the wit, gladdens the heart, and stimulates all that is most generous in human nature.

*– H. Warner Allen*

Quickly, bring me a beaker of wine, so that I may wet my mind and say something clever.

*– Aristophanes*

No, Agnes, a Bordeaux is not a house of ill-repute.

*– George Bain*

Wine, madam, is God's next best gift to man.

*– Ambrose Bierce*

Wine, the most delightful of drinks, whether we owe it to Noah, who planted the vine, or to Bacchus, who pressed juice from the grape, dates from the childhood of the world.

*– Jean-Anthelme Brillat-Savarin*

A wine drinker, being at table, was offered grapes at dessert. "Thank you," he said, pushing the dish away from him, "but I am not in the habit of taking my wine in pills."

*– Jean-Anthelme Brillat-Savarin*

Wine cheers the sad, revives the old, and inspires the youth.

*– Lord Byron*

The dipsomaniac and the abstainer both make the same mistake: they both regard wine as a drug and not as a drink.

*– G. K. Chesterton*

Water is for quenching thirst. Wine . . . is a necessary tonic, a luxury, and a fitting tribute to good food.

*– Colette*

It is no small thing to conceive a contempt, so early in life, not only for those who drink no wine at all but also those who drink too much.

— *Colette*

Often, wine has shown me matters in their true perspective, and has, as though by the touch of a magic wand, reduced great disasters to small inconveniences. Wine has lit up for me the pages of literature, and revealed in life romance lurking in the commonplace.

— *Alfred Duff Cooper*

Wine is the intellectual part of any meal . . . food is the material underpinnings.

— *Alexandre Dumas*

If food is the body of good living, wine is its soul.

— *Clifton Fadiman*

Wine is alive, and when you offer it to your fellow man you are offering him life. More than that, you are calling out more life in him, you are engaging in what might be called a creative flattery, for you are asking him to summon up his powers of discrimination, to exercise his taste, or perhaps merely to evince curiosity of a desire to learn. I know no other liquid that, placed in the mouth, forces one to think.

— *Clifton Fadiman*

A bottle of wine begs to be shared; I have never met a miserly wine lover.

— *Clifton Fadiman*

I can no more think of my own life without thinking of wine . . . than I can remember living before I breathed. In other words, wine is life, and my life and wine are inextricable.

— *M. F. K. Fisher*

Good wine, well drunk, can lend majesty to the human spirit. The rules are simple, and if followed will add pleasure to the simplest palate, the simplest meal, and make it grow.

*– M. F. K. Fisher*

There is a communion of more than our bodies when bread is broken and wine is drunk.

*– M. F. K. Fisher*

Wine is constant proof that God loves us, and loves to see us happy.

*– Benjamin Franklin*

Fine wine must be treated like a lovely woman in bed.

*– French proverb*

Wine is food.

*– Oliver Wendell Holmes*

Bacchus opens the gates of the heart.

*– Horace*

Wine is like sex in that few men will admit not knowing all about it.

*– Hugh Johnson*

Wine makes a man more pleased with himself. I do not say that it makes him more pleasing to others.

*– Samuel Johnson*

What is better than to sit at the end of the day and drink wine with friends, or substitutes for friends?

*– James Joyce*

... the wine of Paradise will never inebriate though you drink it for ever.

*– The Koran*

# Make Mine Wine

Ordering wine in a restaurant can sometimes be intimidating because there's an audience—one's dining partner(s), not to mention the waitperson. Here are a few tips to make things easier for the neophyte.

All but the most modest restaurants have a wine list, or at least a blackboard listing their wines. Some restaurants offer only "house wines" (one each, red and white), usually available by glass or carafe. House wines can be perfectly fine, but can also be dreck. Ask the server what the house wine is—brand name, vintage, and style (Zinfandel, Chardonnay, Merlot). Don't be afraid to ask for a taste of a house wine before ordering it.

Most wine lists arrange the wines by color (red or white) and/or region or country (American, French, Italian). The best wine lists indicate information such as the wine's name, vintage, and region ("1991 Dehlinger Reserve Pinot Noir, Russian River Valley"). Some number their wines, a help if you don't know how to pronounce a wine—you can simply order number 28.

The standard markup for wines in restaurants is two to two and a half times the retail price.

In better restaurants, a *sommelier* (wine steward) can assist you in choosing a wine or answer questions you may have. A good *sommelier* will make you feel comfortable rather than uninformed. In the majority of restaurants, a server performs the *sommelier*'s duties.

The server or *sommelier* brings the wine to the table and presents it to whoever ordered it so he/she can examine the label to be sure it's the wine that was ordered. The server will then open the wine and present the cork. An educated nose will detect malodorousness, although sniffing the cork seems pretentious to some and it certainly isn't necessary. However, it's a good idea to examine the cork to be sure the bottom is wet—a sign that the wine was stored properly on its side. A moldy or crumbly cork signals deterioration. Order another bottle.

The *sommelier* then pours a small amount of wine for the person who ordered it. Gently swirl the wine in the glass to release the aroma, smell the wine, and then take a sip—smell and taste are the best criteria of whether or not a wine is sound. If it doesn't have any rank flavors or odors (such as vinegar), it's most likely fine. Returning a wine simply because you don't like it as much as you thought you would isn't appropriate. Remember that a wine's flavor and aroma expand and develop as it aerates. After tasting and approving the wine, simply say thank you to the server, a signal that the wine may be poured for the other diners. Lastly, don't make the tasting process a long, involved procedure—the *sommelier* or server has other tables to attend.

Some restaurants allow patrons to bring their own wine, particularly if it's a special or rare bottle. Call the restaurant beforehand and ask if it's allowable, and, if so, the amount of the "corkage fee," a charge for opening and serving a diner's own wine.

There is a devil in every berry of the grape.

*— The Koran*

To offer wine is the most charming gesture of hospitality, and a host brings out for his guests the finest he has. Whether there are four wines or one, the gesture is the same.

*— Alexis Lichine*

When you ask one friend to dine,
Give him your best wine!
When you ask two,
The second best will do!

*— Henry Wadsworth Longfellow*

Wine was born, not invented. . . . Like an old friend, it continues to surprise us in new and unexpected ways.

*— Salvatore P. Lucia, M.D.*

A meal without wine . . . is breakfast!

*— Molly Mann*

Wine is like music—you may not know what is good, but you know what you like!

*— Justin Meyer*

Wine is the only natural beverage that feeds not only the body, but the soul and spirit of man. . . .

*— Robert Mondavi*

Never refuse wine. It is an odd but universally held opinion that anyone who doesn't drink must be an alcoholic.

*— P. J. O'Rourke*

The juice of the grape is the liquid quintessence of concentrated sunbeams.

*— Thomas Love Peacock*

Wine lets no lover unrewarded go.

*— Alexander Pope*

As in lovemaking, reading is a damn poor substitute for experience in the gentle art of [wine]tasting. It is one of those things you find out by yourself.

*— James Norwood Pratt*

## Wine Bottle Sizes

In the United States, the standard wine bottle is 750 ml (milliliters), which is almost exactly equivalent to an American fifth (⁴/₅ of a quart, or 25.6 ounces). In answer to the stricter driving/alcohol limits in many states, the wine industry is introducing a new 500-ml bottle, which is about 17 ounces (two thirds of a standard bottle). Other bottle sizes are: split (one fourth of a standard wine bottle); half-bottle (just what it says); magnum (equivalent to two standard bottles in one); Jeroboam (four standard bottles); gallon (five standard bottles); Rehoboam (six standard bottles); Methuselah (eight standard bottles in one); Salmanazar (twelve in one); Balthazar (sixteen in one); and Nebuchadnezzar (twenty in one).

If God forbade drinking, would He have made wine so good?

*— Armand-Jean du Plessis Richelieu*

Excellent wine generates enthusiasm. And whatever you do with enthusiasm is generally successful.

*— Philippe de Rothschild*

A glass of good wine is a gracious creature, and reconciles poor mortality to itself, and that is what few things can do.

*— Sir Walter Scott*

Wine is best because it is the safest, pleasantest and most wholesome of all beverages. It is safer than water or milk, you cannot get typhoid or T.B. from any wine, be it old or young, cheap and nasty, or rare and costly. . . .

*– André Simon*

Wine is to the parched mind of man what water is to the sun-drenched plain. It releases the brakes of his self-consciousness and softens the hard-baked crust of dust so that the seeds below may send forth sweet flowers.

*– André Simon*

Wine makes every meal an occasion, every table more elegant, every day more civilized.

*– André Simon*

No meal is ever dull when there is wine to drink and talk about.

*– André Simon*

Food without wine is a corpse; wine without food is a ghost; united and well matched they are as body and soul, living partners.

*– André Simon*

Nature could not care less about wine. From her point of view, the most important part of the grape is the seeds, which ensure the survival of the species.

*– Edward Steinberg*

. . . with inimitable fragrance and soft fire . . . wine is bottled poetry.

*– Robert Louis Stevenson*

A bottle of good wine, like a good act, shines ever in the retrospect.

*– Robert Louis Stevenson*

A waltz and a glass of wine invite an encore.

*– Johann Strauss*

This wine should be eaten, it is too good to be drunk.

*– Jonathan Swift*

Wine remains a simple thing, a marriage of pleasure.

*– André Tchelistcheff*

Better to die of good wine and good company than of slow disease and doctors' doses.

*– William Thackeray*

It's a naive domestic Burgundy without any breeding, but I think you'll be amused by its presumption.

*– James Thurber*

A meal without wine is as a day without sunshine.

*– Louis Vaudable*

Wine is a bride who brings a great dowry to the man who woos her persistently and gracefully; she turns her back on a rough approach.

*– Evelyn Waugh*

You Americans have the loveliest wines in the world, you know, but you don't realize it. You call them "domestic" and that's enough to start trouble anywhere.

*– H. G. Wells*

*See also* APHRODISIACS; BEER; BRANDY; CHAMPAGNE; COCKTAILS; DRINKING; LIQUOR; PORT; TOASTS

# Reading List

*Words are my passion, and it has long been a habit to include quotes in my cookbooks. Truth be known, I began collecting aphorisms almost twenty years ago — long before I ever contemplated compiling them for a book, which is why it never occurred to me to note the book source of the quotes I scribbled on infinite scraps of paper over the years. So, although I fervently racked my memory, this list is undoubtedly incomplete. Still, it's a very long list — so long, in fact, that it was an editorial decision to include only the author and book title, for it was clear that the typical bibliographic format would take over twice as many pages. We all thought that you, dear reader, would much rather have those valuable pages devoted to the almost seven hundred quotable notables in this tome.*

Ackerman, Diane. *A Natural History of the Senses*
Allen, Brigid. *Food, An Oxford Anthology*
Allen, Fred. *Much Ado About Me*
Allen, H. Warner. *A Contemplation of Wine*
Allen, Tim. *Don't Stand Too Close to a Naked Man*
Allen, Woody. *Getting Even*
Allende, Isabel. *Eva Luna*
Arnim, Mary Elizabeth, Countess von. *Elizabeth and Her German Garden*
Austen, Jane. *The Works of Jane Austen: Three Great Novels*
Bailey, Pearl. *Pearl's Kitchen*
Bain, George. *Champagne Is for Breakfast*
Baker, Russell. *Growing Up*
———. *Russell Baker's Book of American Humor*
Barry, Dave. *Dave Barry Is Not Making This Up*
———. *Dave Barry's Greatest Hits*
Beard, James. *Beard on Pasta*
———. *Delights and Prejudices*
Beard, James, and Alexander Watt. *Paris Cuisine*
Beck, Simone, and Paul Grimes. *Food and Friends: Recipes and Memories from Simca's Cuisine*
Becker, Marion Rombauer. *The Joy of Cooking*
Beeton, Mrs. *Mrs. Beeton's Cookery and Household Management*
Bemelmans, Ludwig. *La Bonne Table*
Benning, Lee Edwards. *The Cook's Tales*
Berto, Hazel. *Cooking with Honey*

Bierce, Ambrose. *The Devil's Dictionary*
Bombeck, Erma. *At Wit's End*
———. *If Life Is a Bowl of Cherries, What Am I Doing in the Pits?*
Boyd, Lizzie. *British Cookery*
Bracken, Peg. *The I Hate to Cook Almanac, A Book of Days*
Brenner, Robert. *Excursions into the Interior of Russia*
Brillat-Savarin, Jean-Anthelme. *Physiologie de Goût (see M. F. K.*
   *Fisher's Translation of Brillat-Savarin's* The Physiology of Taste)
Broun, Heywood. *The Collected Edition of Heywood Broun*
Brown, Rita Mae. *Rubyfruit Jungle*
Buchwald, Art. *Is It Safe to Drink the Water?*
Butler, Samuel. *The Way of All Flesh*
Byron, Lord. Byron's Poetry: *Authoritative Texts, Letters and*
   *Journals*
Campbell, Robert. *Alice in La-La Land*
Capon, Robert Farrar. *Food for Thought*
Capote, Truman. *A Capote Reader*
———. *A Christmas Memory*
Carper, Jean. *The Food Pharmacy Guide to Good Eating*
Carroll, Lewis. *Alice's Adventures in Wonderland*
———. *Through the Looking-Glass*
Chalmers, Irena. *The Great Food Almanac*
Chandler, Raymond. *The Chandler Collection*
———. *Pearls Are a Nuisance*
Chekhov, Anton. *The Siren*
Chesterton, G. K. Wine, *Water, and Song*
———. *The Wisdom of Father Brown*
Child, Julia. *Julia Child's Kitchen*
Christie, Agatha. *Agatha Christie A to Z: The Essential Reference to*
   *Her Life and Writings*
Ciardi, John. *The Hopeful Trout and Other Limericks*
Claiborne, Craig. *Craig Claiborne's The New York Times Food*
   *Encyclopedia*
Colette. *Prisons et Paradis*
Collin, Rima and Richard. *The New Orleans Cookbook*
Colwin, Laurie. *More Home Cooking: A Writer Returns to the Kitchen*
Connolly, Cyril. *The Unquiet Grave*
Cooke, Alistair. *Talk About America*
Corbitt, Helen. *Helen Corbitt Cooks for Company*
Courtine, Robert. *The Hundred Glories of French Cooking* (translated
   by Derek Coltman)
Coward, Noël. *A Collection of Short Stories by Noël Coward*
Craig, Diana. *A Miscellany of Cook's Wisdom*
Crisp, Quentin. *The Naked Civil Servant*

Dadd, Debra Lynn. *Nontoxic, Natural and Earthwise: How to Protect from Harmful Products and Live in Harmony with the Earth*

Danziger, Edward G. *Papa D: A Saga of Love and Cooking*

David, Elizabeth. *English Bread and Yeast Cookery*

———. *French Provincial Cooking*

Davidson, Alan. *A Kipper with My Tea*

de Gouy, Louis P. *The Gold Cook Book*

de Groot, Roy Andries. *In Search of the Perfect Meal*

de la Mare, Walter. *The Complete Poems of Walter de la Mare*

———. *Eighteen Eighties Essays*

De Quincey, Thomas. *Confessions of an English Opium Eater*

Deval, Jacqueline. *Reckless Appetites*

De Vries, Peter. *Comfort Me with Apples*

Diat, Louis. *Cooking à la Ritz*

Dickens, Charles. *American Notes, and Pictures from Italy*

———. *Great Expectations*

Dickinson, Emily. *The Poems of Emily Dickinson*

Dinesen, Isak. *On Modern Marriage and Other Observations*

Dumas, Alexandre PÈRE. *Le Grand Dictionaire de Cuisine*

Duras, Marguerite. *Practicalities*

Durrell, Lawrence. *The Black Book*

———. *Pope Joan*

DuSablon, Mary Anna. *America's Collectible Cookbooks*

Eliot, George. *Daniel Deronda*

Eliot, T. S. *Selected Prose of T. S. Eliot*

Elster, Charles Harrington. *There Is No Zoo in Zoology*

Emerson, Ralph Waldo. *The Essays of Ralph Waldo Emerson*

Ensrud, Barbara. *Wine with Food*

Ephron, Delia. *Hanging Up*

Ephron, Nora. *Crazy Salad: Some Things About Women*

———. *Heartburn*

Escoffier, Auguste. *Le Guide Culinaire*

Esquivel, Laura. *Like Water for Chocolate*

Evans, Bergen. *The Natural History of Nonsense*

Fadiman, Clifton. *Dionysus: A Case of Vintage Tales About Wine*

———. *Party of One*

Fern, Fanny. *Ruth Hall and Other Writings (American Woman Writers Series)*

Ferrary, Jeannette. *Between Friends: M. F. K. Fisher and Me*

Field, Eugene. *Poems of Childhood*

Fisher, M. F. K. *An Alphabet for Gourmets*

———. *The Art of Eating*

———. *M. F. K. Fisher's Translation of Brillat-Savarin's The Physiology of Taste*

Fitzgerald, F. Scott. *The Great Gatsby*
———. *The Short Stories of F. Scott Fitzgerald*
Fitzgibbon, Theodora. *The Food of the Western World*
———. *Irish Traditional Food*
———. *The Pleasures of the Table*
Fleming, Ian. *Diamonds Are Forever*
Forster, E. M. *Howard's End*
———. *A Room with a View*
Frank, Anne. *Anne Frank: The Diary of a Young Girl*
Frumkes, Lewis Burke. *The Logophile's Orgy*
Funk, Wilfred. *Word Origins and Their Romantic Stories*
Fussell, Betty. *I Hear America Cooking*
Fussell, Paul. *Class: A Guide Through the American Status System*
Geist, William. *City Slickers*
Gibbons, Euell. *Stalking the Blue-Eyed Scallop*
———. *Stalking the Wild Asparagus*
Giobbi, Edward. *Italian Family Cooking*
Graham, Sheila. *Hollywood Revisited: A Fiftieth Anniversary Celebration*
Greene, Bert. *Bert Greene's Kitchen Bouquets*
———. *The Grains Cookbook*
———. *Greene on Greens*
———. *Honest American Fare*
Greene, Gael. *Bite, A New York Restaurant Strategy*
Greene, Graham. *End of the Affair*
Greene, Graham, and Henry J. Donaghy. *Conversations with Graham Greene*
Greenwood, Kerry, and Jenny Pausacker. *Recipes for Crime*
Grigson, Jane. *British Cookery*
———. *Food with the Famous*
———. *Jane Grigson's Vegetable Book*
———. *The Mushroom Feast*
Halpern, Daniel. *Not for Bread Alone*
Hamerton, Philip G. *Intellectual Life*
Hanh, Thich Nhat. *The Heart of Understanding*
Hardy, Thomas. *The Collected Novels of Thomas Hardy*
Havoc, June. *Early Havoc*
Hazan, Marcella. *The Classic Italian Cookbook*
Hearon, Reed, and Karen Capucilli. *Salsa*
Heatter, Maida. *Maida Heatter's Book of Great Chocolate Desserts*
Hemingway, Ernest. *The Hemingway Reader*
———. *A Moveable Feast*
Hendrickson, Robert. *American Literary Anecdotes*
Henry, O. *The Best of O. Henry*

Herbert, George. *The Poems of George Herbert*
Herbst, Ron, and Sharon Tyler Herbst. *Wine Lover's Companion*
Herbst, Sharon Tyler. *Breads*
———. *The Food Lover's Guide to Chocolate and Vanilla*
———. *The Food Lover's Guide to Meat and Potatoes*
———. *The Food Lover's Tiptionary*
———. *The New Food Lover's Companion*
Hess, John, and Karen Hess. *The Taste of America*
Hooker, Richard J. *Food and Drink in America*
Hope, Bob. *Don't Shoot, It's Only Me*
Huxley, Aldous. *Time Must Have a Stop*
Huxley, Elspeth. *Brave New Victuals*
Jacobs, Jay. *The Eaten Word*
———. *Gastronomy*
———. *A Glutton for Punishment*
James, Henry. *A Little Tour of France*
Jefferson, Thomas. *The Life and Selected Writings of Thomas Jefferson*
Johnson, Hugh. *Hugh Johnson's Modern Encyclopedia of Wine*
Johnson, Ronald. *The American Table*
Johnson, Samuel. *The Selected Writings of Samuel Johnson*
Jones, Evan. *American Food*
———. *Epicurean Delight: The Life and Times of James Beard*
Joyce, James. *Finnegans Wake*
———. *Ulysses*
Kafka, Barbara. *The Opinionated Palate*
Kaufman, George S. *George S. Kaufman and His Collaborators: Three Plays*
Keats, John. *The Poetical Works of John Keats*
Keillor, Garrison. *Lake Wobegon Days*
———. *Leaving Home*
Kennedy, Diana. *The Cuisines of Mexico*
Kerr, Jean. *Please Don't Eat the Daisies*
Khayyám, Omar. *The Rubaiyat*
Kolpas, Norman. *Comforting Foods*
Kroc, Ray, and Robert Anderson. *Grinding It Out: The Making of McDonald's*
Kuralt, Charles. *Life on the Road*
Lacey, Richard W. *Hard to Swallow, A Brief History of Food*
Laden, Alice, and R. J. Minney. *The George Bernard Shaw Vegetarian Cook Book*
Lang, George. *Cuisine of Hungary*
———. *Lang's Compendium of Culinary Nonsense and Trivia*
Lardner, Ring. *Best Short Stories of Ring Lardner*

Lass, Abraham H., David Kiremidjian, and Ruth M. Goldstein. *The Dictionary of Classical, Biblical & Literary Allusions*
Laver, James. *The Age of Optimism: Manners and Morals*
Lear, Edward. *Edward Lear's Book of Nonsense*
Lebowitz, Fran. *The Fran Lebowitz Reader*
Leigh, H. S. *A Day for Wishing*
Leslie, Cole. *Remembered Laughter: The Life of Noël Coward*
Levy, Paul. *Out to Lunch*
Lewis, Edna. *The Edna Lewis Cookbook*
Lichine, Alexis. *Alexis Lichine's Guide to the Wines and Vineyards of France*
Liebling, A. J. *Between Meals*
Llewellyn, Richard. *How Green Was My Valley*
Luchetti, Emily. *Four-Star Desserts*
Lucia, Salvatore P. *A History of Wine as Therapy*
Lunden, Joan. *Joan Lunden's Healthy Cooking*
Macaulay, Rose. *Personal Pleasures*
Macrone, Michael. *By Jove! Brush Up Your Mythology*
Maleska, Eugene T. *A Pleasure in Words*
Marquis, Don. *archy and mehitabel*
Martial. *Epigrammata*
Martin, Judith. *Miss Manners' Guide to Excruciatingly Correct Behavior*
Marx, Groucho. *Groucho and Me*
Maugham, W. Somerset. *A Writer's Notebook*
McCullers, Carson. *The Member of the Wedding*
McCullough, Donald. *After Dinner Grace*
McLaughlin, Michael. *Good Mornings: Great Breakfasts and Brunches for Starting the Day Right*
Meldrum, Douglas G. *The Night 2,000 Men Came to Dinner and Other Appetizing Anecdotes*
Melville, Herman. *Moby Dick*
Mencken, H. L. *The Vintage Mencken*
Meyer, Justin. *Plain Talk About Fine Wine*
Mikes, George. *How to Be an Alien*
Miller, Bryan. *The New York Times Guide to Restaurants in New York City*
Milne, A. A. *The Complete Tales of Winnie-The-Pooh*
Mitcham, Howard. *Creole Gumbo and All That Jazz*
Mitchell, Margaret. *Gone With the Wind*
Mondavi, Robert. *Robert Mondavi Presents Cooking and Entertaining with America's Rising Star Chefs*
Morley, Christopher. *Christopher Morley's New York*
Nachman, Gerald. *The Fragile Bachelor*

Nash, Ogden. *Food*
———. *I'm a Stranger Here Myself*
———. *The Primrose Path*
Oates, Joyce Carol. *American Appetites*
Ogilvy, David. *Ogilvy on Advertising*
Olive, David. *GenderBabble: The Dumbest Things Men Ever Said About Women*
Olney, Judith. *The Joy of Chocolate*
O'Mara, Veronica Jane, and Fionnuala O'Reilly. *A Trifle, A Coddle, A Fry*
O'Neill, Molly. *New York Cookbook*
Orben, Robert. *Big, Big Laughs*
O'Rourke, P.J. *Modern Manners: An Etiquette Book for Rude People*
Orwell, George. *Collected Essays*
———. *Down and Out in Paris and London*
Palin, Michael, and Terry Jones. *The Complete Ripping Yarns*
Panati, Charles. *Extraordinary Origins of Everyday Things*
Parkin, Molly. *Bite of the Apple*
Parton, Dolly. *Dolly: My Life and Other Unfinished Business*
Pawlcyn, Cindy. *Fog City Diner Cookbook*
Peacock, Thomas Love. *The Works of Thomas Love Peacock*
Pennell, Elizabeth Robbins. *My Cookery Books*
Pépin, Jacques. *A French Chef Cooks at Home*
Pepys, Samuel. *The Diary of Samuel Pepys*
Perelman, S. J. *The Rising Gorge*
———. *Strictly from Hunger*
Pessoa, Fernando. *English Poems*
Peterson, James. *Sauces, Classical and Contemporary Sauce Making*
Piggy, Miss. *In the Kitchen with Miss Piggy*
Pizer, Vernon. *Eat the Grapes Downward*
Pope, Alexander. *The Best of Pope*
Post, Emily. *Etiquette*
Pratt, James Norwood. *The Wine Bibber's Bible*
Prokosch, Frederic. *Voices, A Memoir*
Proust, Marcel. *Remembrance of Things Past*
Puck, Wolfgang. *The Wolfgang Puck Cookbook*
Pullar, Philippa. *Consuming Passions*
Quignard, Pascal. *The Salon in Württemberg*
Rabelais, François. *The Complete Works of Rabelais*
Rawlings, Marjorie Kinnan. *Cross Creek*
Repplier, Agnes. *To Think of Tea!*
Revel, Jean-François. *Culture and Cuisine*
Robbins, John. *Diet for a New America*
Robbins, Tom. *Another Roadside Attraction*

Robertson, Laurel. *The New Laurel's Kitchen: A Handbook for Vegetarian Cookery and Nutrition*
Robinson, Jancis. *The Oxford Companion to Wine*
Roden, Claudia. *Coffee: A Connoisseur's Companion*
Roden, Claudia, and Alta Ann Parkins. *Everything Tastes Better Outdoors*
Rogers, Will. *Will Rogers Speaks: Over 1,000 Timeless Quotations for Public Speakers*
Rombauer, Irma. *The Joy of Cooking*
Rooney, Andy. *Most of Andy Rooney*
Root, Waverley. *Eating in America, A History*
――――. *Food*
――――. *The Food of France*
Rorer, Sarah Tyson. *Mrs. Rorer's Philadelphia Cook Book*
Runyon, Damon. *The Damon Runyon Omnibus*
Safire, William. *Take My Word for It*
Saintsbury, George. *Notes on a Cellar-Book*
Saki [H. H. Munro]. *The Match-Maker*
Sax, Richard. *Classic Home Desserts*
Sayers, Dorothy. *Murder Must Advertise*
――――. *Unnatural Death*
Schiavelli, Vincent. *Papa Andrea's Sicilian Table*
Schremp, Gerry. *Kitchen Culture: Fifty Years of Food Fads*
Schulz, Bruno. *The Street of Crocodiles*
Selzer, Richard. *Mortal Lessons*
Sheehy, Gail. *Passages*
Sheraton, Mimi. *The Seducer's Cook Book*
Simic, Charles. *Return to a Place Lit by a Glass of Milk*
Simon, André L. *The Commonsense of Wine*
――――. *A Concise Encyclopedia of Gastronomy*
Simon, Neil. *The Collected Plays of Neil Simon*
Skinner, Cornelia Otis. *Bottoms Up!*
Sokolov, Raymond. *The Saucier's Apprentice*
――――. *Wayward Reporter: The Life of A. J. Liebling*
Spencer, Colin, and Claire Clifton. *The Faber Book of Food*
Staten, Vince. *The Jack Daniel's Old Time Barbecue Cookbook*
Stein, Gerald M. *Caviar! Caviar! Caviar!*
Stewart, Jimmy. *Jimmy Stewart and His Poems*
Stoker, Bram. *Dracula*
Stone, Martin and Sally. *The Brilliant Bean*
Stout, Rex. *Please Pass the Guilt*
――――. *Too Many Cooks*
Swift, Jonathan. *Polite Conversation*
Tarkington, Booth. *Penrod*

Taylor, Robert Lewis. *W. C. Fields, His Follies and Fortunes*
Thatcher, Margaret. *The Downing Street Years*
Thurber, James. *James Thurber: Writings and Drawings*
Till, Antonia (editor). *Loaves & Wishes*
Tinne, Rosie. *Irish Countryhouse Cooking*
Toklas, Alice B. *The Alice B. Toklas Cook Book*
Tolbert, Frank X. *A Bowl of Red*
Trager, James. *The Food Chronology*
Trillin, Calvin. *Alice, Let's Eat*
———. *Third Helpings*
Tucker, Michael. *I Never Forget a Meal: An Indulgent Reminiscence*
Twain, Mark. *A Tramp Abroad*
Vergé, Roger. *Roger Vergé's Entertaining in the French Style*
Villas, James. *American Taste*
Viorst, Judith. *People and Other Aggravations*
Visser, Margaret. *Much Depends on Dinner*
———. *The Rituals of Dinner*
Vreeland, Diana. *D.V.*
Wagner, Jane. *Search for Signs of Intelligent Life in the Universe*
Waldron, Maggie. *Cold Spaghetti at Midnight*
Waters, Alice. *Chez Panisse Cooking*
Watts, Isaac. *Divine Songs for Children*
Waugh, Alec. *The Best Wine Last*
Waugh, Evelyn. *Brideshead Revisited*
———. *When the Going Was Good*
Wells, Patricia. *Simply French: Patricia Wells Presents the Cuisine of Joël Robuchon*
Whitehorn, Katharine. *Observations*
Wilde, Oscar. *The Importance of Being Earnest*
Wilder, Thornton, and Donald Gallup. *The Journals of Thornton Wilder*
Willan, Anne. *Great Cooks and Their Recipes from Taillevent to Escoffier*
Wilson, Tom. *A Day in the Life of Ziggy*
Winokur, Jon. *The Portable Curmudgeon*
Wolfe, Thomas. *The Web and the Rock*
Youngman, Henny. *Henny Youngman's 500: All-Time Greatest One-Liners*

# Index by Author